The Princeton Review®

550 AP®
WORLD HISTORY
Practice Questions

The Staff of the Princeton Review

PrincetonReview.com

Random House, Inc. New Y

The Princeton Review
111 Speen Street, Suite 550
Framingham, MA 01701
E-mail: editorialsupport@review.com

– Poem by Ho Xuan Huong (1772–1822)
– "The Weaver of Designs" by Bernardino de Sahagun from *Florentine Codex*, 1577
– Excerpt from "The White Man's Burden" by Rudyard Kipling, 1899
– Engraving from the Encyclopedie vol 18. Public domain eighteenth century French engraving.
– Excerpt from *Nationalism* by Sir Rabindrauth Tagore, 1918
– Excerpt from Sarojini Naidu, An Indian Nationalist Condemns the British Empire, 1920
– *Justice*, a print by Sir John Tenniel in an issue of Punch Magazine, September 1857
– Excerpt from letter written by Syed Ahmad Khan, 1900
– Excerpt from *The Future of Culture in Egypt* by Taha Husayn, 1938
– Excerpt from Ahmad Lutfi as-Sayyid, Memoirs, 1963
– Excerpt from the *Rock and Pillar Edicts of Asoka Maurya* (304-232 BC)
– Excerpt from Edict of Expulsion of the Jews, 1492
– Excerpt The Peace of Westphalia, 1648
– Excerpt from The General Act of the Conference of Berlin, 1885
– Excerpt from Thomas Paine's *Rights of Man*, 1791
– Excerpt from the Balfour Declaration, 1917
– Excerpt from *Nationalism* by Sir Rabindranath Tagore, 1918.
– Excerpt from *Women In Asia: Restoring Women to History* by Barbara N. Ramusack and Sharon Sievers. Indiana University Press, 1999
– Excerpt from *Chinese Women Yesterday and Today* by Florence Ayscough. Published by Jonathan Cape, London, 1938.
– Page from *Ling Long* women's magazine, published in Shanghai from 1931 to 1937.
– "The Examples" by Nguyen Quang Thieu from *The Women Carry the River Water: Poems*, 1997.
– Excerpt from 'The New Vietnam" by Phan Boi Chau, 1907
– Statement by Le Duan at The Vietnamese Women's Fourth Congress, 1974

ISBN: 978-0-8041-2441-6
eBook ISBN: 978-0-8041-2444-7
ISSN: 2330-698X

Editor: Selena Coppock
Production Editor: Kathy Carter
Production Artist: Craig Patches

Printed in the United States of America on partially recycled paper.

10 9 8 7 6 5 4 3 2 1

Editorial
Rob Franek, Senior VP, Publisher
Mary Beth Garrick, Director of Production
Selena Coppock, Senior Editor
Calvin Cato, Editor
Kristen O'Toole, Editor
Meave Shelton, Editor
Alyssa Wolff, Editorial Assistant

Random House Publishing Team
Tom Russell, Publisher
Nicole Benhabib, Publishing Director
Ellen L. Reed, Production Manager
Alison Stoltzfus, Managing Editor
Erika Pepe, Associate Production Manager
Kristin Lindner, Production Supervisor
Andrea Lau, Designer

Acknowledgments

The Princeton Review would like to give thanks to Merav Ceren, Cynthia Cowan, Danny Poochigian, and Chris Stobart for their hard work and dedication to the development and release of this book.

Contents

Part I
Using This Book to Improve Your AP Score

- Preview: Your Knowledge, Your Expectations
- Your Guide to Using This Book
- How to Begin
- Diagnostic Test
- Diagnostic Test: Answers and Explanations

PREVIEW: YOUR KNOWLEDGE, YOUR EXPECTATIONS

Your route to a high score on the AP World History Exam depends a lot on how you plan to use this book. Start thinking about your plan by responding to the following questions.

1. Rate your level of confidence about your knowledge of the content tested by the AP World History Exam:

   A. Very confident—I know it all
   B. I'm pretty confident, but there are topics for which I could use help
   C. Not confident—I need quite a bit of support
   D. I'm not sure

2. If you have a goal score in mind, circle your goal score for the AP World History Exam:

   5   4   3   2   1   I'm not sure yet

3. What do you expect to learn from this book? Circle all that apply to you.

   A. A general overview of the test and what to expect
   B. Strategies for how to approach the test
   C. The content tested by this exam
   D. I'm not sure yet

YOUR GUIDE TO USING THIS BOOK

This book is organized to provide as much—or as little—support as you need, so you can use this book in whatever way will be most helpful for improving your score on the AP World History Exam.

- The remainder of **Part I** will provide guidance on how to use this book and help you determine your strengths and weaknesses, plus a diagnostic test, so you can see what areas you should focus on in your AP World History review.

- **Part II** of this book will
  o provide information about the structure, scoring, and content of the AP World History Exam.
  o help you to make a study plan.
  o point you towards additional resources.

- **Part III** of this book will explore various strategies:
  o how to attack multiple-choice questions
  o how to write effective essays
  o how to manage your time to maximize the number of points available to you

- **Part IV** of this book covers the content you need for your exam. The content has been split into the six periods that the College Board tests on the AP World History Exam. This section contains drills for each period, plus detailed answers and explanations. If you are taking an AP World History course at your high school, your teacher may not have time to cover all topics in every period. Since our drills are divided by period, you can hone in on any topics that you may not have had time to explore and discuss in class. In addition, Part IV contains a final chapter that is comprised entirely of practice essays. We also provide detailed explanations and scoring rubrics for these practice essays.

You may choose to use some parts of this book over others, or you may work through the entire book. Your approach will depend on your needs and how much time you have. Let's now look at how to make this determination.

HOW TO BEGIN

1. **Take a Test**

    Before you can decide how to use this book, you need to take a practice test. Doing so will give you insight into your strengths and weaknesses, and the test will also help you create an effective study plan. If you're feeling test-phobic, remind yourself that a practice test is a tool for diagnosing yourself—it's not how well you do that matters but how you use information gleaned from your performance to guide your preparation.

    So, before you read further, take the AP World History Diagnostic Test starting on page 7 of this book. Be sure to do so in one sitting, under realistic testing conditions, following the instructions that appear before the test.

2. **Check Your Answers**

    Using the answer key on page 35, count how many multiple-choice questions you got right and how many you missed. Don't worry about the explanations for now, and don't worry about why you missed questions. We'll get to that soon.

3. **Reflect on the Test**

    After you take your first test, respond to the following questions:

    *   How much time did you spend on the multiple-choice questions?

    *   How much time did you spend on each free response question?

    *   How many multiple-choice questions did you miss?

    *   Do you feel you had the knowledge to address the subject matter of the essays?

    *   Do you feel you wrote well-organized, thoughtful essays?

4. **Read Part II and Complete the Self-Evaluation**

    Part II of this book (About the Exam) will provide information on how the test is structured and scored. It will also set out areas of content that are tested.

    As you read Part II, re-evaluate your answers to the questions above. At the end of Part II, you will revisit and refine the questions you answer above. You will then be able to create a study plan, based on your needs and time available, that will allow you to use this book most effectively.

5. **Engage with Parts III and IV as Needed**

Strategy chapters will help you think about your approach to the question types on this exam. Part III will open with a reminder to think about how you approach questions now and then close with a reflection section asking you to think about how/whether you will change your approach in the future.

Part IV is comprised entirely of drills (both multiple-choice and essay) and detailed answers and explanations. As we mentioned earlier, these drills are divided by period (per the College Board's breakdown of the six periods tested on the AP World History Exam). In addition to doing content review on your own (in your AP World History class and/or books from your local library or school), you should test your knowledge in context. That is, practice for the AP World History Exam by tackling drills and practice tests.

6. **Keep Working**

There are other resources available to you, including a wealth of information on AP Central. You can continue to explore areas that can stand to improve and engage in those areas right up to the day of the test.

Diagnostic Test

AP® World History Exam

DO NOT OPEN THIS BOOKLET UNTIL YOU ARE TOLD TO DO SO.

At a Glance

Total Time
55 minutes
Number of Questions
70
Percent of Total Grade
50%
Writing Instrument
Pencil required

Instructions

Section I of this examination contains 70 multiple-choice questions. Fill in only the ovals for numbers 1 through 70 on your answer sheet.

Indicate all of your answers to the multiple-choice questions on the answer sheet. No credit will be given for anything written in this exam booklet, but you may use the booklet for notes or scratch work. After you have decided which of the suggested answers is best, completely fill in the corresponding oval on the answer sheet. Give only one answer to each question. If you change an answer, be sure that the previous mark is erased completely. Here is a sample question and answer.

Sample Question   Sample Answer

Chicago is a
(A) state
(B) city
(C) country
(D) continent

Use your time effectively, working as quickly as you can without losing accuracy. Do not spend too much time on any one question. Go on to other questions and come back to the ones you have not answered if you have time. It is not expected that everyone will know the answers to all the multiple-choice questions.

About Guessing

Many candidates wonder whether or not to guess the answers to questions about which they are not certain. Multiple-choice scores are based on the number of questions answered correctly. Points are not deducted for incorrect answers, and no points are awarded for unanswered questions. Because points are not deducted for incorrect answers, you are encouraged to answer all multiple-choice questions. On any questions you do not know the answer to, you should eliminate as many choices as you can, and then select the best answer among the remaining choices.

GO ON TO THE NEXT PAGE.

This page intentionally left blank.

GO ON TO THE NEXT PAGE.

WORLD HISTORY

SECTION I

Time—55 minutes

70 Questions

Directions: Each of the questions or incomplete statements below is followed by four suggested answers or completions. Select the one that is best in each case and then fill in the corresponding oval on the answer sheet.

Note: This examination uses the chronological designations B.C.E. (before the common era) and C.E. (common era). These labels correspond to B.C. (before Christ) and A.D. (anno Domini), which are used in some world history textbooks.

1. All of the following ancient civilizations developed near river valleys EXCEPT

   (A) Sumerian
   (B) Egyptian
   (C) Chavin
   (D) Shang

2. The two major religions practiced in Classical India were

   (A) Hinduism and Buddhism
   (B) Islam and Buddhism
   (C) Islam and Hinduism
   (D) Catholicism and Hinduism

3. Which of the following was NOT characteristic of early civilizations?

   (A) Caravan trade
   (B) Urban centers
   (C) Growing populations
   (D) Agricultural surplus

4. The location and architecture of buildings in major Mayan cities such as Palenque are most likely based on

   (A) defensibility from attack by sea
   (B) astronomical observations and phenomena
   (C) accessibility of major trade routes
   (D) haphazard, population-driven expansion

5. The Silk Roads, the largest trade network of the ancient world, were controlled by

   (A) India
   (B) Christians
   (C) China
   (D) Buddhists

6. Which of the following is an accurate characterization of trade along the overland route between the Roman Empire and India through the first two centuries C.E.?

Roman Empire	India
(A) Silver and gold	Silk and cotton cloth
(B) Horses	Olive oil and pepper
(C) Indigo	Silver and gold
(D) Olive oil and pepper	Silver and gold

7. The Hebrews were unique in ancient civilization for their

   (A) large, centralized state
   (B) belief in monotheism
   (C) strong military tradition
   (D) relative equality of social classes

8. Which of the following is an accurate statement about the ancient Greeks?

   (A) The Greeks incorporated the gods of the Persians after the Persian Wars.
   (B) It is the commitment to arts and sciences begun in Greece's Golden Age that would become cornerstones of Western culture.
   (C) Greece's philosophers concentrated on the afterlife, beginning new religions.
   (D) During the Golden Age of Pericles, the Greeks abolished slavery.

GO ON TO THE NEXT PAGE.

Source: Encyclopedie: Classical Orders, engraving from the Encyclopédie vol. 18. Public domain eighteenth century French engraving.

9. The columns illustrated above are architectural contributions from which civilization?

(A) China
(B) Persia
(C) Sumer
(D) Greece

10. Ashoka Maurya is responsible for which religion's expansion beyond India and into many parts of Southeast Asia?

(A) Hinduism
(B) Daoism
(C) Buddhism
(D) Christianity

11. Which of the following is an important contribution of the Lydians?

(A) Their dualistic beliefs inspired the Zoroastrian religion.
(B) Their development of a written alphabet was adapted by the Phoenicians.
(C) Their introduction of coined money facilitated development of global trade.
(D) Their defeat by the Aryans began the formation of the modern state of India.

12. Emperor Justinian of Byzantium preserved Roman customs in which of the following ways?

(A) He unified the Byzantine Empire by making the Roman Catholic Church the official state church when the Western Roman Empire crumbled.
(B) He codified Roman legal principles in the Justinian Code, even as those principles fell out of use in the West.
(C) He pursued an aggressive foreign policy of conquering the Germanic tribes who held the Western Roman Empire.
(D) He mandated the use of Latin in all official government documentation and commercial transactions in the Eastern Roman Empire.

13. Which of the following contributed significantly to the decline of both the Han and Gupta empires?

(A) Conflict with nomadic invaders
(B) Population growth leading to overcrowding
(C) Tax revolts by the upper class
(D) Government corruption

GO ON TO THE NEXT PAGE.

14. Which of the following was NOT a major effect of movement along the Silk Road?

    (A) The spread of epidemic diseases throughout Europe and Asia
    (B) The use of a common language among the countries along the road
    (C) The exchange of religious ideas between the East and West
    (D) The transmission of artistic influences among cultures

15. Along the trade routes of the post-classical period spread

    (A) disease
    (B) religion
    (C) technology
    (D) all of the above

16. All of the following were contributions from cultures Muslim invaders absorbed from civilizations they were in contact with EXCEPT

Civilization	Contribution
(A) India	System of numbers
(B) Greece	Anatomy
(C) Japan	Philosophy
(D) Greece	Astronomy

17. Which of the following is not one of the Five Pillars of Islam?

    (A) Pilgrimage to Mecca
    (B) Confession
    (C) Charitable giving
    (D) Fasting

18. The Islamic *ummah* was

    (A) the concept of community of believers which transcended clan boundaries
    (B) the name given to the group of clergy of the new faith
    (C) the name given to the battle which resulted in Muhammad's successful return to Mecca
    (D) the writings which explained Muhammad's dreams, which a sub-sect of Islam is based upon

19. The image above, of the Alhambra in Andalusia, Spain, shows the influence of which widespread religion?

    (A) Christian
    (B) Jewish
    (C) Islamic
    (D) Buddhist

20. Which of the following is true about the declining role of women in the Islamic Abbasid era?

    (A) Men were permitted to have more than one wife.
    (B) Abbasid caliphs instituted harems in the court.
    (C) Women were kept secluded from civil life.
    (D) All of the above.

GO ON TO THE NEXT PAGE.

Expansion of Seventh Century Empire

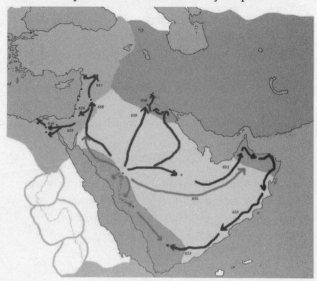

21. The map above shows which seventh century empire's expansion?

    (A) Islamic
    (B) Byzantine
    (C) Sassanid
    (D) Western Roman

22. Which of the following is an example of how Muslim culture influenced Western Europe in the era of the Crusades?

    (A) Castle fortifications
    (B) The game of chess
    (C) Coffee
    (D) All of the above are examples of ways in which Muslim culture influences Western Europe.

23. Orthodox Christianity split from Roman Catholicism in 1054 C.E. in part due to the former's

    (A) belief in papal infallibility
    (B) tradition of allowing priests to marry
    (C) belief in the Virgin Mary
    (D) more "law-centric" interpretation of scripture

Alhambra's Courtyard of the Lions

24. The fourteenth century palace in Spain shown above is an example of

    (A) the wealth and power of the Roman emperor
    (B) cross-cultural interaction
    (C) architectural wonders lost to destruction by invaders
    (D) religious conflict

25. Which of the following correctly chronicles the regions to which Islam spread from the Arabian Peninsula?

    (A) Somali Coast, Southeast Asia, Iberian Peninsula
    (B) Central Asia, Eastern Europe, Somali Coast
    (C) Eastern Europe, Southeast Asia, Somali Coast
    (D) Somali Coast, Central Asia, Southeast Asia

GO ON TO THE NEXT PAGE.

26. Which of the following most accurately describes the development of Incan political structure from the 12th to 15th centuries C.E.?

    (A) A collection of city-states united in a loose confederation before being conquered by the Aztecs.

    (B) A small city-state expanded via conquest under a strong military leader.

    (C) Coastal villages developed naval power that centralized to protect maritime trade.

    (D) Popularly elected monarchy developed into military dictatorship.

27. The Ming Dynasty adopted which of the following belief systems for which of the following reasons?

    (A) Islam, because it was the faith of Mongols who invaded during this period

    (B) Catholicism, due to the arrival of Jesuit missionaries

    (C) Neoconfucianism, to build a more competent and effective bureaucracy

    (D) Taoism, in line with a more isolationist foreign policy

28. Which of the following correctly compares the Muscovite Russians and Ottoman Turks?

    (A) Each benefited from Mongolian khanates previously unifying territorial holdings.

    (B) The rise of each to power was facilitated by schisms in Christianity and Islam, respectively.

    (C) The Muscovite Russians benefited from Afro-European trade, while the Ottoman Turks did not.

    (D) The Muscovite Russians used their naval prowess to engage in trade, while the Ottoman Turks focused on naval conquest.

29. Epidemics in sixteenth-century Mesoamerica led to

    (A) the largest decline in history in global population, by percentage

    (B) an increase in wages for workers who survived the epidemics

    (C) a shift in Europeans' focus to conquest of North America

    (D) the decline of African slavery in the region

30. From 1600 to 1700, sugar was

    (A) less profitable than tobacco in the Caribbean

    (B) the leading product in Atlantic trade

    (C) produced largely without slave labor

    (D) considered the easiest crop to produce

31. Northern Europe's population increased in the 16th and 17th centuries in part thanks to the

    (A) end of religious civil war in England

    (B) expulsion of the Moors from Spain during the Reconquista

    (C) conclusion of the Crusades

    (D) introduction of the potato from South America as a staple crop

32. Which of the following statements about the Songhai in the sixteenth century is accurate?

    (A) This dynasty's founding emperor completed the Great Wall of China.

    (B) This dynasty unified several smaller kingdoms into early outlines of modern-day China.

    (C) This Islamic kingdom in West Africa was a major part of the trans-Saharan salt and gold trade.

    (D) This West African kingdom rose to power as a result of the Portuguese slave trade.

GO ON TO THE NEXT PAGE.

33. Babur led his Mughal army to conquer India chiefly in order to

    (A) build a powerful military empire
    (B) unify India under Hinduism
    (C) extend religious tolerance to the region
    (D) lay siege to holy sites such as the Taj Mahal

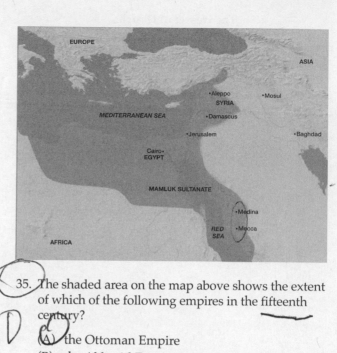

34. The building shown above is an example of

    (A) communal urban housing in the Ottoman Empire
    (B) food storage outbuildings in Western Europe
    (C) homes of the peasant class in rural Southeast Asia
    (D) African dwellings adapted for the American South

35. The shaded area on the map above shows the extent of which of the following empires in the fifteenth century?

    (A) the Ottoman Empire
    (B) the Abbasid Empire
    (C) the Caliphate of Cordoba
    (D) the western of two Mamluk Sultanates

36. The "Columbian Exchange" brought

    (A) Spanish gold to America and American diseases to Spain
    (B) Native American slaves to Africa and African guns to the Americas
    (C) European diseases to America and American crops to Europe
    (D) American horses to Europe and European turkeys to America

37. The expansion of global trade in the 16th and 17th centuries contributed to China's becoming a major holder of the world's silver because

    (A) China's exports outstripped its imports
    (B) China's South American colonies were rich silver producers
    (C) Britain paid large quantities of silver for Chinese opium
    (D) Britain paid for the rights to use the lucrative trading port of Hong Kong

GO ON TO THE NEXT PAGE.

The Weaver of Designs

"She concerns herself with using thread, works with thread. The good weaver of designs is skilled—a maker of varicolored capes, an outliner of designs, a blender of colors, a joiner of pieces, a matcher of pieces, a person of good memory. She does things dexterously. She weaves designs. She selects. She weaves tightly. She forms borders. She forms the neck…"

Source: Bernadino de Sahagun, *La Historia Universal de las Cosas de Nueva España.*

38. The above sixteenth-century quote from Spaniard Bernardino de Sahagún refers to a woman from which civilization?

    (A) France
    (B) Aztec
    (C) The Low Country
    (D) China

Careful, careful where are you going:
You group of know-nothings!
Come here and let your older sister teach you to write poems.
Young bees whose stingers itch rub them in wilted flowers.
Young goats who have nothing to do with their horns butt
    them against sparse shrubbery.

39. The eighteenth-century poem above was written by a woman of which region?

    (A) China
    (B) Japan
    (C) Vietnam
    (D) Arabia

40. Which of the following statements about slavery in the pre-modern world is NOT accurate?

    (A) All pre-modern societies except India used slave labor.
    (B) In Greece, slaves were most often foreigners or prisoners of war.
    (C) In the Islamic world, slaves of kings could rise to high-level positions.
    (D) In China, laws restricted slavery to foreigners and criminals.

41. The European maritime activity at the end of the fifteenth century led to all of the following EXCEPT

    (A) the creation of a new international venue for the exchange of foods, diseases, and manufactured goods
    (B) the opening of some parts of the world to European colonization
    (C) the formation of a far-reaching world economy
    (D) the destruction of Indian and Chinese maritime trade

42. North American European colonies differed from Latin American colonies in that

    (A) the North American colonists tended to integrate with the native populations more than did colonists in Latin America
    (B) later North American migration served as a pressure-release valve for Europeans seeking religious persecution
    (C) north American colonists were uniquely driven by the search for wealth
    (D) latin American colonists treated the area as an agricultural laboratory, bringing European crops, especially the sweet potato, to the New World

43. How was the process of industrialization similar in Russia and Japan?

    (A) Both countries emancipated their work forces.
    (B) Both countries adopted Western characteristics.
    (C) Both countries depended on the steel industry.
    (D) Both countries began to industrialize in the early nineteenth century.

GO ON TO THE NEXT PAGE.

44. Which of the following was a characteristic regarding gender roles in the early days of the Industrial Revolution?

    (A) Japanese women abandoned their traditional roles as housewives and mothers.
    (B) British women lost work to domestic manufacturing.
    (C) Married women began to join the medical profession in significant numbers.
    (D) Russian women began working outside the home in banking.

45. Which of the following did most industrializing countries quickly develop?

    (A) Unions
    (B) Steel manufacturing
    (C) Railroads
    (D) Suffrage rights

46. Japan's industrialization process was initially limited by which of the following?

    (A) Its banking system
    (B) Its lack of government support
    (C) Its lack of a labor pool
    (D) Its geography

47. All of the following were contributing factors to Great Britain's Industrial Revolution EXCEPT

    (A) changing philosophies on the role of women
    (B) agricultural innovations such as crop rotation and the application of fertilizer
    (C) the introduction of the enclosure movement
    (D) technological developments such as the steam engine

48. Which of the following is true about Egypt's industrialization process in the early nineteenth century?

    (A) Egypt distanced itself from the Ottoman Empire
    (B) Lower classes began to enjoy new freedoms
    (C) Egypt freed itself from Western influence
    (D) Egypt narrowed the technological gap between the Muslim world and the West

49. How were immigration patterns of the nineteenth century to Hawaii similar to those to Latin America in the seventeenth century?

    (A) Africans were brought to plantations as slaves.
    (B) Due to depletion of the native population, huge numbers of laborers immigrated.
    (C) Spanish Jesuits arrived to convert the native population.
    (D) Jewish immigrants fleeing pogroms arrived in large numbers.

50. Which of the following is NOT true about population patterns in the nineteenth century?

    (A) Death rates were affected by the Columbian trade.
    (B) Families became smaller.
    (C) Family patterns remained unchanged.
    (D) Cities expanded significantly.

51. Why were the Opium Wars of the nineteenth century fought?

    (A) China began a War Against Drugs within its borders to end the use of opium.
    (B) India fought England for control of the world's opium trade routes.
    (C) Japan fought to gain access to poppy fields in India.
    (D) England began a war for the right to trade opium in China.

52. Which of the following is true about the end of the trans-Atlantic slave trade?

    (A) Great Britain resisted closing the trade routes.
    (B) The end of the trans-Atlantic slave trade happened around the time Russian serfs were emancipated.
    (C) African kings successfully petitioned European powers to end the trade.
    (D) The United States saw the end of the trade as a moral imperative.

GO ON TO THE NEXT PAGE.

53. Which of the following countries most resisted European intervention in the early nineteenth century?

    (A) Brazil
    (B) Egypt
    (C) Japan
    (D) Russia

54. Great Britain's first Industrial Revolution was fueled primarily by

    (A) steel
    (B) rubber
    (C) shipbuilding
    (D) textiles

55. Latin American wars of independence in the early nineteenth century had which of the following results?

    (A) Entire populations were forcibly converted to Roman Catholicism.
    (B) The existing social structure remained largely in place.
    (C) Most soon abolished slavery and established racial equality.
    (D) They produced Latin America's Industrial Revolution.

    "Take up the White Man's burden—
    Send forth the best ye breed—
    Go send your sons to exile
    To serve your captives' need
    To wait in heavy harness
    On fluttered folk and wild—
    Your new-caught, sullen peoples,
    Half devil and half child"

    Source: Rudyard Kipling, *The White Man's Burden*, 1899.

56. The quotation above by a late nineteenth-century British author illustrates

    (A) the racism involved in the conquest of South America
    (B) social Darwinism's influence in justifying imperialism
    (C) explorers' views on encountering natives for the first time in Canada
    (D) crusaders' justification for the wholesale slaughter of non-Christians

57. Dissatisfaction over the agreements ending the First World War led to all of the following EXCEPT

    (A) Germany's Beer Hall Putsch
    (B) Hitler's occupation of the Rhineland
    (C) American reluctance to join the United Nations
    (D) China's May Fourth Movement

58. Mao Zedong's Great Leap Forward in 1958 was primarily intended to

    (A) compete with the Americans and Soviets in the Space Race
    (B) revolutionize the civil service
    (C) achieve village-based industrialization
    (D) ensure popular compliance with anti-religious policies

59. Industrialization and rural exodus in Latin America in the twentieth century drove the trend of

    (A) Abolition and slave emancipation
    (B) Declining health care standards
    (C) Wage inflation
    (D) Hyperurbanization

60. Massive labor migrations to economically developed countries in the twentieth century occurred primarily because of

    (A) falling birth rates in developed countries
    (B) epidemics depopulating crowded urban areas
    (C) rural crime and civil unrest
    (D) strikes in developed countries creating the need for replacement workers

GO ON TO THE NEXT PAGE.

"Concerned that in situations of poverty women have the least access to food, health, education, training and opportunities for employment and other needs... Parties shall take all appropriate measures to eliminate discrimination against women in order to ensure to them equal rights with men in the field of education and in particular to ensure, on a basis of equality of men and women...The same conditions for career and vocational guidance, for access to studies and for the achievement of diplomas in educational establishments of all categories in rural as well as in urban areas; this equality shall be ensured in pre-school, general, technical, professional and higher technical education, as well as in all types of vocational training.... The elimination of any stereotyped concept of the roles of men and women at all levels and in all forms of education by encouraging coeducation and other types of education which will help to achieve this aim and, in particular, by the revision of textbooks and school programmes and the adaptation of teaching methods..."

61. Which of the following most likely produced the twentieth-century document quoted above?

   (A) The United Nations
   (B) NATO
   (C) Maoist China
   (D) The Soviet Union

62. Martin Luther King, Jr., Nelson Mandela, and Aung San Suu Kyi each drew their political philosophy and protest tactics in part from the work of

   (A) Thich Quang Duc
   (B) Mother Teresa of Calcutta
   (C) Mahatma Gandhi
   (D) Shaka kaSenzangakhona

63. The European Union was founded primarily in order to

   (A) guard against Soviet takeover of Western European nations
   (B) facilitate economic development and intra-European trade
   (C) more closely parallel the organization of the United States
   (D) wrest global economic dominance from the United States

64. All of the following countries experienced social unrest and student protest movements in the 1960s similar to those in the United States EXCEPT

   (A) Israel
   (B) Iran
   (C) The Soviet Union
   (D) Switzerland

65. In late-twentieth century sub-Saharan Africa, political stability often failed in part because

   (A) Apartheid spread from South Africa to other surrounding nations
   (B) former colonial puppet rulers repeatedly attempted to regain power
   (C) efforts to form an African National Congress proved prohibitively complicated
   (D) colonizers ignored longstanding ethnic conflicts when drawing boundaries had predicted

66. Which of the following correctly lists three leaders who rose in opposition to colonial rule of their home countries?

   (A) Macario Sakay, Ngo Dinh Diem, U Wisara
   (B) Edmund Andros, George Washington, Francisco Madero
   (C) Chandrashekar Azad, Touissant L'Ouverture, Marquess Dalhousie
   (D) Ho Chi Minh, Jomo Kenyatta, Kwame Nkrumah

GO ON TO THE NEXT PAGE.

67. Which of the following statements correctly describes global affairs at the dawn of the twenty-first century?

(A) Rapid innovation in transportation and communication have accelerated the pace and intensity of international interactions.

(B) Interethnic conflict has largely been resolved through the United Nations and its support of nationalist independence movements.

(C) Global terrorism that accelerated in the late twentieth century led to a worldwide economic downturn.

(D) The spread of science and secularism sent belief in world religions into serious decline.

68. In the twentieth century, the phrase "mutually assured destruction" most accurately referred to

(A) the threat to Berliners of taking down the Berlin Wall while the city was still divided between Soviet and Allied leadership

(B) the danger of continuing to pollute the environment as the ozone layer became depleted

(C) the result, for upper and lower classes alike, of fraudulent banking practices and market speculation

(D) the consequences of anything worse than proxy war between the U.S.S.R. and United States in the nuclear age

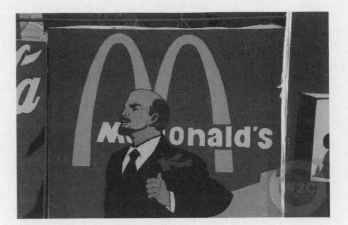

69. The image above reflects

(A) Lenin's opposition to Western influences

(B) an irony in the globalization of American culture

(C) the Communist Party's endorsement of egalitarian fast food

(D) American advertising promoting a culture of conformity in the 1950s

70. During the Cold War, Latin America was primarily

(A) a source of oil to replace that cut off by O.P.E.C. during the 1970s

(B) an arena for proxy conflicts between the United States and U.S.S.R.

(C) uninvolved, as the continent was too underdeveloped to be of interest

(D) governed by stable democracies with burgeoning civic involvement

END OF SECTION I

WORLD HISTORY
SECTION II

You will have 10 minutes to read the contents of this green insert. You are advised to spend most of the 10 minutes analyzing the documents and planning your answer for the document-based question essay in Part A. You may make notes in this green insert. At the end of the 10-minute period, you will be told to break the seal on the pink free-response booklet and to begin writing your answers on the lined pages of the booklet. Do not break the seal on the pink booklet until you are told to do so. Suggested writing time is 40 minutes for the document-based essay question in Part A and 40 minutes for each of the essay questions in Part B and Part C.

BE SURE TO MANAGE YOUR TIME CAREFULLY.

Write your answers in the <u>pink</u> booklet with a <u>pen</u>. The green insert may be used for reference and/or scratchwork as you answer the free-response questions, but no credit will be given for the work shown in the green insert.

DO NOT OPEN THIS BOOKLET UNTIL YOU ARE TOLD TO DO SO.

GO ON TO THE NEXT PAGE.

WORLD HISTORY
SECTION II
Part A
(Suggested writing time—40 minutes)
Percent of Section II score—33 1/3

Directions: The following question is based on the accompanying Documents 1–7. (The documents have been edited for the purpose of this exercise.) Write your answer on the lined pages of the Section II free-response booklet.

This question is designed to test your ability to work with and understand historical documents. Write an essay that:

- Has a relevant thesis and supports that thesis with evidence from the documents.
- Uses all of the documents.
- Analyzes the documents by grouping them in as many appropriate ways as possible. **Does not simply summarize the documents individually**.
- Takes into account both the sources of the documents and the authors' points of view.
- Explains the need for one type of additional document.

You may refer to relevant historical information not mentioned in the documents.

1. Using the following documents, analyze the rise of nationalism in Egypt and India following World War I. Identify an additional type of document and explain how it would help your analysis of causes for the nationalist feelings in these nations.

   Historical Background: In 1947 British-controlled South Asia was partitioned to form the Islamic state of Pakistan and the secular state of India. In North Africa, Egypt gained partial independence from Great Britain in 1922, but the British kept control of the Suez Canal until 1954.

GO ON TO THE NEXT PAGE.

Document 1

Excerpt from: *Nationalism*, by Sir Rabindranath Tagore, 1918.

Rabindranath Tagore, Bengali poet, playwright, and novelist, who was one of the earliest non-European recipients of the Nobel Prize for literature, wrote the following:

Has not this truth already come home to you now when this cruel war has driven its claws into the vitals of Europe? When her hoard of wealth is bursting into smoke and her humanity is shattered on her battlefields? You ask in amazement what she has done to deserve this? The answer is, that the West has been systematically petrifying her moral nature in order to lay a solid foundation for her gigantic abstractions of efficiency. She has been all along starving the life of the personal man into that of the professional.

Document 2

Source: Mahatma Gandhi, 1909.

We hold the civilization that you support to be the reverse of civilization. We consider our civilization to be far superior to yours. If you realize this truth, it will be to your advantage and, if you do not, according to your own proverb, you should only live in our country in the same manner as we do. You must not do anything that is contrary to our religions. It is your duty as rulers that for the sake of the Hindus you should eschew beef, and for the sake of Mahomedans you should avoid bacon and ham. We have hitherto said nothing because we have been cowed down, but you need not consider that you have not hurt our feelings by your conduct. We are not expressing our sentiments either through base selfishness or fear, but because it is our duty now to speak out boldly. We consider your schools and courts to be useless. We want our own ancient schools and courts to be restored. The common language of India is not English but Hindi. You should, therefore, learn it. We can hold communication with you only in our national language.

Document 3

Source: Sarojini Naidu, *An Indian Nationalist Condemns the British Empire*, 1920.

I speak to you today as standing arraigned because of the blood-guiltiness of those who have committed murder in my country. I need not go into the details. But I am going to speak to you as a woman about the wrongs committed against my sisters. Englishmen, you who pride yourselves upon your chivalry, you who hold more precious than your imperial treasures the honour and chastity of your women, will you sit still and leave unavenged the dishonour, and the insult and agony inflicted upon the veiled women of the Punjab?

The minions of Lord Chelmsford, the Viceroy, and his martial authorities rent the veil from the faces of the women of the Punjab. Not only were men mown down as if they were grass that is born to wither; but they tore asunder the cherished Purdah, that innermost privacy of the chaste womanhood of India. My sisters were stripped naked, they were flogged, they were outraged. These policies left your British democracy betrayed, dishonored, for no dishonor clings to the martyrs who suffered, but to the tyrants who inflicted the tyranny and pain. Should they hold their Empire by dishonoring the women of another nation or lose it out of chivalry for their honor and chastity? The Bible asked, "What shall it profit a man to gain the whole world and lose his own soul?" You deserve no Empire. You have lost your soul; you have the stain of blood-guiltiness upon you; no nation that rules by tyranny is free; it is the slave of its own despotism.

GO ON TO THE NEXT PAGE.

Document 4

Source: *Punch* Magazine, England.

JUSTICE.

Justice, a print by Sir John Tenniel in a September 1857 issue of *Punch*

Document 5

Source: Syed Ahmad Khan, educator and founder of the Muhammadan Anglo-Oriental College, undated letter to a fellow Muslim, published two years after Khan's death. *Several Notable Letters of Sir Syed Ahmad Khan*, India, 1900.

If the Muslims do not take to the system of education introduced by the British, they will not only remain a backward community, but will sink lower and lower until there will be no hope of recovery left to them.

If the choice were to lie between giving up and preserving Islam, I would have unhesitatingly chosen Islam. That, however, is not the choice. The adoption of the new system of education does not mean the renunciation of Islam. It means its protection. We are justly proud of the achievements of our forefathers in the fields of learning and culture, but these achievements were possible only because they were willing to act upon the teachings of the Prophet Muhammad. The Prophet said that knowledge is the heritage of the believer and that he should acquire it wherever he can find it. He also said that the Muslims should seek knowledge even if they have to go to China, which at that time was one of the most civilized countries in the world, but it was a non-Muslim country and could not teach the Muslims anything about their own religion. Did the early Muslims not take to Greek learning avidly? Did this in any respect undermine their loyalty to Islam?

Europe has made such remarkable progress in science that it would be suicidal not to make an effort to acquire that knowledge. How can we remain true Muslims or serve Islam if we sink into ignorance?

GO ON TO THE NEXT PAGE.

Document 6

Source: Taha Husayn, Muslim literary figure and Egyptian nationalist, *The Future of Culture in Egypt*, Egypt, 1938.

We Egyptians must not assume the existence of intellectual differences, weak or strong, between the Europeans and ourselves or infer that the East mentioned by Kipling* in his famous verse "East is East and West is West, and never the twain shall meet" applies to us or our country.

We want to be like the European nations in military power in order to repel the attack of any aggressor and to be able to say to our English friends, "Thank you, you may go, for we can now defend the Suez Canal." Who wants the end must want the means: who wants power must want the elements constituting it: who wants a strong European-type army must want European training.

We also need economic independence. I do not mean we should be independent of Arabia, Syria, and Iraq, but independent of Europe and America. We must therefore use the same means that the Europeans and Americans use to defend their national economies.

   *English novelist, journalist, and longtime resident of South Asia.

Document 7

Source: Ahmad Lutfi as-Sayyid, founder of the Egyptian Peoples Party in 1907, *Memoirs*, Egypt, 1965.

Among our forefathers were those who maintained that the land of Islam is the fatherland of all Muslims. However, that is a colonialist formula used to advantage by every colonizing nation that seeks to expand its possessions and to extend its influence daily over neighboring countries.

Today the [traditional Islamic] formula has no reason to exist. We must replace this formula with the only doctrine that is in accord with every Eastern nation that possesses a clearly defined sense of fatherland. That doctrine is nationalism.

Our love of Egypt must be free from all conflicting associations. We must suppress our propensity for anything other than Egypt because patriotism, which is love of fatherland, does not permit such ties.

Our Egyptian-ness demands that our fatherland be our qibla* and that we not turn our face to any other.

   *Marks the direction of Mecca, to which a Muslim turns in prayer.

END OF PART A

GO ON TO THE NEXT PAGE.

WORLD HISTORY

SECTION II

Part B

(Suggested planning and writing time—40 minutes)

Percent of Section II score—33 1/3

Directions: You are to answer the following question. You should spend 5 minutes organizing or outlining your essay. Write an essay that:

- Has a relevant thesis and supports that thesis with appropriate historical evidence.

- Addresses all parts of the question.

- Uses historical context to show change over time and/or continuities.

- Analyzes the process of change and/or continuity over time.

2. Describe the continuities and changes in Africa's relationship with Europe between the fifteenth and the nineteenth centuries C.E.

END OF PART B

GO ON TO THE NEXT PAGE.

Part C
(Suggested planning and writing time—40 minutes)
Percent of Section II score—33 1/3

Directions: You are to answer the following question. You should spend 5 minutes organizing or outlining your essay. Write an essay that:

- Has a relevant thesis and supports that thesis with appropriate historical evidence.
- Addresses all parts of the question.
- Makes direct, relevant comparisons.
- Analyzes relevant reasons for similarities and/or differences.

3. Describe the progression and effects of the Industrial Revolution in either Japan OR Belgium, as compared to its progress and effects in surrounding nations. Be sure to address both similarities and differences in your analysis.

STOP

END OF EXAM

Completely darken bubbles with a No. 2 pencil. If you make a mistake, be sure to erase mark completely. Erase all stray marks.

1.

YOUR NAME: _____
(Print)
          Last   First   M.I.

SIGNATURE: _____ DATE: ____ / ____ / ____

HOME ADDRESS: _____
(Print)
                    Number and Street

_____
        City   State   Zip Code

PHONE NO.: _____

5. YOUR NAME

First 4 letters of last name				FIRST INIT	MID INIT
Ⓐ	Ⓐ	Ⓐ	Ⓐ	Ⓐ	Ⓐ
Ⓑ	Ⓑ	Ⓑ	Ⓑ	Ⓑ	Ⓑ
Ⓒ	Ⓒ	Ⓒ	Ⓒ	Ⓒ	Ⓒ
Ⓓ	Ⓓ	Ⓓ	Ⓓ	Ⓓ	Ⓓ
Ⓔ	Ⓔ	Ⓔ	Ⓔ	Ⓔ	Ⓔ
Ⓕ	Ⓕ	Ⓕ	Ⓕ	Ⓕ	Ⓕ
Ⓖ	Ⓖ	Ⓖ	Ⓖ	Ⓖ	Ⓖ
Ⓗ	Ⓗ	Ⓗ	Ⓗ	Ⓗ	Ⓗ
Ⓘ	Ⓘ	Ⓘ	Ⓘ	Ⓘ	Ⓘ
Ⓙ	Ⓙ	Ⓙ	Ⓙ	Ⓙ	Ⓙ
Ⓚ	Ⓚ	Ⓚ	Ⓚ	Ⓚ	Ⓚ
Ⓛ	Ⓛ	Ⓛ	Ⓛ	Ⓛ	Ⓛ
Ⓜ	Ⓜ	Ⓜ	Ⓜ	Ⓜ	Ⓜ
Ⓝ	Ⓝ	Ⓝ	Ⓝ	Ⓝ	Ⓝ
Ⓞ	Ⓞ	Ⓞ	Ⓞ	Ⓞ	Ⓞ
Ⓟ	Ⓟ	Ⓟ	Ⓟ	Ⓟ	Ⓟ
Ⓠ	Ⓠ	Ⓠ	Ⓠ	Ⓠ	Ⓠ
Ⓡ	Ⓡ	Ⓡ	Ⓡ	Ⓡ	Ⓡ
Ⓢ	Ⓢ	Ⓢ	Ⓢ	Ⓢ	Ⓢ
Ⓣ	Ⓣ	Ⓣ	Ⓣ	Ⓣ	Ⓣ
Ⓤ	Ⓤ	Ⓤ	Ⓤ	Ⓤ	Ⓤ
Ⓥ	Ⓥ	Ⓥ	Ⓥ	Ⓥ	Ⓥ
Ⓦ	Ⓦ	Ⓦ	Ⓦ	Ⓦ	Ⓦ
Ⓧ	Ⓧ	Ⓧ	Ⓧ	Ⓧ	Ⓧ
Ⓨ	Ⓨ	Ⓨ	Ⓨ	Ⓨ	Ⓨ
Ⓩ	Ⓩ	Ⓩ	Ⓩ	Ⓩ	Ⓩ

IMPORTANT: Please fill in these boxes exactly as shown on the back cover of your test book.

2. TEST FORM

_____

3. TEST CODE

4. REGISTRATION NUMBER

⓪	Ⓐ	Ⓙ	⓪	⓪	⓪	⓪	⓪	⓪	⓪	⓪	⓪
①	Ⓑ	Ⓚ	①	①	①	①	①	①	①	①	①
②	Ⓒ	Ⓛ	②	②	②	②	②	②	②	②	②
③	Ⓓ	Ⓜ	③	③	③	③	③	③	③	③	③
④	Ⓔ	Ⓝ	④	④	④	④	④	④	④	④	④
⑤	Ⓕ	Ⓞ	⑤	⑤	⑤	⑤	⑤	⑤	⑤	⑤	⑤
⑥	Ⓖ	Ⓟ	⑥	⑥	⑥	⑥	⑥	⑥	⑥	⑥	⑥
⑦	Ⓗ	Ⓠ	⑦	⑦	⑦	⑦	⑦	⑦	⑦	⑦	⑦
⑧	Ⓘ	Ⓡ	⑧	⑧	⑧	⑧	⑧	⑧	⑧	⑧	⑧
⑨			⑨	⑨	⑨	⑨	⑨	⑨	⑨	⑨	⑨

6. DATE OF BIRTH

Month		Day		Year	
◯ JAN					
◯ FEB	⓪	⓪	⓪	⓪	
◯ MAR	①	①	①	①	
◯ APR	②	②	②	②	
◯ MAY	③	③	③	③	
◯ JUN		④	④	④	
◯ JUL		⑤	⑤	⑤	
◯ AUG		⑥	⑥	⑥	
◯ SEP		⑦	⑦	⑦	
◯ OCT		⑧	⑧	⑧	
◯ NOV		⑨	⑨	⑨	
◯ DEC					

7. GENDER
◯ MALE
◯ FEMALE

1. Ⓐ Ⓑ Ⓒ Ⓓ
2. Ⓐ Ⓑ Ⓒ Ⓓ
3. Ⓐ Ⓑ Ⓒ Ⓓ
4. Ⓐ Ⓑ Ⓒ Ⓓ
5. Ⓐ Ⓑ Ⓒ Ⓓ
6. Ⓐ Ⓑ Ⓒ Ⓓ
7. Ⓐ Ⓑ Ⓒ Ⓓ
8. Ⓐ Ⓑ Ⓒ Ⓓ
9. Ⓐ Ⓑ Ⓒ Ⓓ
10. Ⓐ Ⓑ Ⓒ Ⓓ
11. Ⓐ Ⓑ Ⓒ Ⓓ
12. Ⓐ Ⓑ Ⓒ Ⓓ
13. Ⓐ Ⓑ Ⓒ Ⓓ
14. Ⓐ Ⓑ Ⓒ Ⓓ
15. Ⓐ Ⓑ Ⓒ Ⓓ
16. Ⓐ Ⓑ Ⓒ Ⓓ
17. Ⓐ Ⓑ Ⓒ Ⓓ
18. Ⓐ Ⓑ Ⓒ Ⓓ

19. Ⓐ Ⓑ Ⓒ Ⓓ
20. Ⓐ Ⓑ Ⓒ Ⓓ
21. Ⓐ Ⓑ Ⓒ Ⓓ
22. Ⓐ Ⓑ Ⓒ Ⓓ
23. Ⓐ Ⓑ Ⓒ Ⓓ
24. Ⓐ Ⓑ Ⓒ Ⓓ
25. Ⓐ Ⓑ Ⓒ Ⓓ
26. Ⓐ Ⓑ Ⓒ Ⓓ
27. Ⓐ Ⓑ Ⓒ Ⓓ
28. Ⓐ Ⓑ Ⓒ Ⓓ
29. Ⓐ Ⓑ Ⓒ Ⓓ
30. Ⓐ Ⓑ Ⓒ Ⓓ
31. Ⓐ Ⓑ Ⓒ Ⓓ
32. Ⓐ Ⓑ Ⓒ Ⓓ
33. Ⓐ Ⓑ Ⓒ Ⓓ
34. Ⓐ Ⓑ Ⓒ Ⓓ
35. Ⓐ Ⓑ Ⓒ Ⓓ
36. Ⓐ Ⓑ Ⓒ Ⓓ

37. Ⓐ Ⓑ Ⓒ Ⓓ
38. Ⓐ Ⓑ Ⓒ Ⓓ
39. Ⓐ Ⓑ Ⓒ Ⓓ
40. Ⓐ Ⓑ Ⓒ Ⓓ
41. Ⓐ Ⓑ Ⓒ Ⓓ
42. Ⓐ Ⓑ Ⓒ Ⓓ
43. Ⓐ Ⓑ Ⓒ Ⓓ
44. Ⓐ Ⓑ Ⓒ Ⓓ
45. Ⓐ Ⓑ Ⓒ Ⓓ
46. Ⓐ Ⓑ Ⓒ Ⓓ
47. Ⓐ Ⓑ Ⓒ Ⓓ
48. Ⓐ Ⓑ Ⓒ Ⓓ
49. Ⓐ Ⓑ Ⓒ Ⓓ
50. Ⓐ Ⓑ Ⓒ Ⓓ
51. Ⓐ Ⓑ Ⓒ Ⓓ
52. Ⓐ Ⓑ Ⓒ Ⓓ
53. Ⓐ Ⓑ Ⓒ Ⓓ
54. Ⓐ Ⓑ Ⓒ Ⓓ

55. Ⓐ Ⓑ Ⓒ Ⓓ
56. Ⓐ Ⓑ Ⓒ Ⓓ
57. Ⓐ Ⓑ Ⓒ Ⓓ
58. Ⓐ Ⓑ Ⓒ Ⓓ
59. Ⓐ Ⓑ Ⓒ Ⓓ
60. Ⓐ Ⓑ Ⓒ Ⓓ
61. Ⓐ Ⓑ Ⓒ Ⓓ
62. Ⓐ Ⓑ Ⓒ Ⓓ
63. Ⓐ Ⓑ Ⓒ Ⓓ
64. Ⓐ Ⓑ Ⓒ Ⓓ
65. Ⓐ Ⓑ Ⓒ Ⓓ
66. Ⓐ Ⓑ Ⓒ Ⓓ
67. Ⓐ Ⓑ Ⓒ Ⓓ
68. Ⓐ Ⓑ Ⓒ Ⓓ
69. Ⓐ Ⓑ Ⓒ Ⓓ
70. Ⓐ Ⓑ Ⓒ Ⓓ

Diagnostic Test
Answers and
Explanations

ANSWER KEY

1.	C	36.	C
2.	A	37.	A
3.	A	38.	B
4.	B	39.	C
5.	C	40.	A
6.	A	41.	D
7.	B	42.	B
8.	B	43.	A
9.	D	44.	B
10.	C	45.	C
11.	C	46.	D
12.	B	47.	A
13.	A	48.	A
14.	B	49.	B
15.	D	50.	C
16.	C	51.	D
17.	B	52.	B
18.	A	53.	C
19.	C	54.	D
20.	D	55.	B
21.	A	56.	B
22.	D	57.	C
23.	B	58.	C
24.	B	59.	D
25.	D	60.	A
26.	B	61.	A
27.	C	62.	C
28.	A	63.	B
29.	A	64.	C
30.	B	65.	D
31.	D	66.	D
32.	C	67.	A
33.	A	68.	D
34.	D	69.	B
35.	D	70.	B

EXPLANATIONS

1. **C**   The Sumerian civilization (A) rose in the southern part of Mesopotamia, between the Tigris and Euphrates River. The Egyptians (B) settled in the Nile River Valley. The Shang (D) rose in the Hwang Ho, or Yellow, River Valley. The Chavin of the Andes in what is today South America (C), like the Olmec who settled in modern-day Mexico, did not settle in a river valley.

2. **A**   Hinduism and Buddhism developed in India. Islam would not rise in the Middle East until the first half of 600 C.E. The earliest reference to Catholicism, a branch of Christianity, is found in Smyrna, an ancient city in modern-day Turkey.

3. **A**   Remember that you're looking for the one that *isn't* true. Early civilizations such as those in Mesopotamia (Sumer, Babylon), Egypt, China, and the Indus River Valley were all characterized by urban centers, growing populations, and highly developed writing systems. Caravan trade would come in time, as civilizations grew larger and began to form connections.

4. **B**   The Mayans were skilled astronomers and appear to have constructed their cities at Palenque, Tikal, and elsewhere based on astronomical phenomena, such as the sun's movement across the sky at the solstices. During the time of the Maya, the threat of invaders was always land-based, so cross off (A). Trade was not a major concern, so cross off (C). Above all else, though, the Mayans' major architectural projects were highly planned, nothing haphazard about it, so cross off (D).

5. **C**   China controlled the Silk Roads.

6. **A**   The Roman Empire exported gold, silver, and olive oil, though the oil wasn't so popular in India. India exported silk and cotton, along with indigo and spices such as pepper.

7. **B**   The Hebrews were the first monotheistic faith. Christianity began as an offshoot. Later, Islam grew in a place with many polytheistic faiths. The Hebrews had a state off and on, and so did not have a large, centralized government (A). They did not have a strong military tradition (the Trojans did) (C). Gender roles were strict in Hebrew society, with women subservient to men (D).

8. **B**   Greece's pursuit of knowledge and art created the foundation of Western culture, though it wasn't a straight road. During the Renaissance, a new interest in the knowledge that the Greeks acquired hundreds of years prior brought the scientific and artistic curiosity of the Greeks back to public interest. The Greeks had their own religion, so they didn't incorporate Persian gods (A). The unique thing about Greeks was that they concentrated on this life, instead of the afterlife like its contemporary civilizations (China and India) did (C). The Greeks relied on slaves for labor, though (D).

9. **D** Think about who'd be building buildings (since you need columns for keeping things standing), and you'd want to get rid of the Sumerians (C), since that'd be a bit out of era. Then think of the architecture of specific places today. These columns would be at home in the West, and the Greeks are the foundation for Western civilization, so you'd want to go with them. The architecture in Chinese (A) and Persian (B) societies looks different, so use Process of Elimination (POE) to cut those guys out.

10. **C** The name "Maurya" should tip you off that Ashoka was Indian (remember the Maurya and Gupta dynasties?), so get rid of Daoism (B), since you should associate it with China, and Christianity (D) (which didn't exist during Ashoka's time anyway). Ashoka is famous as a great conqueror who became so remorseful after his bloody conquest of a great civilization (Kalinga), he converted to Buddhism.

11. **C** The Lydians (ca. 1200–546 B.C.E.) introduced coined money, moving trade past the barter system and allowing for standardized pricing and for saving (and, eventually, banking) money. While the Zoroastrian religion is dualistic, this does not relate to the Lydians or their beliefs, so cross off (A). Written alphabets, likewise, are associated with the Phoenicians, but it was the Phoenicians who invented the first one, not the Lydians, so cross off (B). Finally, while the Aryan conquest did lay some of the foundations for the modern Indian state, this is not related to the Lydians, who lived in Anatolia, or modern-day Turkey, so cross off (D).

12. **B** The Justinian Code, or the Corpus Juris Civilis, was issued from 529 to 534 C.E. by Justinian I, and included references to the writing of many Roman jurists and legal scholars. By that time, the Western Roman Empire and the legal systems that had governed it, had been fragmented by war and tribal conquest for a century. Cross off (A) because Constantine made Christianity the state religion two centuries prior to Justinian's rule, and the Western Roman Empire had crumbled a century before Justinian's rule. Cross off (C) because Justinian just didn't do that. Cross off (D) because, while most official business was done in Latin, even in the Eastern Roman Empire, Justinian had nothing to do with that trend, which long predated his rule.

13. **A** The Han and Gupta Dynasties both suffered from conflict with invading nomads—the Han with the Xiong-nu, who invaded as Han government was collapsing, and with the Gupta it was the White Huns, who were expelled in a costly campaign during the dynasty's s waning decades. While Han China suffered from overcrowding, this was not a significant problem for the Gupta, so cross out (B). Similarly, government corruption afflicted the Han Dynasty, but the Gupta did not have this as a major challenge, so cross out (D). The Han and the Gupta both had tax problems— the Han with tax collection among peasants, and the Gupta with insufficient taxes to support military defense—but (C) correctly describes neither dynasty (but explains one cause of the Western Roman Empire's decline around the same time), so cross off (C).

14.   **B**   The countries in Africa, Europe, and Asia through which the Silk Road traveled have always used a variety of different languages, and even languages common to some areas were not shared by others. Travel along the Silk Road did, however, contribute to the spread of diseases, such as the bubonic plague, as well as the spread of religious ideas, including Islam and Buddhism, and the transmission of artistic influences, creating styles such as the Greco-Buddhist style of painting—so cross out (A), (C), and (D).

15.   **D**   Just as with trade routes throughout history, the routes of the post-classical period acted as highways of information. Paper, for example, developed in China, spread to the Muslim troops fighting on China's western border, and then dispersed to Europeans through trade and religious wars. The trade routes prove to also transport the Black Death (bubonic plague) to Europe.

16.   **C**   In the Abbasid period, Muslim invaders came in touch with the Indian system of numbers, transporting it throughout the world via scholars and merchants. Scholars were also committed to recovering and preserving the learning of the ancient civilizations in the Middle East and Mediterranean they interacted with. Key tomes of Greek learning concerning medicine, algebra, geometry, astronomy, anatomy, and ethics were saved, recopied in Arabic, and dispersed throughout the empire. This is an "except" question, so (C) is correct because the Muslims never invaded Japan and thus Japanese philosophy would not have been incorporated.

17.   **B**   The Five Pillars of Islam are (1) the declaration of faith and trust (shahada), which states "I bear witness that there is no other god but Allah and Muhammad is His messenger," (2) prayer (salat) five times a day, (3) alms-giving (zakat) for those who are financially able, (4) fasting (sawm), especially during the month of Ramadan, and (5) a pilgrimage to Mecca (hajj) at least once in the believer's life.

18.   **A**   Ummah is an Arabic word meaning "nation" or "community," distinct from sha'b, which means a nation based on common ancestry or geography. The ummah were thus greater than just the clans from which Muslims came from. It is commonly used to refer to the collective community of all Muslims.

19.   **C**   Completed towards the end of Muslim rule of Spain by Yusuf I (1333–1353) and Muhammad V, Sultan of Granada (1353–1391), the Alhambra is a reflection of the culture of the last centuries of the Moorish rule of Al Andalus, reduced to the Nasrid Emirate of Granada. The Alhambra is a testament to Moorish culture in Spain and the skills of Muslim, Jewish, and Christian artisans, craftsmen, and builders of their era.

20.   **D**   The Abbasid period introduced the harem and the veiling of women to the Islamic Middle East. Although women had been kept in seclusion since ancient times, the Abbasid caliphs began the harem, and kept their wives and concubines in forbidden quarters. It is important to remember, though, that the Islamic law that Muslim life was built upon did not allow for women's rights to be completely eroded, in comparison to the rights of women in Asia, Europe, and other parts of the Middle East. This same law, however, allowed for men to keep no more than four wives. So the correct answer is (D) since all of the possible answer choices are true.

21. **A** The map shows the Arabian peninsula. If you look closely, you'll see a handful of dates (630, 632, 633, and so on). These are the years that the Islamic Empire began to expand. The Roman and Sassanid Persian Empires had been fighting for centuries (92 B.C.E. to 627 C.E.) by the time of Muhammad. Islamic armies found both these opponents surprisingly weak and relatively easily took control and spread Islam to these regions. The Western Roman Empire refers to the Western half of the former Roman Empire, which quickly declined after the split in 395 C.E., after the death of Theodosius I. Just remember—by the seventh century (the time of Muhammad), the Western Roman Empire was gone, and the Byzantine (also referred to as the Eastern Roman Empire) and the Sassanid were just about on their way out.

22. **D** The castles built by William the Conqueror and his successors in the 11th and 12th centuries throughout Normandy and coastal England show the influence of Muslim techniques of building fortifications. Persian and Arabic words, games such as chess (which came initially from India), chivalric ideals, and foods such as dates, coffee, and yogurt also made their way into popular culture.

23. **B** In contrast to the Roman Catholic emperors of the West, who regarded the pope as the leader of Byzantium's church, secular rulers headed the church (which, remember, was Orthodox). For centuries the two churches managed to tolerate each other, but in time the differences became too great. They disagreed over the sacrament of communion, whether priests should be allowed to marry, and the use of local languages in church. They even were at odds regarding the nature of God, specifically God as a trinity, and they disagreed over the placement of icons during worship. In 1054 C.E., unable to reconcile their differences, the pope excommunicated the patriarch of Constantinople, who did the same to the pope. From this point forward, Orthodoxy influenced the East and Roman Catholicism influenced the West. Remember that the East was more of a secular empire with an official church religion; the West was more of a religious empire with subservient political units.

24. **B** This is the Courtyard of the Lions at the Alhambra palace in Granada, Spain. Granada was under Moorish rule, and this is a prime example of Muslim architecture brought into a heavily Catholic area by conquest. The Roman emperor was not the one who commissioned its creation, so cross off (A). The Alhambra still stands today (which is why we have a picture) and was thus not lost to invaders, so cross off (C). And while Spain was the site of considerable religious conflict in the 15th century, the architecture of this palace is not representative of that conflict in any way, so cross off (D).

25. **D** Islam spread to the Somali Coast by the seventh century, while it was still expanding in the Arabian Peninsula, so cross off (B) and (C). Islam moved into Central Asia during the Abbasid Dynasty, which began in the eighth century, but did not reach Southeast Asia until the eleventh century, so cross off (A) and pick (D). Islam also reached the Iberian Peninsula in the eighth century.

26. **B** The Kingdom of Cuzco was a small city state that expanded by conquest under Pachacuti, a military leader known as "The Earth-shaker." The Incans were never conquered by the Aztecs, so cross off (A). The Incans were not a maritime people, so cross off (C). The Incan ruler was also not popularly elected at any point in their history, so cross off (D).

27. **C** In the fourteenth century, Ming rulers adopted Neoconfucianism, with its emphasis on filial piety, the maintenance of proper roles, and loyalty to one's superiors, in order to improve a weak and ineffective bureaucracy. While Jesuit missionaries did come to China, Catholicism never gained state sponsorship, so cross off (B). While (A) may have been distracting, the Ming dynasty gained control from Mongol invaders, whose Yuan dynasty had crumbled, so the Ming were under no pressure to adopt Islam, which was not even the official faith under the Yuan dynasty—so cross off (A). Taoism, (D), might also have been distracting, but the Ming were not particularly isolationist, so cross that off, too.

28. **A** Both the Muscovite Russians and the Ottoman Turks were able to exert control over a wide range of territory because those territories had previously been unified by Mongol conquerors. When the khanates fell, the Muscovites and the Ottomans rose to claim their lands. Schisms in Christianity and Islam played no role in this, so cross off (B). Ottoman Turks benefited quite a lot from Afro-European trade, sitting at the nexus of that trade, so cross off (C). The Muscovites and Ottomans did not limit their use of naval technology to trade or conquest in either case, so cross off (D).

29. **A** By percent, the epidemics that followed Europeans' first contact with Mesoamerican natives resulted in a larger population decline than the Black Death in Europe or the global flu pandemic in the early twentieth century. Unlike the Black Death, this did not result in an increase in wages for surviving workers—most of the Mesoamerican populations affected were subjugated or enslaved by their European conquerors. So cross off (B). Nor did this deter European interest in Mesoamerica: the British who settled North America did so largely because they had been shut out of Mesoamerica by the Spaniards' early and persistent presence, so cross off (C). Finally, this did not cause the decline of African slavery in the region but rather prompted its introduction. As the native workforce had died, import of African slaves became the preferred solution, much as it soon would in North America, so cross off (D).

30. **B** While there were other products, sugar was the big moneymaker, particularly for Europe's colonies in the Caribbean—so cross off (A) as (B) starts to look good. This was a crop, though, that required tremendous effort and labor—in this case, slave labor—to produce (and had the highest mortality rate of any major crop in the Atlantic), so cross off (C) and (D).

31. **D** The introduction of the potato was a major factor in providing better sustenance to Northern Europeans and became an integral part of their diet. This is why the Irish Potato Famine a few centuries later was so devastating. Religious civil war in England would not end until the late seventeenth century, so cross off (A). Expulsion of the Moors from Spain had no reason to influence population numbers in Northern Europe, as the Moors were driven south into North Africa, so cross off (B). The Crusades, too, were over by the fourteenth century, meaning they could have no direct influence on population numbers during this period, so cross off (C).

32. **C** The Songhai Empire was in sub-Saharan West Africa—cross off (A) and (B). Angola, not the Songhai, was involved with the Portuguese slave trade, so cross off (D).

33. **A** It's as simple as that. He wanted to conquer as much territory as possible, so he built a powerful military. He was Muslim and a man of faith, but his motives were not primarily religious, so cross off (B) and (C). Furthermore, the Taj Mahal wouldn't be built until four generations later by Babur's great-great-great-grandson Shah Jahan, so (D) isn't right, either.

34. **D** It was not uncommon to see slave dwellings built in this distinctly African style in the American South. The broad, over-sized roof offered significant protection from the sun, and the grasses on the roof are typical of African grasslands and of much of the North American coastal South. This would not be urban housing (too space-inefficient), and it bears none of the ornate arches of Muslim architecture, so cross off (A). Western Europe doesn't get enough sun to make roofs like this necessary, so cross off (B). And a home like this in Southeast Asia would be terrible because of regular flooding seasons, so cross off (C).

35. **D** There were two Mamluk Sultanates, one headquartered in Delhi and the other headquartered in Cairo. The Mamluks ruled this territory from 1250 to 1517. The Mamluk Sultanates were chunks of the former Abbasid Empire, so that's not it, and cross off (B). The Ottoman Empire was to the northeast, though it did battle with the Mamluk Sultanate over certain territories, so cross off (A). Finally, Cordoba is in Spain, so cross (C) off, too.

36. **C** While diseases and crops went in both directions, this is a true statement, so choice (C) is correct. It is also true that European germs did significantly more damage to America than American diseases did to Europe. Gold flowed from America to Spain, not really the other way around, so cross off (A)—though the Spanish and others suffered mightily from a previously unknown American disease called syphilis! There was no trade of Native American slaves into Africa: European labor demands in South and Central America meant exporting slaves would be senseless and counterintuitive. Also, the Africans got their guns from the Europeans and were not themselves gun producers. So cross off (B). Finally, horses did not exist in the Americas prior to their introduction by the Spanish, so cross (D) off, too.

37. **A** China sold more than it bought, so it held a lot of (silver) money. What it didn't hold were silver-producing South American colonies, so cross off (B). Or, for that matter, opium to sell to the British—quite the other way around. The Opium Wars of the nineteenth century were about China's buying British opium, so cross off (C). Finally, Hong Kong became a British territory as a result of the First Opium War, long after the trade expansion the question asks about, and was not considered "leased" from the Chinese until 1898, so cross off (D).

38. **B** The quote is from the encyclopedia of Aztec culture written by Spanish missionary Bernardino de Sahagún in the mid-sixteenth century. Remember that weaving is an essential part of Native American culture. Though all civilizations had weavers, the Spanish name mentioned and the era should clue you in that you're looking for places that Spain specifically interacted with at the time.

39.   C   Remember that though China will spread its culture to Korea, Japan, and Vietnam in the postcolonial period, Vietnam is the least assimilated of these groups. One of the greatest differences was how China and Vietnam treated their women, with Vietnamese women given much more freedom (such as the opportunity to educate themselves and become poets). In the poem, written by Ho Xuan Huong, the narrator mocks her male suitors.

40.   A   Slavery was a rather widespread institution, including in India. When a group was conquered, those left behind were very often brought into slavery, though many societies had a formal, structured way for slaves to attain their freedom. Slavery wasn't what we know the institution to be from the United States, usually. In many parts of the world, slaves could become powerful. In China, for example, during the Mongol Yuan dynasty (1271–1368), slaves could have their own slaves.

41.   D   The rise of naval trade in the second part of the fifteenth century and throughout the sixteenth century created a new, global economy, with Spain and Portugal as the prominent controlling powers in the fifteenth century, and England, France, and Holland jumping in when the British defeat the Spanish Armada in 1588. This didn't cover all the world economy, though. Chinese and Japanese coastal waters boasted ships from throughout Asia, and Muslim merchants were essential for trade with Africa, especially in the east of the continent.

42.   B   The differences between the Latin American and North American colonies are mostly found in what the goals of these territories were. In both places, the search for gold and wealth drove initial discoveries, but as time went on, North American colonies, especially those of England, became places where those looking for a fresh start turned to for salvation. Native American populations were driven west. New crops—especially the potato, sweet potato, tomato, and tobacco—were brought into European life.

43.   A   Industrialization didn't reach either Japan or Russia until the late nineteenth century (D). Japan's industrialization relied on textile mills, while Russia's was widely tied to the steel industry (C). Japan adopted many Western practices, but Russia did not (B). Russia abolished serfdom in 1861, freeing its workforce for other labors, an essential part of industrialization. Japan ended feudalism during the Meiji Restoration (1868) and began adopting Western culture in earnest.

44.   B   In general, as factories became larger parts of the economy, work moved out of the homes, taking work away from women who couldn't follow the employment they had at home to the factories. Japanese, and all women, kept their traditional roles (A). Women couldn't work outside the home, really, so none really joined the medical profession (C). Though banking reform was an important part of Russia's industrialization, women didn't move into the profession (D).

45.   C   Railroads were an essential part of the Industrial Revolution, important for the moving of goods. Russia's trans-Siberian railroad and the United States' transcontinental railroad were prime examples. Russians produced steel (B), unions were initially unique to the West during the industrialization process (A), and suffrage (voting) rights will come a bit later (D).

46. **D** All these elements are important in industrializing countries, but Japan had most of these elements—it developed an efficient banking system (A), was supported (driven, really, in Japan's case) by the government (B), and had freed its lower class from feudalism and so had access to a proper labor pool (C). It lacked access to natural resources, though. This drove Japan's expansionist policies in this era.

47. **A** Major changes in the role of women are out of era, so (A) has to be your answer. The flow of the causes of industrialization in Great Britain related to the agricultural improvements that occurred, such as crop rotation, use of fertilizer, and scientific breeding of animals (B), which led to the enclosure movement (C) as landowners wanted to restrict access to valuable land. Landless laborers moved to the cities and searched for work elsewhere. The steam engine (D) made transportation from factories to markets much easier.

48. **A** Muhammad Ali, an officer in the Ottoman Empire's military during Napoleon's invasion of Egypt, was the driving force behind industrialization in the country. He wanted to distance Egypt from the Empire, and so began westernizing Egypt. He forced peasants to farm cotton, indigo, and other goods the Europeans wanted in order to gain revenue to fund new industries, so (B) doesn't work. Great Britain actually forced Ali to reduce tariffs when he tried to impose protective taxes to stimulate growth in the Egyptian markets, making Egypt MORE reliant on the West (C). Egyptian efforts weren't entirely successful, so the technological gap wasn't really narrowed (D).

49. **B** Western Europeans made it to Hawaii in the eighteenth century. About half of Hawaii's native population fell to diseases such as syphilis and tuberculosis. The Chinese and Japanese began arriving in the next century to fill the labor demands. Africans were not brought as slaves (A), the Jesuits went to China but not Hawaii (C), and Jewish immigrants fleeing pogroms went elsewhere (Latin America, North America) (D).

50. **C** Since sometimes individuals left the family home to seek their fortune in the cities, the structure of the family changed. The foods brought back through the Columbian trade, most significantly the potato and sweet potato, stabilized food sources throughout the rest of the world, so not as many people died (A). Once people moved to the cities (D), the tendency was to make smaller families (B) since you didn't have to have so many kids to work the farm.

51. **D** The Opium Wars were fought so England could trade the highly profitable opium the Chinese were addicted to within China. The Qing dynasty banned the use of opium after addiction skyrocketed. England, however, wanted a product to counterbalance the silver it was pouring into China for goods such as tea and silk.

52. **B** Great Britain actually led the charge to end the slave trade, so (A) and (D) can't work. African kings, especially of coastal kingdoms, tended to take other Africans from the interior of the country and sell them into slavery (C). The slave trade and serfdom both ended in the 1860s.

53.   C   Brazil (A) can be eliminated because the early nineteenth century was a period beset by rebellions and wars that resulted in an almost isolationist foreign policy. Remember that Egypt and Russia actively looked to import Western technologies, so cross off (B) and (D). Choice (C), Japan is the correct answer because it was right at that time--the second half the nineteenth century—that Japan began interactions with Europe.

54.   D   England's rise as a maritime power predated the Industrial Revolution, so cross off (C). Rubber and steel would come later, so cross off (A) and (B). All of the technologies necessary to create the first integrated textile mills came together in Britain in the mid- to late-seventeenth century, spurring Britain's first Industrial Revolution.

55.   B   Not much changed—the poor stayed poor and at the bottom of the social food chain, while the rich and powerful generally stayed rich and powerful, as long as they backed the winning side. Entire populations were not forcibly converted to Roman Catholicism—not least because the overwhelming majority of people in these countries were already Roman Catholic. So cross off (A). While many Latin American countries did abolish slavery in this period, that by no means established racial equality, so cross off (C)—half right is still all wrong! Latin America had its Industrial Revolution beginning in the late 1800s, but this was at best an indirect result of the wars for independence, so cross off (D) in favor of (B).

56.   B   This quotation from Rudyard Kipling's *The White Man's Burden* (1899) exhorts American imperialists in the Pacific to care for the less capable, less civilized ("half devil and half child") peoples they had conquered ("serve your captives' need"). Social Darwinism was the idea that some people were inferior (and had inferior life outcomes) because they were genetically inferior, and that played into justifications for imperial conquest. The conquest of South America, European explorers in Canada, and the Crusades are all the wrong time period, so cross off (A), (C), and (D).

57.   C   Remember that you're looking for the one that isn't true. Read carefully—if this had talked about the League of Nations, it would be right on target, but the United States government did not show the same resistance to the United Nations after World War II. Adolf Hitler resented the Weimar government greatly for its inability to restore Germany's position and territorial interests after the harsh penalties imposed on Germany in the Treaty of Versailles, leading to his attempt to overthrow the Weimar government in 1923's unsuccessful Beer Hall Putsch. (A) is true, so cross it off. It also led to his eventual reconquest of onetime German territories, such as the Rhineland, stripped away by the treaty. (B) is true, so cross it off. Finally, the May Fourth Movement was an anti-imperialist movement in China begun in response to the Treaty of Versailles's granting the disputed province of Shandong to the Japanese, rather than the Chinese, from whom the Germans had taken it. (D) is true, so cross it off.

58. C   Village-based industrialization was the key to Chairman Mao's vision of a modern communist state in China—this was his Great Leap Forward. China was not a part of the Space Race, so cross off (A). While Chinese communism was indeed anti-religious, this was not the purpose of the Great Leap Forward, so cross off (D). And China achieved a highly effective civil service organization centuries before Mao, so cross off (B).

59. D   Think about it this way: If people are leaving rural areas, where are they going? Thanks to industrialization, people had more incentive to move to cities, and cities had increasing capacity to support them, so urban population growth reached staggering proportions in twentieth-century Latin America. Over a long enough period, many factors lead to wage inflation, but a sharp population influx initially depresses wages because workers are easy to come by, so cross off (C). Health care standards have, on balance, risen considerably as better technology enabled better care, so cross off (B). And (A) is mismatched to the time period—Latin American countries ended slavery at various points throughout the nineteenth century, so cross that off, too.

60. A   The primary reason for massive labor migrations in economically developed countries in the twentieth century was the opportunity created by falling birth rates that often accompany economic development. It wasn't that there were fewer workers because they were dying—so cross off (B)—it's that, relatively speaking, fewer workers were being born. Neither rural crime and unrest nor workers' strikes were significant factors in these migrations, so cross off (C) and (D). Note, this also isn't a rural vs. urban question, so (B) and (C) aren't directly relevant, another reason to cross them off.

61. A   This quotation comes from the United Nations' 1979 Convention on the Elimination of All Forms of Discrimination against Women. NATO would not have produced this document, as it was a military alliance, so cross off (B). The document also lacks the overtly communist language that would be expected from the Soviet Union or Maoist China, so cross off (C) and (D). Instead, this convention is characteristic of the human rights-oriented approach taken by the U.N. to global inequalities.

62. C   The common factor here is the philosophy of passive resistance and nonviolent protest advocated by Mahatma Gandhi. None of the three activists mentioned in the question ever self-immolated (burned themselves to death), so cross off (A)—Thich Quang Duc self-immolated in Saigon in 1963 to protest the Vietnam War. "Protest" and "Mother Teresa" don't go together at all, so cross off (B). Finally, Shaka kaSenzangakhona, better known as Shaka Zulu, was a brutal military leader of the Zulu, with political philosophies very unlike those of Gandhi, King, Mandela, or Suu Kyi, so cross off (D).

63. B   The common currency and forum for setting compatible economic policies were intended to improve economic cooperation and trade among European states. Its founders' motives were not as antagonistic as (D), so cross that off. The point was improving trade, not mimicking the United States, so cross off (C). Finally, this was not about guarding against Soviet takeover—this is more nearly a description of NATO (though not a perfect one), so cross off (A).

64. C   Student protests and social unrest were a worldwide epidemic in the 1960s. Israel, Iran, and Switzerland all experienced such movements, so cross off (A), (B), and (D).

65.	D	European colonizers drew territorial boundaries arbitrarily, without regard for the populations living on the land they divided. This meant warring tribes and ethnic groups were sometimes thrown together as other tribal and ethnic groups found their lands divided. Apartheid did not spread, so cross off (A). While some former rulers who had collaborated with colonial governments attempted to reassert their power, this was a limited phenomenon and was not a major cause in political instability in sub-Saharan Africa, so cross off (B). The African National Congress is not an organization of African nations, but rather the ruling political party of South Africa, so cross off (C).

66.	D	These are the leaders of anti-colonial independence movements in (North) Vietnam, Kenya, and Ghana, respectively. Cross off Choice (A) because Ngo Dinh Diem was no anti-colonialist but a collaborator with the French and American agendas in Vietnam. Cross off Choice (B) because Edmund Andros was a British colonial governor forced to flee from America at the end of the seventeenth century. Cross off Choice (C) because the Marquess Dalhousie was Governor-General of the East India Company, the colonial authority in British India.

67.	A	The test will be very careful and conservative with a question this modern, but (A) offers a safe, accurate statement: Advances in transportation and communication (such as the Internet!) have accelerated how often and how involved interactions among countries have become. Interethnic conflict is still very much a problem, particularly in Africa but elsewhere as well, despite the efforts of the United Nations, so cross off (B). (C) is exactly the kind of politically charged statement that is unlikely to be a right answer, but while global terrorism and the worldwide economic downturn have both been major issues in the early twenty-first century, they are not linked in this way, so cross off (C). Finally, though science and secularism did spread into the dawn of the twenty-first century, the major world religions have seen no serious decline in adherents, so cross off (D).

68.	D	Basic idea: If two countries have nukes, then neither will really want to go to war with the other, since starting a war means both will end up dead. Mutually assured destruction, then, was the best deterrent to nuclear war. To avoid going to war with each other directly, the U.S.S.R. and United States engaged in proxy wars, such as in Korea or Vietnam, in which each backed a side but the nations were not themselves in conflict. Mutually assured destruction didn't have anything to do with the Berlin Wall, the environment, or banking, so cross off Choices (A), (B), and (C).

69.	B	The globalization of American culture in the twentieth century was such a powerful and pervasive force that Moscow, Lenin's capital after 1918, was the first city in the former Soviet Union to get a McDonalds in 1990. The image shows Lenin in a supportive stance, so cross off (A), even if (A) describes how Lenin might really have felt. Cross off (C) because egalitarianism was not really the chief concern here. Finally, American advertising in the 1950s would not show Lenin approving of something as all-American as McDonald's, so cross off (D).

70.	B	During the Cold War, Latin America experienced a number of communist and socialist movements, some of which succeeded in seizing power (Cuba, anyone?), and the Soviet Union and United States backed opposite sides in a number of these conflicts (Nicaragua, anyone?). Those governments were not particularly democracies with burgeoning civil involvement—some were brutal military dictatorships, so cross off (D). While there is oil in South America, O.P.E.C.'s embargo on oil to the United States was not primarily related to the Cold War, so cross (A) off, too. But South America was very much in the mix, so cross off (C).

ESSAYS

Part A

BASIC CORE (competence) (0–7 points)

1. Has acceptable thesis (1 point)

- The thesis must appear at the beginning, in the intro, or at the end, in the conclusion, of the essay
- The thesis can be found in multiple sentences throughout the essay. The thesis must refer to the unique and similar causes in both Egypt and India for nationalism
- A thesis that is split among multiple paragraphs is unacceptable
- Don't just restate the prompt; that doesn't count for this point
- The thesis CANNOT count for any other points

2. Understands the basic meaning of the documents (1 point)

(May misinterpret one document)

- Make sure to mention all 7 documents
- Demonstrate the basic meaning of at least 6 of the documents
- Don't just repeat what's in the document. Give the document context—who is saying it and why

3. Supports thesis with appropriate evidence from all or all but one document (2 points)

For 2 points, evidence must be drawn from 6 of the 7 documents and address the question

For 1 point, evidence must be drawn from 5 of the 7 documents and address the question

4. Analyzes point of view in at least two documents (1 point)

Remember that POV means who the particular person is, why he/she may have that particular POV.

Give more analysis than just who the person is—explain who he/she is speaking to (his/her audience), the tone, the context, and how all those elements may come together to explain *why* the author is writing this document

5. Analyzes documents by grouping them in two or three ways, depending on question (1 point)

- Group in at least two ways. Examples: pro-nationalist and anti-nationalist, by religious group, by social group
- Noting the Indian and the Egyptian documents does NOT count as a grouping, but noting nationalist Egyptian and anti-nationalism Egyptian documents, and the same for the Indian documents *is* acceptable

6. Identifies and explains the need for one type of appropriate additional document or source (1 point)

- Explain how this extra document could contribute to the analysis as a whole
- Examples:
    - Egyptian women's POV
    - British officials
    - Anti-nationalist Egyptian or Indian advocates

Subtotal—7 points

EXPANDED CORE (excellence) (0–2 points)

Expands beyond the basic core of 0–7 points. You can't get these points unless you hit all of the seven points above.

Examples

- Has a clear, analytical, and comprehensive thesis
- Show careful and insightful analysis of the documents
    - Put the documents in historical context
    - Analyze all 7 documents
- Use the documents persuasively as evidence
- Analyze the point of view of most or all of the documents
    - Think about the author's background, intended audience, or the historical context
- Analyze the documents in additional ways—grouping, comparisons
    - Include groups beyond the two required
    - Contribute additional analysis of subgroups within a larger grouping
- Bring in relevant "outside" historical content
- Explain, don't just identify, why additional types of document(s) are needed
    - Identify more than one kind of document that could give better context
    - Give a sophisticated explanation of why the addition is necessary
    - Mentions of why the additional documents are necessary are woven throughout the essays and part of the larger analysis
- Write a clear and comprehensive conclusion that brings the argument into a meaningful perspective

Subtotal—2 points

TOTAL—9 points

Part B

This essay asks you to explain the **continuities and changes over time** that Africa's relationship with Europe underwent between the 1400s and 1800s. A great way to tackle the Change and Continuity over Time essay prompts is to describe how the region in question was in the beginning of the period the prompt states, give some big reasons for why changes occurred, and then state what was the end result of those changes at the end of the time period given, while taking care to mention what may have remained the same.

For instance, regarding this prompt, you will want to start with how 1450 witnessed the tapering off of the Crusades, which had targeted North Africa, and how the primary interest Europe had with Africa was its trade connections. Trade in salt, slaves, ivory, and gold, flowed upwards from sub-Saharan Africa, through the Saharan trade routes in kingdoms like Mali or Songhay, to North African ports where it was picked up by Italian merchants and sent off through them towards Europe. The only European nation with a great interest in Africa was Portugal, and the Portuguese were interested in Africa not only for trade, but also for bases for their voyages of discovery.

Now you should give some examples of causes of changes that caused the region in question to change, explaining how these causes affected change and what their immediate results were. One example would be the voyages undertaken in the Age of Discovery, when the Portuguese, following their eastern approach, started sailing around the coast of Africa in their attempt to reach the Indies. Portuguese ports dotted the coasts of Africa along the route to India and, through these, direct contact and trading began to take off in earnest. Not to be outdone, the Dutch as well set up their Cape Colony in South Africa as a base for their own voyages to the East Indies.

Another pertinent, and important, vehicle for change would thus be the trade that opened up from these ports. By establishing their network of ports on the coasts of Africa, the Portuguese had effectively cut out the Muslim middlemen, who were at that point being sponsored by the anti-European Ottomans, from their trade routes into Europe. The trade that flowed through these ports ended up linking Africa to the triangular trade system in the Atlantic, and certainly helped to finance the technological developments that were underway in Europe. Through such trade came contact between cultures. Christian missionaries arrived in Africa, converting those who would listen. The kingdom of the Congo was indeed converted to Catholicism by Portuguese missionaries and would remain in Portugal's orbit for centuries. While such penetration was limited to the coasts, there was certainly more interaction than there was before.

Finally, a good essay would continue with discussing the impact of Enlightenment thought and the Scientific Revolution on Europe's relations with Africa. Remember that Africa's hostile climate, difficult topography, and numerous natives ensured that European attempts at going deeper into the continent were frustrated, and often not judged worthy of the costs. But the Enlightenment's emphasis on human rights and the eventual ban of the Slave Trade that the British implemented in 1807 started reducing commercial ties to Africa in earnest, as routes to the East mitigated Africa's importance as a stopping point and New World production had supplanted Africa's contribution to global trade networks. But the result of the Scientific Revolution was the Industrial Revolution, and Europe, stripped of its New World colonies through their successful independence movements, now desired the raw materials and markets available in unexplored, and unclaimed, Africa. These new medicines, new weapons, and determined explorers allowed Europe to flesh out the "dark continent" and open it up fully once, and for all.

The end result of all this was that by the end of the 1800s, Africa had been completely dominated by European powers, with the exceptions of the countries of Liberia, a land settled by freed American slaves, and Ethiopia, which had defeated Italy's attempt at conquering the territory in the Battle of Adowa in 1896. Europeans, using machine guns and quinine, literally carved up the entire continent between seven colonial powers—Portugal, Great Britain, France, Germany, Italy, Spain, and Belgium—in the Berlin Conference in 1884. What was once a relationship that was rather distant and not well-integrated turned into a scenario in which Europeans completely dominated the entire continent.

Part C

Remember that this essay asks you to **compare and contrast** either Japan or Belgium with its surrounding nations, so make sure you choose just one of these countries to do a comparison with its neighbors.

Let's start with Belgium. Belgium industrialized rather soon after the United Kingdom's monopoly on industrial technologies lifted. Indeed, Belgium itself did not even become formally independent from the Netherlands until 1839, well into the period of the first Industrial Revolution. As such, it started industrializing sooner than nearby, larger, stronger European powers like Austria or Russia, but was limited by its rather small size, as the UK, France, and Prussia (Germany) would come to have much greater industrial, and therefore military power. To try to ensure its place among leading nations, Belgium also joined in the Scramble for Africa, participating in the Berlin Conference of 1884, in which its king, Leopold II, managed to acquire the Congo for himself as his own domain. Leopold's administration of the Congo was so abhorrent and poor, however, that the Belgian parliament in 1908 took direct control of the land and placed it back under direct governmental authority. Nevertheless, despite having such a sizeable colony, Belgium still was too small to be a true force in European affairs, and in both World War I and II, the country was overrun by Germany, and defended by the United Kingdom and France.

Now, onto Japan. On account of the closed-door policies of the Tokugawa Shogunate, Japan had remained quite unconnected to the world at large, having only very minimal contact with the Dutch. As such, the Japanese had little contact with the industrializing west, eagerly assimilating whatever knowledge they could from the single Dutch ship permitted per year. All that changed when Commodore Perry arrived in 1853, and forced the Tokugawa government to open itself to foreign influence with the Treaty of Kanagawa, signed in 1854. From this point, the Tokugawa government committed itself to the odious "unequal treaties" similarly imposed upon China by the British and French and United States after its defeat in the Opium Wars. Rather than become another China, however, forward-thinking Japanese daimyo saw that the key to retaining Japan's independence would be to forcibly modernize and be strong enough to achieve parity with the West. Thus, the Meiji Restoration occurred in 1868, in which the Tokugawa Shogunate was abolished, and the Meiji emperor was given back executive powers. Under his rule, Japan embraced Western technologies and practices, bringing in foreign experts to help modernize the country. The government invested in factories and railroads, and Japan industrialized rather quickly. An excellent essay will mention that unlike China, which sputtered in its attempts at modernizing, the Japanese central government put down rebellions sparked in reaction to the quickening pace of modernization—rebellions headed by disaffected Samurai whose positions had been abolished by the government. With its progress undeterred, Japan was able to throw off the unequal treaties imposed by the West and started to impose its will on foreign countries, fighting wars against China (the First Sino-Japanese War 1894–95) and Russia (The Russo-Japanese War 1904–05) for the hegemony of East Asia. Japan managed to win both of these wars, annexing Taiwan in 1895, and Korea in 1910. On account of its strength, Japan also was approached by Great Britain with the offer of an alliance in 1902, which was the first equal military alliance between a Western and non-Western country. Indeed, Japan's defeat of Russia in 1905 ensured it a place among the Great Powers of the world, and certainly in East Asia, as according to its obligations in the treaty, joined World War I on the Allied side.

HOW TO SCORE THE DIAGNOSTIC TEST

Section I: Multiple Choice

$$\underline{\hspace{3cm}} \times 0.8571 = \underline{\hspace{3cm}}$$

Number of Correct   Weighted
(out of 70)   Section I Score
       (Do not round)

Section II: Free Response

(See if you can find a teacher or classmate to score your essays using
the guidelines in Chapter 2.)

Question 1 $\underline{\hspace{3cm}} \times 2.2222 = \underline{\hspace{3cm}}$
     (out of 9)   (Do not round)

Question 2 $\underline{\hspace{3cm}} \times 2.2222 = \underline{\hspace{3cm}}$
     (out of 9)   (Do not round)

Question 3 $\underline{\hspace{3cm}} \times 2.2222 = \underline{\hspace{3cm}}$
     (out of 9)   (Do not round)

**AP Score
Conversion Chart
World History**

Composite Score Range	AP Score
77–120	5
64–76	4
48–63	3
34–47	2
0–33	1

Sum   = $\underline{\hspace{3cm}}$
Weighted Section II
Score (Do not round)

COMPOSITE SCORE

$$\underline{\hspace{3cm}} + \underline{\hspace{3cm}} = \underline{\hspace{3cm}}$$

Weighted   Weighted   Composite Score
Section I Score   Section II Score   (Round to nearest
                                         whole number)

Part II
About the
AP World
History Exam

- The Structure of the AP World History Exam
- How the AP World History Exam Is Scored
- Overview of Content Topics
- How AP Exams Are Used
- Other Resources
- Designing Your Study Plan

THE STRUCTURE OF THE AP WORLD HISTORY EXAM

The AP World History Exam is divided into two sections: multiple-choice and free-response essays. Section I of the test is comprised of 70 multiple-choice questions to be answered in 55 minutes. Section II of the test begins with a ten-minute reading period (time to review the documents you must use for the first essay question), followed by a two-hour period to write three essays.

HOW THE AP WORLD HISTORY EXAM IS SCORED

Once the multiple-choice section of your test has been scanned and your essays scored by readers, ETS (your local testing giant) applies a mysterious formula that converts your raw score numbers to a 120-point scale. Somehow they turn 70 possible multiple-choice points into 60 points, and 27 possible essay points into another 60 points.

But that's not all the magic they do. They then take your score (up to 120 points) and convert it to the standard AP 1 to 5 score that you see when you rip open the test results that come in the mail. Seems like a little bit of a letdown to do all this work for a 4, doesn't it? However, a 4 or a 5 is the score that will most likely get you what you want from the college or university you'll attend—college credit for World History. A 3 is considered passing and might get you college credit; then again, it might not. Therefore, your goal is to get at least a 3, preferably a 4 or 5. If you receive below a 3, it is highly unlikely that you will get college credit for your high school AP course, but you still get a grade for that class. A good grade in an AP class always looks good on your transcript.

The tricky part about the 1 to 5 scoring system is that it is designed to compare you to everyone else who took the AP World History Exam during a given year. But if the test that year was particularly tough, the top 25 percent or so of scorers will still score 4's and 5's. In other words, if all the scaled (0–120) scores are somewhat low, the top end will still earn high marks. Of course, the opposite is also true—if everyone does an excellent job, some people will end up with 2's and 1's.

What Do The Scores Mean?

Qualification	Score	% of Testers
Extremely well qualified	5	6.9%
Well qualified	4	15.7%
Qualified	3	30.5%
Possibly qualified	2	29.4%
No recommendation	1	17.4%

Student score distributions from the May 2012 College Board AP World History Exam.

OVERVIEW OF CONTENT TOPICS

The AP World History Exam divides all history into six major periods from about 10,000 years ago to the present. On the multiple-choice section of the test, the distribution of questions is as follows:

Period	Date Range	Percent of Questions
Period 1: Technological and Environmental Transformations	c. 8000 B.C.E. to c. 600 B.C.E.	5%
Period 2: Organization and Reorganization of Human Societies	c. 600 B.C.E. to c. 600 C.E.	15%
Period 3: Regional and Transregional Interactions	c. 600 C.E. to c. 1450	20%
Period 4: Global Interactions	c. 1450 to c. 1750	20%
Period 5: Industrialization and Global Integration	c. 1750 to c. 1900	20%
Period 6: Accelerating Global Change and Realignments	c. 1900 to the present	20%

Now, you may be wondering why the first period spans thousands of years while the last period spans a little more than 100 years. When more and more societies came into being and got more complex, world history also got more complex. Also, we have more historical accounts and documents to study from recent history than we do from ancient history, so we simply know more about what happened in the last 100 years. Even though there are 8,000 years in the first period, 800 in the third period, and just over 100 in the last period, you can study each period for the same amount of time. The review of history included in this book divides world history into the periods covered on the exam in order to help guide your study.

By the Way
While the multiple-choice section of the test asks questions from each of the above periods, these questions do not appear in any particular order. In other words, when you take the multiple-choice part of the exam, you'll jump from the Roman Empire to the present back to the Middle Ages back to the present and so on. Some students find it a challenge to shift gears rapidly from hunter-gatherers to NAFTA to Galileo, so be sure to do a few trial runs on the practice test in this book and other practice materials (from the College Board website and elsewhere).

Free-Response Questions (a.k.a. the Essays)

In the free-response section of the exam, you are asked to write three essays, each in response to a question. The questions are as follows:

The document-based question or DBQ: As the name implies, the DBQ is based on a collection of four to ten documents that you must use in order to answer the question. Luckily, you will have 10 minutes at the start of the essay portion of the test to read the given documents prior to writing your essay. That may not sound like a lot right now, but don't worry. Chapter 2 will tell you exactly what to do with those 10 minutes.

The continuity and change-over-time essay: Again, as the name implies, you need to answer a question about how something changed over a certain period of time and how it remained the same. These questions tend to deal with large global issues such as technology, trade, culture, migrations, or biological developments. Chapter 2 will also help you get organized for this essay.

The comparative essay: The comparative essay typically asks you to compare how two societies responded to a major theme or event.

What Do They Want From Me?

What is the AP World History Exam really testing? In a nutshell: Can you make connections between different societies over different periods of time? In other words, for any given period of history, can you explain who was doing what? How did what they were doing affect the rest of the world? What changed about the society during this period of time? To show what you know about world history, keep this big-picture perspective in mind as you study and answer multiple-choice questions or construct essays. To help you do this, keep an eye out for certain recurring themes throughout the different time periods. Specifically, be on the lookout for the following:

- How did people interact with their environment? Why did they live where they did? How did they get there? What tools, technology, and resources were available to them? How was the landscape changed by humans?
- What new ideas, thoughts, and styles came into existence? How did these cultural developments influence people and technology (for example, new religious beliefs or Renaissance thought)?
- How did different societies get along—or not get along—within a time period? Who took over whom? How did leaders justify their power? Who revolted or was likely to revolt? And were they successful?
- How did economic systems develop and what did they depend on in terms of agriculture, trade, labor, industrialization, and the demands of consumers?
- Who had power and who did not within a given culture and why? What was the status of women? What racial and ethnic constructions were present?

HOW AP EXAMS ARE USED

Different colleges use AP Exams in different ways, so it is important that you go to a particular college's web site to determine how it uses AP Exams. The three items below represent the main ways in which AP Exam scores can be used:

- **College Credit**. Some colleges will give you college credit if you score well on an AP Exam. These credits count towards your graduation requirements, meaning that you can take fewer courses while in college. Given the cost of college, this could be quite a benefit, indeed.

- **Satisfy Requirements**. Some colleges will allow you to "place out" of certain requirements if you do well on an AP Exam, even if they do not give you actual college credits. For example, you might not need to take an introductory-level course, or perhaps you might not need to take a class in a certain discipline at all.

- **Admissions Plus**. Even if your AP Exam will not result in college credit or even allow you to place out of certain courses, most colleges will respect your decision to push yourself by taking an AP Course or even an AP Exam outside of a course. A high score on an AP Exam shows mastery of more difficult content than is taught in many high school courses, and colleges may take that into account during the admissions process.

OTHER RESOURCES

There are many resources available to help you improve your score on the AP World History Exam, not the least of which are your teachers. If you are taking an AP class, you may be able to get extra attention from your teacher, such as obtaining feedback on your essays. If you are not in an AP course, reach out to a teacher who teaches American History, and ask if the teacher will review your essays or otherwise help you with content.

Another wonderful resource is AP Central, the official site of the AP Exams. The scope of the information at this site is quite broad and includes the following information:

- Course Description, which includes details on what content is covered and sample questions
- Full-length practice test
- Essay prompts from previous years
- AP World History Exam Tips

The AP Central home page address is: http://apcentral.collegeboard.com/apc

The AP World History Exam Course home page address is http://apcentral.collegeboard.com/apc/public/courses/teachers_corner/4484.html

Finally, The Princeton Review offers tutoring for the World History Exam. Our expert instructors can help you refine your strategic approach and add to your content knowledge. For more information, call 1-800-2REVIEW.

DESIGNING YOUR STUDY PLAN

As part of the Introduction, you identified some areas of potential improvement. Let's now delve further into your performance on the Diagnostic Test, with the goal of developing a study plan appropriate to your needs and time commitment.

Read the answers and explanations associated with the multiple-choice questions (starting at page 33). After you have done so, respond to the following questions:

- Review the Overview of Content Topics on page 55 and, next to each one, indicate your rank of the topic as follows: "1" means "I need a lot of work on this," "2" means "I need to beef up my knowledge," and "3" means "I know this topic well."

- How many days/weeks/months away is your AP World History Exam?

- What time of day is your best, most focused study time?

- How much time per day/week/month will you devote to preparing for your AP World History Exam?

- When will you do this preparation? (Be as specific as possible: Mondays and Wednesdays from 3 to 4 pm, for example)

- Based on the answers above, will you focus on strategy (Part III) or content (Part IV) or both?

- What are your overall goals in using this book?

Part III
Test-Taking Strategies for the AP World History Exam

PREVIEW ACTIVITY

Review your responses to the first three questions on page 2 of the Introduction and then respond to the following questions:

- How many multiple-choice questions did you miss even though you knew the answer?

- On how many multiple-choice questions did you guess blindly?

- How many multiple-choice questions did you miss after eliminating some answers and guessing based on the remaining answers?

- Did you find any of the free response questions easier or harder than the others—and, if so, why?

HOW TO USE THE CHAPTERS IN THIS PART

For the following Strategy chapters, think about what you are doing now before you read the chapters. As you read and engage in the directed practice, be sure to appreciate the ways you can change your approach.

Chapter 1
How to Approach Multiple-Choice Questions

WELL, WHAT DO YOU KNOW?

As we mentioned in the introduction, to do well on the multiple-choice section of the AP World History Exam, you need to know two things: (1) world history (à la Advanced Placement), and (2) how to show that you know world history. One way to prove that you know world history is by correctly answering the number of multiple-choice questions necessary to score 3 or above.

Obvious, right? Then why is it that lots of students who know world history don't get a great score on the test? Could it be because there are 70 questions to answer in 55 minutes? Or is it because they know the history but don't know how to wade through the answer choices efficiently?

Students often don't perform to the best of their ability on the AP World History Exam because in addition to knowing the history, they need to know how to analyze the questions, get rid of the bad answer choices, and find the correct answer in a short period of time. That's what this chapter is all about.

Guessing on the AP Exams

As of May 2011, the AP exams no longer subtract one quarter of a point for incorrect answers—the infamous "guessing penalty." Instead, students are assessed only on the total number of correct questions. It is really important to remember that if you are running out of time, you need to fill in all the bubbles before the time for the multiple-choice section is up. Even if you don't plan to spend a lot of time on every question and even if you have no idea what the correct answer is, you need to fill something in. We don't recommend random guessing as an overall strategy, but taking smart guesses at the right time can substantially increase your raw score on the multiple-choice section of the test. Let's see when guessing can help you.

There are four answer choices for each multiple-choice question. If you were able to eliminate just one wrong answer for each question on the entire multiple-choice section, random odds say you would get one-fourth of the questions correct. That's about 17 questions. Even if you get rid of just one wrong answer from each question throughout the test, you begin to gain points. When you get to questions in which you can't eliminate any options, use what we call your letter of the day (LOTD). Selecting the same answer choice each time you guess will increase your odds of getting a few of those skipped questions right.

And Furthermore

Guessing also raises your score because it saves you time. Seventy questions in 55 minutes is a lot. In fact, it's about 45 seconds per question. How can you possibly answer that many questions in that short a period of time? Two ways: Guess and Go, or Don't.

Guess and Go

Consider the following thought processes of two AP World History test takers on this question:

1. Signed in 1215 C.E., England's Magna Carta was a document that

    (A) increased the wealth of the European nobility
    (B) established England as a monarchy under King Richard
     guaranteed individual liberties to all men
    (D) contained articles that were the foundation for modern justice

Student One	Student Two
The Magna Carta—*I know it was that charter in England in the 1200s that made the king accountable for his actions, so the answer can't be (A) so cross it off. Who was that king? Was it John? I think so. That gets rid of (B). Now, is it more accurate to say that the original document guaranteed individual liberties to all men or that some of the articles became foundations for modern justice. Individual liberties for all men…hmmm…foundations for modern justice. Both sound possible. Was it liberties for all men? I thought so but maybe not or not all men or not at the time. Did the Magna Carta influence modern justice? I think so but in what way exactly? Could it be described as foundational to modern justice? Hmmm….*	*The* Magna Carta—*that charter in England in the 1200s that made the king accountable for his actions. Cross off (A). The king was…John…yeah, King John. That gets rid of (B). (C)…hmmm…did the Magna Carta guarantee individual liberties to all men? Maybe, not sure so leave it. (D)…did it contain articles that became foundations of modern justice? Could have. Guaranteed for all men or foundations of modern justice? I'm not sure, but I think (C) is too strong—guaranteed for all men. I'll guess (D).*
	Next question. The printing press was invented by Gutenberg sometime near the Reformation. Cross off (A) and (C)…

In the above scenario, Student One continues to deliberate between (C) and (D) while Student Two goes on to the next question. What's the difference? Student Two did all the work she could, considered the remaining options, then took a smart guess and moved on. Student One did all the work he could, and then got stuck trying to make a decision between the two remaining options. As the test progresses, Student One will lag further and further behind Student Two, not because he knows less world history, but because he is less willing to take that guess and move on. To do well on the AP World History Exam, you need to do what you can but then be willing to take your best guess and move on to the next question.

Three Out of Every Four Choices Are Bad

Imagine that you are an AP World History Exam writer (you never know, it could happen). As you begin, you first formulate the question portion of the question (or the stem), and then craft your correct answer. But your work does not stop there.

Once you are satisfied with the correct answer, you need to create three wrong answer choices. How would you come up with respectable wrong answer choices quickly? Probably by looking at closely related facts or words that remind you of the question, or by thinking of almost-true and partially true answers. In other words, you create distractor answers that appear to be likely options. Distractors are meant to trip up a test taker who doesn't know the history, doesn't know how to wade through multiple-choice answers, or is rushing to finish.

For example, let's say you have crafted a question about a similarity between Christianity and Islam.

2.   The spread of Islam and the spread of Christianity were
     similar in that members of both religions

     (A)
     (B)
     (C)
     (D) actively strived to convert members of other belief
          systems

Now that you have your question and your correct answer, what wrong answers could be inserted that might attract a tester who is unsure of the correct response? You could insert something that is true about one religion but not necessarily of the other. For example, look at choices (A) and (B).

2. The spread of Islam and the spread of Christianity were
    similar in that members of both religions

    (A) were required to make a journey to the Holy Land
        once in the course of their lifetimes
    (B) believed that their main prophet (Jesus for
        Christians, Mohammad for Muslims) was the
        one true son of God
    (C)
    (D) actively strived to convert members of other belief
        systems

(A) is true of Islam but not Christianity, and (B) is true of Christianity but not Islam. What else could you fill in? Something that is true of both religions but does not answer the question. To do this, you must make sure that part of the answer choice (often the second half) makes that choice clearly wrong. For example, look at answer choice (C).

2. The spread of Islam and the spread of Christianity were
    similar in that members of both religions

    (A) were required to make a journey to the Holy Land
        once in the course of their lifetimes
    (B) believe that their main prophet (Jesus for
        Christians, Mohammad for Muslims) was the
        one true son of God
    (C) ascribed to a monotheistic view in which the only
        way to salvation is through the rejection of all
        other beliefs, both sacred and secular
    (D) actively strived to convert members of other belief
        systems

Notice how (C) begins with something that is true of both religions, but then incorrectly describes rejecting beliefs that are both sacred and secular. It also does not have to do with the spread of the religions. A tester who reads this question in a hurry might see the following:

> *Islam and…Christianity were similar…(C), ascribe to a
> monotheistic view. That's it.*

You get the idea. Why are we making you create AP World History questions? So that you can avoid the mistakes you are expected to make on the exam. How often have you read the answer choices to a question, assuming each is a plausible answer but only one of them is right? When you do that, you spend a whole lot of time considering the options. For example, consider the following:

> *(A), Were required to make a journey to the Holy Land once in the course of their lifetimes. Well, I know that Muslims have to. Did early Christians have to? I don't think so, but maybe. I guess it's possible. What about (B)? Major prophet...Jesus or Mohammad, son of God. Well, Jesus, yes. Mohammad was the main prophet...do Muslims consider him the son of God? I don't know for sure. I don't think so, but I guess it is possible too. Well, how about (C)? Ascribe to a monotheistic view...yes...salvation through the rejection of other beliefs? Hmmm...both sacred and secular. Hmmm...well, the first part is true. I'm not so sure about that second part, but maybe it was true. I don't know what the rule was about secular beliefs. Then again, the question is about the spread of religion, so it really doesn't answer the question. What about (D)? Actively strive to convert members. Well, yes, I think both of these religions did that. That's a possibility.*

Processing each answer choice as if it is a good possibility leads to considering far too many things that a critical eye would see as wrong right away. Instead, work through this question assuming each answer is wrong until proven right.

> *(A), Were required to make a journey to the Holy Land...Muslims yes, but I don't think Christians. Cross it off. (B), Jesus or Mohammad, one true son of God. True for Jesus, I don't think so for Mohammad. Cross it off. (C), Monotheistic, yes, reject other beliefs, not sure, skip it and come back. (D), Actively strive to convert members of other belief systems. Definitely.*

Notice how you can process answers much more quickly and efficiently when you are reading them with a critical eye? Different approaches may very well get you to the correct answer, but it will take a whole lot longer. You could also get caught up in a wrong answer, spending too much time trying to figure out why it might be right instead of remembering that it is probably wrong. On the other hand, reading with a critical eye allows you to cross off answers more aggressively, so by the time you get to (D), you feel pretty sure that it is the answer. And what if we had crossed off all the answer choices? No problem. Just start over and read a little more carefully. It is better to be a little too aggressive than to consider every answer choice a viable option.

Process of Elimination

Every time you read an AP World History Exam question, remember that three out of four answer choices you are reading are wrong. Use the Process of Elimination (POE) to get rid of what you know is wrong as you go through the choices. Then deal with any answer choices you have left. For most questions, you will be able to eliminate one to two answer choices relatively quickly. That leaves you with a few answer choices to consider and take a better-than-blind guess among. We will talk more about POE throughout the rest of this chapter. Just remember to read answer choices as "wrong until proven right" and you'll be on your way to showing what you know on the multiple-choice part of this test.

If you can't eliminate any answers, it's best to skip the question altogether. Mark these skipped questions in some distinctive way so that you can come back to them later if you have time, and make sure you leave a space on your answer sheet. Always keep in mind that the multiple-choice section is difficult, if not impossible, for most students to finish—a score of 50 is good! Focus on accuracy as you work through this section.

HOW TO CRACK AP WORLD HISTORY MULTIPLE-CHOICE QUESTIONS

To do well on the multiple-choice section of the exam, you need to solve each question step by step. The best way to learn this process is to take a look at a sample AP World History Exam question.

3.   When the Europeans arrived in sub-Saharan Africa in the 1400s and 1500s, the African slave trade was

(A) just beginning
(B) well established and about 500 years old
(C) still under the control of Muslim traders
(D) not economically viable and did not interest the Europeans

Step 1: Read the Question and Put It in Your Own Words

First you must make sure that you understand what the question is asking. Read the sample question again. What is it really asking? If you are having trouble figuring it out, answer the questions *When?*, *Who?*, *What?* For example, in the above question about slave trade, you can answer in the following way:

When? *1400–1599*

Who? *Europeans and sub-Saharan Africa*

What? *Slave trade*

Then, rephrase the question so that it is clear to you.

What was up with the African slave trade in the 1400–1500 period?

Step 2: Answer in Your Own Words

Once you've rewritten the question, take a moment to call up the relevant history that you know. If it is a topic you know well, it will be easy to come up with an answer. If you can't come up with a full answer, think of a few key points that you do know about the topic. Here's an example of what you might know about the slave trade from 1400–1500.

It already existed in both Africa and Europe, so it wasn't new.

If you can't answer the question completely, you can still use what you do know to get rid of wrong answer choices using the Process of Elimination.

Step 3: Process of Elimination

Even if you do not know exactly what was going on with the slave trade in the 1400s and 1500s, you can use the little you do know to eliminate wrong answer choices. Remember to read each answer choice with a critical eye, looking for what makes it wrong. Cross off the choices that you know are wrong; leave ones that you are uncertain about or you think are right.

Let's review what we know so far about the question. When? *1400–1599*. Who? *Europeans in Africa*. What? *Slave trade*. What do you know about slave trade in 1400–1599? It was not new. Armed with this information, take a look again at the answer choices.

(A) just beginning
(B) well established and about 500 years old
(C) still under the control of Muslim traders
(D) not economically viable and did not interest the Europeans

Take a look at answer choice (A). Was it just beginning? No. Cross off (A)—this cannot be the answer to the question. You may not be sure about (B) or (C), but what about (D)? Was slavery economically viable or interesting to Europeans? It must have been or it would not have become so extensive. Your common sense tells you that (D) cannot be the answer, so cross it off and move along. If you have no idea between (B) and (C), at least it's now a 50-50 shot, so what should you do? Guess and move on.

Step 4: Guess and Go

After using POE, you have a 50-50 shot of guessing the right answer on our sample question. Let's look at answer choice (C). The Europeans arrived on the west coast of sub-Saharan Africa while the Muslims were on the east coast. Remember the Indian Ocean trade and the Swahili culture? If that is the case, then (C) cannot be the answer. The answer must be (B): well established and about 500 years old.

Can you see how taking a moment to frame the question can help you find the right answer quickly and easily? Knowing just some of the information can be enough to get you to a smart guess. This does not mean that you should not learn as much of the history as possible. The more you know, the easier it will be to eliminate wrong answer choices and zero in on the correct answer. However, using the steps and POE will help you get to the right answer quickly by making the most of the information you know.

Step by Step by Step by Step

Let's walk through the Four Steps to solving an AP World History multiple-choice question again.

4. Matrilinearity was found in which of the following societies?

   (A) Rome
   (B) Sumer
   (C) Bantu
   (D) Byzantium

Step 1: Read the Question and Put It in Your Own Words

What does matrilinearity mean? Matri is like matriarch—has to do with females or females as leaders. Linear means in a line like lineage.

When? *Looks like early times*

Who? *Female rulers*

What? *Early rulers who were woman*

So in which society did the rulers come from the female line?

Step 2: Answer in Your Own Words

Not sure. Definitely not Rome, probably not Byzantium either. They had major male-dominance going on.

Step 3: Process of Elimination

I know that (A) and (D) are out, so I'll cross them off. (B) and (C) remain.

Step 4: Guess and Go

I don't know about any of these three societies, so I'll guess (C).

As it happens, you're right—the answer is (C): Bantu. Even if you didn't pick (C), if you eliminated as many as you could and then wasted no further time fretting over the unknowns before you picked one and moved on, then you did the right thing. Good job!

Your Turn

Now it's your turn. Use the Four Steps to solve the following multiple-choice question.

5. Which of the following is an example of Chinese influence in Japan during the sixth, seventh, and eighth centuries?

    (A) The expansion of European culture to the island of Japan

    (B) The adoption by Japan of the Chinese civil service exam for government employees

    (C) The Taika Reforms enacted after the death of Prince Shotoku

    (D) The conversion of most Japanese Shinto to Buddhism

Step 1: Read the Question and Put It in Your Own Words

Step 2: Answer in Your Own Words

Step 3: POE

Step 4: Guess and Go

Here's How to Crack It

First, note that the question is asking for an example of China's influence on Japan during the sixth, seventh, and eighth centuries (there is your When? and Who?). What do you know about Japan during this time period? China had just started to influence Japan. Lots of reforms took place, but Japan didn't adopt everything Chinese—for example, Confucianism. Knowing that, let's use POE.

(A) is about European culture. Had European culture touched Japan at this time? No, it had barely touched China let alone Japan, so cross off (A). (B) is out if you remember that Japan did not embrace Confucianism, and that Confucianism was a big part of Chinese government and the Chinese civil service exam. You may not remember anything about the Taika Reforms, but you might recall that while the Japanese embraced Buddhism, they did not give up Shinto but rather practiced both simultaneously. That eliminates (D). Your answer must be (C).

So Far, So Good EXCEPT...

Not all questions are asked in a straightforward manner on the AP World History Exam. Consider the following example:

6. All of the following are results of the bubonic plague, which swept through China and Europe from the 1200s to the 1600s, EXCEPT

(A) social unrest
(B) tremendous population loss
(C) a decrease in wages
(D) less rigidity between social classes

Approach these questions using the same Four Steps. During Step 1, rephrase the question to make it clear what you have to do to find the right answer.

Step 1: Read the Question and Put It in Your Own Words

When? *1200–1699. Into the Age of Exploration, Renaissance*

Who? *China/Europe*

What? *Bubonic plague. Lots of people died, had an impact on everyone*

Four of the following things happened because of bubonic plague. Which one didn't?

Step 2: Answer in Your Own Words

I know a lot of people died and there were not enough people to work, and that everyone had to draw together to get things done, but I forget what else happened.

Step 3: POE

Remember that on EXCEPT or NOT questions, three of the answer choices are true while one is not true. Instead of trying to choose the answer, make a note next to each as to whether it is true or not. Then pick the "not."

(A) social unrest	not sure
(B) tremendous population loss	T
(C) a decrease in wages	not sure
(D) less rigidity between social classes	T

Step 4: Guess and Go

Because you are looking for the answer that is not true, cross out (B) and (D). Now consider (A) and (C). Could social unrest have been the result of thousands of people dying? Sounds plausible, so cross off (A). Consider that you can pick (C) confidently if you remember that the massive labor shortage actually raised the average wage for both farm laborers and skilled artisans.

By the way, the bubonic plague led to less rigidity between social classes because it decimated the population of all social classes, and therefore people needed to learn new skills (beyond their traditional classes) to make up for the loss of people in other social classes. This led to an overlap in social and economic classes.

When to Bail

Remember that you are on a fairly tight time schedule for this test. You need to make sure that you spend your time on questions that will pay off. If you read a question and have absolutely no idea what is being asked or know as soon as you read a question that you do not know the subject matter, mark it in some way, and then move on. Better to skip a few along the way than to run out of time before you get to questions at the end that you know about. After you go through the section once, you can always return to any remaining questions.

Notice that Steps 1 and 2 can vary quite a bit based on the question. Also, the more you can frame the history in Step 2, the easier it will be to cross off wrong answer choices and zero in on the right answer. For example, instead of just saying that the What? in the last question was the bubonic plague, we took a minute to add what that meant at the time: lots of people died, had an impact on everyone. Taking a moment to think of this additional information helped get to the answer quickly and easily.

Practice Set 1

Step 1 and Step 2

Take a few moments to practice Steps 1 and 2. The better you are at interpreting questions and coming up with your own answers before you get to the answer choices, the easier it will be to POE and Guess and Go!

---

1. During the Cold War era, the United States and the Soviet Union were reluctant to become involved in direct military conflict mainly because of

Step 1: Read the Question and Put It in Your Own Words

Step 2: Answer in Your Own Words

nuclear fall out

---

2. In the sixteenth and seventeenth centuries, European mercantilism in Latin America led to

Step 1: Read the Question and Put It in Your Own Words

Step 2: Answer in Your Own Words

Nationalist movements

3.   One way in which the Maya, the Songhai, and the
     Gupta cultures were similar is that they

Step 1: Read the Question and Put It in Your Own Words

Step 2: Answer in Your Own Words

4.   The teachings of Confucius encouraged people to

Step 1: Read the Question and Put It in Your Own Words

Step 2: Answer in Your Own Words

Step 3 and Step 4

Here are the answer choices that go with the questions you just worked through. Now that you've framed the history, use that information to POE and Guess and Go. Be sure to check EVERY answer before picking one! Answers can be found on pages 86–89.

1. During the Cold War era, the United States and the Soviet Union were reluctant to become involved in direct military conflict mainly because of

   (A) pressure from many of the nonaligned nations
   (B) the role of the United Nations as peacekeeper
   (C) increased tensions in the Middle East
   (D) the potential for global nuclear destruction

2. In the sixteenth and seventeenth centuries, European mercantilism in Latin America led to

   (A) the exploitation of people and resources
   (B) the European Renaissance
   (C) the Protestant Reformation
   (D) the growth of democratic forms of government

3. One way in which the Maya, the Songhai, and the Gupta cultures were similar is that they

   (A) developed great civilizations without major influence from Western Europe
   (B) emerged as a result of nationalist movements of the twentieth century
   (C) thrived due to a prosperous trade economy with Portugal and other European nations
   (D) became dependent on slave trade in order to maintain enough laborers to tend to their profitable sugar cane crop

4. The teachings of Confucius encouraged people to

   (A) embrace a heliocentric view of the solar system
   (B) follow a code of moral conduct
   (C) accept the teachings of the Pax Romana
   (D) worship the one true God who watches over and cares for his people

CHECK YOUR ANSWERS ON PAGES 86–89 BEFORE MOVING ON!

Take a Picture

You will occasionally see a question that asks you to interpret an illustration such as a painting, poster, political cartoon, or map. Treat these questions as you would any other. Just follow the steps and don't read too much into the illustration. Try the following example:

The above poster was most likely used as

(A) British propaganda during the Boer War
(B) American propaganda during World War II
(C) British propaganda during World War I
(D) American propaganda during World War I

In the space on the next page, solve this question using the Four Steps. Study the poster for clues as to the When? Who? and What?

Step 1: Read the Question and Put It in Your Own Words

Step 2: Answer in Your Own Words

Step 3: POE

Step 4: Guess and Go

Here's How to Crack It

The question asked what the poster was used for. You probably guessed the What? to be propaganda. For the When? and Who?, look at the words at the top of the poster. Did you remember that Hun was the term used by the British in reference to the Germans? If you did, you could eliminate (B) and (D) for having nothing to do with the British. Even if you didn't recognize that term, look at the smaller type underneath—England? Belgium? Whatever else it might be, it's definitely not the American KKK and Reconstruction. Because the British were referencing the Germans, the answer must be (C) British propaganda during World War I. If you knew that the term Hun referred to the Germans in WWI, but did not remember who said it, you could have eliminated all but (C) and (D) and then taken a smart guess.

What He Said

Sometimes you will be given a quotation and asked to either interpret the quote or identify the person who said it. As always, use the steps to frame your answer and take a smart guess. Try the next one using the Four Steps.

"Which, O Bhikkhus, is this Middle Path the knowledge of which the Tathagata has gained, which leads to insight, which leads to wisdom, which conduces to calm, to knowledge, to the Sambodhi, to Nirvana?"

The person who would most likely be associated with this quote is a

(A) Muslim
(B) Christian
(C) Polytheist
(D) Buddhist

Here's How to Crack It

Many times the key to solving a quotation comes from only one or two words of the quotation. In this case, the word is Nirvana. Nirvana has to do with what religion? If you remember, great. If you cannot remember exactly which religion strives for Nirvana, you probably know that it is Eastern. Let's say you remember that it is one of the Indian religions. What answers can you eliminate? (B) and (C). From there, take a smart guess between Muslim and Buddhist. The answer is (D): Buddhist.

Not So Bad, Huh?

That's pretty much all you need to know to score your best on the multiple-choice section of the exam. Oh yeah, that, and a bunch of history. Most of the rest of your work in this book will be about reviewing the history. Remember, however, what we said at the beginning of this book—knowing the history is really important, but knowing how to demonstrate that you know it is just as important. That's where your multiple-choice strategy comes in.

As you practice, remember to process everything using the Four Steps.

Step 1: Read the Question and Put It in Your Own Words

Step 2: Answer in Your Own Words

Step 3: Process of Elimination (POE)

Step 4: Guess and Go

Practice Set 2

Now that you have the basics of cracking these types of questions let's practice.

1. The primary purpose of the Dawes Plan was to

    (A) contain the spread of communism to newly
        formed nations in sub-Saharan Africa through
        direct economic support
    (B) ensure that Latin American nations maintained
        economic ties with the United States
    (C) allow Germany to rebuild its economy while also
        fulfilling its reparation responsibilities after
        World War I
    (D) temporarily occupy Japan as it transitioned from a
        monarchy to a democracy after World War II

2. The concept of bushido is most similar to

    (A) feudalism
    (B) chivalry
    (C) manorialism
    (D) meritocracy

3. The Han dynasty (200 B.C.E. to 200 C.E.) had a stable
    government for centuries, due in part to all of the
    following EXCEPT

    (A) the strong military force with which the
        government, under the leadership of Asoka, the
        Warrior Emperor, expelled the Hun invasion
    (B) the adoption and growth of the Confucian system
        of civil administration
    (C) the Mandate of Heaven, which inclined Emperors
        to rule fairly and justly
    (D) the creation and exportation of goods such as
        paper, silk, and gun powder along the Silk Road

4. Common to Latin American revolutions before 1915 was

    (A) the influence of European intellectual movements
    (B) the important role played by women in instituting change
    (C) the installation of representative democracies in nearly all new nations
    (D) the importance of foreign intervention in the success of revolutions

5. The Peace of Augsburg was an example of

    (A) a gentlemen's agreement
    (B) mutual defense
    (C) enlightened absolutism
    (D) religious tolerance

6. Which of the following is an accurate list of the permanent members of the United Nations Security Council?

    (A) China, Japan, United States, Russia, Great Britain
    (B) China, Russia, United States, France, Great Britain
    (C) Russia, Japan, United States, Italy, Great Britain
    (D) Russia, China, United States, France, Italy

7. The Siege of Vienna was important because it

    (A) marked the beginning of the end of Ottoman military conquests in Europe
    (B) was the first attempt of the Ottoman Empire to advance into Western Europe
    (C) precipitated a Christian Crusade to retake Vienna from the Turks
    (D) was the first time a secret alliance between European nations was tested

8. All of the following are examples of attempts by early humans to gain control over nature EXCEPT

    (A) constructing sundials
    (B) plowing fields
    (C) domesticating animals
    (D) settling in river basins

9. The establishment of the Hanseatic League (1241 c.e.) was significant because it

   (A) set a precedent for large, European trading operations
   (B) organized to become the first joint-stock company
   (C) comprised nearly 50 port cities along the Mediterranean Sea
   (D) held exclusive rights to trade along the Silk Road

10. "Sing, O goddess, the anger of Achilles son of Peleus, that brought countless ills upon the Achaeans. Many a brave soul did it send hurrying down to Hades, and many a hero did it yield a prey to dogs and vultures, for so were the counsels of Jove fulfilled from the day on which the son of Atreus, king of men, and great Achilles, first fell out with one another."

   The above quote is from which of the following texts?

   (A) The Vedas
   (B) Homer's Iliad
   (C) Hobbes' Leviathan
   (D) The Code of Hammurabi

CHECK YOUR ANSWERS ON PAGES 89–91 BEFORE MOVING ON!

ANSWER KEY

Practice Set 1

Step 1 and Step 2

1.   Try to anticipate the answer on this one even before you look at the answer choices. Why would two superpowers not want to fight each other?

Step 1: Read the Question and Put It in Your Own Words

Why were the United States and the Soviet Union reluctant to get into direct military conflict during the Cold War?

Step 2: When? Who? What?

When? The Cold War era

Who?   The United States and the Soviet Union

What? Reluctance to get involved militarily

Try to think of everything you know about "military conflict" during the time period of the Cold War. The Cold War was after World War II, right? How did World War II end in Japan? Remember the Cuban Missile Crisis? That was during the Cold War. What did that involve?

2.   Notice that this question tells you that European mercantilism occurred during the sixteenth and seventeenth centuries. A lot of times, questions give you information. Look at the questions themselves as clues.

Step 1: Read the Question and Put It in Your Own Words

When? The sixteenth and seventeenth centuries

Who?   Europeans doing, Latin Americans receiving

What? Mercantilism

What did European mercantilism in Latin America lead to in the sixteenth and seventeenth centuries?

Step 2: Answer in Your Own Words

If you remember what mercantilism was, this question is a gift. If you don't remember mercantilism, think about everything you know about Europe's involvement in Latin America during the sixteenth and seventeenth centuries.

3.   Sometimes you'll get questions that seemingly don't give you very many clues in the question to work with.

Step 1: Read the Question and Put It in Your Own Words

When? The question doesn't say, but it certainly isn't contemporary (the verb were) and it doesn't refer to the same time period. When the test writers ask you to compare cultures, remember that those cultures may have existed during different time periods.

Who?   The Maya, the Songhai, and the Gupta

What?   Similarities. Any similarity. Just one. That's all you need.

How were the Maya, Songhai, and Gupta cultures similar?

Step 2: Answer in Your Own Words

It's hard to anticipate what the answer is going to be, but even if you don't remember the details of all three cultures, if you remember one or two, you should focus on the details that you remember so that you can pick an answer choice that is consistent with what you do know.

4.   Sometimes questions rely on very specific knowledge of just one thing. In this case, it's just one person.

Step 1: Read the Question and Put It in Your Own Words

When? The question doesn't tell us, but we know it was during and possibly after the life of Confucius.

Who?   Confucius

What?   Teachings and encouragement

Confucius encouraged people to do what?

Step 2: Answer in Your Own Words

Even though this question seems like it doesn't give you very much information, it does if you remember some basics. If you recall that Confucius lived in China and lived a long time ago, that's enough to start focusing on the answer. All you have to do is think of everything you know about traditional China and you can start to zero in on an answer.

Step 3 and Step 4

Now evaluate the answer choices and use POE to get rid of bad answers.

1. **D**   Focus on answer choices that make the most sense. You should certainly be attracted to answer choice (D), because even if you don't remember much about the Cold War, it just makes sense that global nuclear destruction would make two countries reluctant to fight. If you recall that the two superpowers had nuclear weapons and that WWII, which preceded the Cold War, ended with the

United States dropping atomic bombs on Japan, answer choice (D) should definitely stick out. (A) doesn't make much sense, because "nonaligned nations" means that they didn't take sides in the Cold War, which means that they probably didn't impact it very much. You might be attracted to (B), but if you recall that both the United States and the Soviet Union were members of the United Nations Security Council, making the organization somewhat useless in addressing Cold War concerns, so this answer choice doesn't make much sense. Finally, (C) definitely describes an event that was true during the Cold War era, but it wasn't the cause for the reluctance for direct military conflict. Direct military conflict in the Middle East was somewhat common, just not between the Soviet Union and United States (except, to a certain degree, in Afghanistan). Make sure you focus on the who in the question. Even if you aren't sure of why answer choices (A) through (C) are incorrect, it's hard to argue with answer choice (D). When you find an answer choice that has to be true, it probably is. Because only one answer choice can work, the other three can be eliminated.

2. **A**   Mercantilism was all about exploitation. The policy advocated the creation of colonies for the purpose of increasing exports from the mother country while not technically increasing imports to the mother country (mercantilist countries essentially stole resources from the colonies). If you remember anything at all about mercantilism, you gotta go with (A). Even if you don't remember anything about mercantilism, you still should go with (A) because you should know that Europe colonized Latin America.

    All of the other answer choices can be eliminated if you focus on the When?, Who?, and What? of the question. (B) can be eliminated because the European Renaissance had nothing to do with Latin America. (C) can be eliminated because the Protestant Reformation was an event that primarily affected Europe, not Latin America—and not because of Latin America, either. You can be even more comfortable crossing off (C) if you also remember that Latin America is extremely Catholic as opposed to Protestant. Finally, cross off (D); democracies didn't start developing until long after the sixteenth and seventeenth centuries. It wasn't until after the American and French Revolutions that democratic movements started to get rolling, and it wasn't until the twentieth century that democracies started taking root in Latin America.

3. **A**   Even if you just remember one of the three civilizations, you can get this question correct because (A) applies so clearly to any one of them. If you remember that the Maya, for example, existed for centuries before the first Europeans arrived in the New World, you're done. Even if you're not sure about the other three answer choices, (A) is definitely true. The same, of course, is true of the Songhai in Africa and the Gupta in India.

    The other answer choices make no sense even if you remember the When? and What? of just one of the cultures. All of the cultures existed long before the twentieth century, so get rid of (B). None of the cultures traded with Portugal. Think of the time periods here. The Gupta Empire existed in the fourth through sixth centuries C.E. Portugal had been part of the Roman Empire and wasn't even a country, but more of a region, and was being invaded by Visigoths during this time period. As for (D), you can eliminate it as soon as you see "sugar cane" as a profitable crop because it doesn't fit with any of the cultures.

4. **B**   If you remember anything about Confucius or traditional China, (B) is the obvious choice here; Confucius' code of conduct clearly dominated the culture of traditional China.

The other answers have no connection with Confucianism. (A) is out, because Ptolemy of Alexandria (second century c.e.) and Copernicus (sixteenth century c.e.) were the two figures most closely associated with the heliocentric model. (C) is about the Pax Romana, which describes the period of stability in the Roman Empire between the reigns of Augustus (27 b.c.e.–14 c.e.) and Marcus Aurelius (161–180 c.e.). As for (D), Confucianism is generally considered a system of ethics, not a religion in the strictest sense.

Practice Set 2

1. **C** Germany could not repay its war debts to France and England (no surprise given the state of the economy), so France sent troops into the Ruhr Valley where German steel was manufactured. This further compromised Germany's ability to fulfill its obligations, and again brought Europe to the brink of war. Charles Dawes (an American banker) developed a more flexible repayment schedule for Germany based on economic growth. The Dawes Plan also gave low-interest loans to Germany to help jump-start key industries.

   This is a bit of a factoid (don't get it confused with the Dawes Act, which is something completely different!), but remember that anything you can think of that's related may help you cross out answers. If you remember that this had to do with America and Europe, you could go ahead and cross out at least (A), (B), and (D). If you know the Dawes Plan related to World War I, you have another good reason to get rid of (D), which describes something that happened after World War II.

2. **B** Bushido is a term associated with the shogunate period in Japan. The aristocratic-warrior class of the samurai followed a strict code of honor known as bushido. It is most similar to chivalry, because both stressed discipline, respect, and bravery.

   Using POE, you can get rid of (A) and (C) because even though the code of bushido was practiced during Japanese feudalism, it isn't the same thing as feudalism or manorialism, both of which were also practiced in Europe. Feudalism and manorialism were social and political structures, ways of organizing society, not what would be described as "concepts." Also, guilds are organizations, not "concepts." While (D) is a concept, so that's good, it has nothing to do with bushido.

3. **A** Asoka ruled the Mauryan empire in India during the third century b.c.e. The Han Dynasty, on the other hand, was in China. Its stability was due to all three reasons in the incorrect answer choices.

   Using POE, you can eliminate any answer choices that were true of the Han dynasty. (B) was definitely true of the Han dynasty (and through much of China's history). The adoption of Confucianism as the basis of state administration led to the creation of a highly skilled government bureaucracy, which of course led to stability. (C) is incorrect: According to the Mandate of Heaven, a king or emperor ruled only with the approval of Heaven, and would continue to prosper only if they ruled justly and wisely. The Mandate was a belief which arose during the earlier Zhou dynasty and was influential in the Han dynasty and beyond. And finally, choice (D) helped to expand and stabilize the economy of Han China, and the ensuing prosperity further promoted China's stability.

4. **A** The Enlightenment in Europe had a profound effect on educated people beyond Europe's shores, especially in Europe's colonies. The writings of intellectuals such as Locke, Rousseau, and Montesquieu impacted the American Revolution, French Revolution, and Latin American revolutions.

Even if you're not sure of the right answer, you can eliminate the wrong answer choices that don't make sense, or that are inconsistent with what you remember about history. Eliminate (B); Latin American society was highly patriarchal, as were most societies prior to 1915. That leaves you with (A), (C), and (D). (C) can be eliminated: Many Latin American nations became dictatorships. (D) can be eliminated because the revolutionaries were born in Latin America and succeeded with the support of popular uprisings, not foreign armies. That leaves you with (A), which makes a lot of sense. The Enlightenment inspired revolutions in general, such as the American Revolution and the French Revolution. It just makes sense, then, that it also impacted the Latin American independence movements of the nineteenth century, especially when you consider that San Martin and Bolivar were educated peninsulares, who were well-schooled in European affairs.

5. **D** During the mid-fifteenth century, Charles V had a difficult time preventing Protestantism from spreading through the Holy Roman Empire. In 1555, he and the prevailing German princes signed the Peace of Augsburg, which allowed each prince to choose the religion his subjects would follow.

Using POE, you can eliminate (C) because enlightened absolutism is an oxymoron—an internally contradictory idea. (A) would mean the Peace of Augsburg was an informal agreement, and (B) makes it sound like a military strategy—neither of these is true, as it was a formal agreement to end religious conflict.

6. **B** If you don't remember all the permanent members, use POE with the ones of which you are sure. The United States is in all the choices so that won't help. You probably know that Japan is not a permanent member because the council was established right after WWII and Japan was not high on anyone's list at that time. In fact, Japan was occupied by the United States and forced to demilitarize, so it certainly would not be on the security council. Eliminate (A) and (C). That leaves you with (B) and (D), Great Britain versus Italy. Again, because of when the council was formed, your best guess is (B), Great Britain. Remember that Great Britain still had an empire through the 1940s.

7. **B** In 1529, Ottoman Turks tried (unsuccessfully) to capture the Austrian city of Vienna. Beginning in the 1300s, the Turks began to make inroads into Europe, first in the Balkans, then by taking Constantinople (which then became Istanbul), and then conquering parts of Romania and Hungary.

To use POE, try to remember that the Siege of Vienna occurred in the sixteenth century. That means that (C), the Crusades, is out because they began in 1096 and ended in 1302. (A) is also out because the Ottoman influence in Europe lasted into the twentieth century. (D) has to go because, first of all, it doesn't make sense because there's no way the test writers could know if and when all secret alliances were tested because some of them are "secret" and perhaps still unknown. (D) also doesn't work because the siege of Vienna had nothing to do with Austria's alliances (secret or otherwise)—the Ottomans wanted to make inroads into Western Europe for their own expansionist purposes, not because they were trying to test alliances in Europe.

8. **D**   Settling in a river basin exemplifies how nature often controlled where people needed to live in order to survive, not the other way around. This is especially true if you remember that civilizations continued to settle in river basins even though they were often devastated by unpredictable floods.

To use POE, first remember that three of the answer choices are examples of peoples' attempts to control nature and one is not—your answer is the one that is not an example of this. (B) and (C) are direct efforts to use or harness natural resources in order to grow or otherwise provide food. (A) is more subtle—while sundials did not give humans control over the elements of time, they did give humans the knowledge required to use patterns of time for their own purposes.

Tip: Notice how one answer is not like the others; comparing answers is a great way to see small, yet crucial, differences that can help you eliminate wrong answers. (A), (B), and (C) are all material things or techniques, while (D) denotes a different kind of activity.

9. **A**   The Hanseatic League was a major trading operation comprised dozens of northern European cities. The existence of the league helped pull Europe out of the relative isolation it experienced under feudalism during the Middle Ages by increasing contact among different parts of Europe, which then led to increased trade between Europe and other parts of the world. By establishing a monopoly on trade in northern Europe, the Hanseatic League helped contribute to a culture of expansionism and mercantilism, which of course dominated developments during the Age of Exploration.

Using POE, you can eliminate (B) because a "league" isn't a company but rather an association, and joint-stock companies didn't come onto the scene until after the Commercial Revolution in the sixteenth century (the Muscovy Company—founded in 1555—and the Dutch and British East India Companies—both chartered in the 1600s—were among the first). If you can remember the "where" of the Hanseatic League, that will help you quickly eliminate (C) and (D) because the league was in northern Europe and primarily served as a way of regulating trade among northern European ports.

10. **B**   This one might be tough if you're not familiar with the details of any of these texts, but you can still use clues from the passage. We know there's a reference to a goddess, and there are other characters that seem godlike ("hero" and "king of men"). We also know there's a group referred to as the Achaeans. The quote also has a poetic quality to it—"Sing, O goddess" and "Many a brave soul did it send" aren't exactly everyday ways of speaking.

Through POE, we can probably eliminate (D) because it doesn't sound like a legal code. You can get rid of (C) if you know that Hobbes was an English writer during the Enlightenment who wrote about things like the social contract and free will; this doesn't seem to fit. That leaves you with (A) and (B). The Vedas, if you recall, is a collection of the essential beliefs and mythologies of Hinduism. The Iliad is a poem of ancient Greek mythology. Poetic language fits both, and both traditions have gods, so it's a toss-up, unless you remember that Achilles (as in Achilles heel) is a Greek warrior. You may remember that Achaeans were Greeks (recall the Achaean League). Whenever you have quotations, look for clues that help you identify the culture. Then go with the author who is from that culture.

Chapter 2
How to
Approach
Essays

HOW TO BE A WRITER…AN AP WORLD HISTORY ESSAY WRITER, THAT IS

Once you complete the multiple-choice part of the test, you'll get a short break while tests are collected and essay booklets are handed out. Then comes the essay portion of the exam. You'll be given a ten-minute reading period prior to the start of the essay-writing section, and then two hours to write three essays. While you are given approximate guidelines, you are not told how long to spend on each essay or when to move on to the next essay.

What's in a Name?

The three essays you'll need to write are the document-based question (or DBQ), the change-over-time essay, and the comparative essay. You can probably gather from the names what you need to do in each essay—the document-based question provides you with a set of documents on which to base your essay; the change-over-time essay asks you to analyze the changes and continuities that occurred within a certain period of time; and the comparative essay asks you to compare and contrast two episodes, cultures, religions, or other historical phenomenon from a given period.

Writing a thesis for an AP World History Exam essay is a little different from other theses you may have learned to write in English class. For now, let's take a minute to look at the basic format you should use for all of your AP World History Exam essays.

What Are You Talking About?

The key to writing a good AP World History Exam essay is to tell the reader what you are going to talk about before you talk about it. The AP World History Exam refers to this as your thesis. In fact, writing a good thesis is worth 1 to 2 of 9 possible points on each essay, and it is the first thing that the essay grader will look for. The scoring rubric (the guidelines readers use to score your essays) requires readers to answer the following questions about each of your essays:

- Do you have a comprehensive, analytical, and explicit thesis?
- Is your thesis acceptable?

So What Does an Analytical Thesis Look Like?

Put simply, an analytical thesis includes a clear description of why the central claim of your essay is correct. These statements alone would not receive points for "adequacy."

- Buddhism's spread through China was very important to the development of Chinese culture.
- In the area of trade, North America and Latin America underwent significant change between 1750 and the present.

These vague, general, and weak statements add nothing to your essay, and leave the reader with a laundry list of questions that remain unanswered: What exactly does the term "Buddhism" denote here? What, exactly, "spread"? When did this occur? In what context? "Very important" how? What were Buddhism's specific effects? What specific aspects of culture did it touch on, and how do we know?

Clear, explicit theses will use specific details to delimit the scope of the discussion. The first thesis would be vastly improved by the addition of more details such as in the following statement:

- As Buddhism began to spread from India through China in the first century c.e., the influence of its religious principles in a society troubled—at least among lower classes—by warfare and want is demonstrated by the Confucianists' negative reaction to it as well as the lasting political effects it left in its wake.

Why is this better than the first version? Yes, it has more words, but what do those extra words do? The reader now has more details regarding what spread, when this spread took place, what the context of that spread was, and what kind of support will be referenced in the rest of the essay. Most importantly, it answers the question, "Why was the spread of Buddhism important?" The reader now knows that Buddhism was important because it caused meaningful changes in different areas of Chinese society, which the essay should describe in more detail.

Remember also that a thesis isn't just one sentence; it can be a group of statements. Therefore, you can start with a more general sentence, but you have to then follow it up with additional sentences that provide all the necessary elements described above. Together, these statements must

- state your claim clearly
- define terms, context, and chronology of the events under discussion
- describe why your claim is true

Lastly, a clear, analytical thesis isn't there just for the reader's benefit. A strong analytical thesis serves as a map that you should follow as you write the remainder of the essay. If your thesis at first is too vague, it may be that you haven't thought through what you want to say yet, so take more time to organize your ideas. Once you craft a strong thesis, make sure that the rest of your essay supports the basic ideas your thesis introduces.

So What Is "Acceptable"?

To write a solid, acceptable thesis for each of your essays, remember to do three things: Give 'Em What They Want, Show 'Em Where You Got It, and Help 'Em Get There.

The two most common essay cues you will see are "analyze" and "compare and contrast." Sometimes you will see both in the same essay question.

To really analyze you must explain how and why something happens and what the impacts of that something were. For example, to return to the spread of Buddhism in China—analysis of this process would include explaining how it spread to China, why it was appealing to the Chinese, and finally, how it impacted Chinese society over both the short and long term.

To "compare and contrast" deals with similarities and differences; however, it is not enough to point out what is similar or different: Buddhism existed in both India and China. It is far more important to explain what causes the similarities and differences—in essence, to analyze why: Because of Buddhism's appeal to the lower classes, it spread throughout India and China; however, acceptance differed because it was perceived as a threat to the Confucian order in China.

Give 'Em What They Want

Your essay reader is trained to look for certain specific criteria in your essay. To make sure that she finds what she's looking for (and to ensure that you get credit for including all that stuff), begin by using the question to develop a thesis that includes key phrases from the question AND sets up the structure of your argument. For example, a typical question is as follows:

3.   Compare and contrast the impact of nationalism in Europe versus the impact of nationalism in the European colonies throughout the nineteenth and twentieth centuries.

Do not just reword the question by using a simple introductory sentence such as the following statement: There were many similarities and differences between nationalism in Europe and its colonies.

This sentence is a waste of space that doesn't tell the reader anything. Instead, your first sentence should clearly indicate what is to come in the rest of the thesis and the body of the essay and why nationalism was important.

The opening sentence of your thesis might read something like this:

Nationalism was a driving force throughout much of the nineteenth and twentieth centuries, but it had a very different flavor in Europe than in most European colonies.

Notice the key phrases that were included in the sentence: Nationalism, Europe, European colonies, and nineteenth and twentieth centuries. Also note that the sentence is worded to imply contrast. Just to make sure that all aspects of the question are covered, the next sentence could read as follows:

> *While nationalism for both groups meant pride in and commitment to one's own "nation," nationalism in Europe—which often meant racism or desire for domination—became synonymous with national expansion and conquest of other peoples, while nationalism in the colonies meant self-determination—freedom from European rule, and the nation's right to determine its own destiny.*

This sentence continues the contrast, but opens with a comparison, so as not to overlook the similarities in the responses of the two countries (something you must do to get a good score).

Try It

To make sure you include all the necessary elements in the opening sentence of your thesis, circle each key phrase as you process the question. Try it on the following example:

2. Choose TWO of the areas listed below and discuss the impact of the spread of Islam from its inception to 1450 on each area. Be sure to describe each area prior to the introduction of Islam as your starting point.

    Sub-Saharan Africa   The Middle East
    The Byzantine Empire   Spain (the Iberian
    Western Europe   Peninsula)
    China   India
                                Northern Africa

Did you circle key words and phrases like spread of Islam, inception to 1450, impact on each area? Once you circle the key phrases and select your countries/areas, try writing your opening sentence below.

_____

_____

_____

Your opening sentence should read something like the following:

From its inception to the early 1400s and beyond, the spread of Islam had a major impact on both the Iberian Peninsula (Spain) and the Middle East.

Show 'Em Where You Got It

Because you are writing an essay about something from history, the essay must be based on historical fact as opposed to your opinion. Once you let your reader know what you are going to say, you need to support what you are going to say by adding evidence. You've already done half the work by circling the key phrases. Once you know what the key phrases are, make sure that you introduce some evidence for each one. For example, look again at the first two sentences of our nationalism thesis:

> *Nationalism was a driving force throughout much of the nineteenth and twentieth centuries, but it had a very different flavor in Europe than in most European colonies. While nationalism for both groups meant pride in and commitment to one's own "nation," nationalism in Europe—which often meant racism or desire for domination—became synonymous with national expansion and conquest of other peoples, while nationalism in the colonies meant self-determination—freedom from European rule, and the nation's right to determine its own destiny.*

The second sentence in our thesis alludes to historical events—colonization and expansion was the result of European nationalism, while independence movements were the result of colonial nationalism. Because the thesis is just an intro to the body of the essay, you don't need to go into detail, but you do need to begin to pull in evidence at this stage of the game. The next sentence could go on to state more specifically some of the results of nationalism for each group.

Different but Equal

Each type of essay also requires something slightly different for its thesis. For example, most change-over-time questions ask that you detail the starting point for changes as well as the changes themselves. Therefore, you need to include a statement about the starting point and evidence to support your statement.

Provide information about starting points for change for the Islam example from above.

_____

_____

_____

_____

Depending on the countries or regions you chose, your essay should now read something like this:

> The spread of Islam had a major impact on both the Iberian Peninsula (Spain) and the Middle East from its inception to the early 1400s and beyond. Despite the relatively early split into two camps—the Shia and the Sunni—over a disagreement about who should succeed Mohammad as the leader of the faith, Islam spread rapidly throughout the Middle East, due in part to the fact that although Muslims were intent on converting those they conquered, they were also flexible and tolerant of different forms of religious expression. By the middle of the eighth century, Muslims held parts of southern Iberia and southern parts of Italy and were intent on moving further into Europe, which threatened the Christians who dominated most of the regions to the north.

If this were a document-based question, your evidence would be documents rather than historical information you know.

Help 'Em Get There

The last sentence in your thesis can be as important as the first because it helps the reader get from your intro into the bulk of what you have to say. Make the transition to the body of the essay with a sentence that opens with something like, "To better understand these changes…" or "To better understand these documents…" Consider the following example:

> To better understand how nationalism led to the struggle for independence in many European colonies, one must first examine how nationalism, among other factors, led to the establishment of many of these colonies.

In the space below, try writing a transitional sentence for the essay on Islam:

_____

_____

_____

_____

_____

Your sentence could read something like the following:

To better understand the impact of Islam on both the Middle East and Spain during this period, one must first take a look at what these areas were like prior to the introduction of Islam.

As you know, each type of essay requires a slightly different kind of thesis. Keep this page marked for future reference. Here is a quick summary of the specs for each type of thesis you will write.

DBQ Thesis
- Open with something like, "After reviewing these documents, it is clear that..."
- Rephrase the question as an answer; include all key phrases.
- Address each part of the question with a statement and a document reference or an example (compare, contrast, and change over time as appropriate).
- Make the transition to the body of the essay by citing the additional document: "To better understand how these documents relate to each other, a document about *x* would be useful..."

Change-Over-Time Thesis
- Rephrase the question as an answer; include all key phrases.
- Address each part of the question with a statement and evidence.
- Make the transition to the body of the essay with a sentence like, "To better understand these changes..."

Comparative Thesis
- Restate the question as an answer; include all key phrases.
- Address each part of the question with a statement and evidence.
- Include both similarities and differences.
- Make the transition to the body of the essay with a sentence like, "To better understand the similarities and differences between these two societies..."

But What About the Rest?

Of course, the thesis is only the beginning of your essay, but getting the beginning right can really make writing the rest of the essay much easier. There are some basic rules of writing essays for standardized tests that will help you score your best. Here are the points to keep in mind while writing each AP World History Exam essay.

- Essays should be a minimum of 4 to 6 paragraphs: Opening (thesis), Body, Body, Body, Closing.
- Use transitional words and trigger words to highlight important points.

Good Transitional Words

Contrast or Change	Similarity or Continuity
but, however, although, though in contrast, alternatively	*since, moreover, similarity, as well as, still, likewise, therefore*

- Write neatly. An essay that cannot be read will not receive a good score.
- If you don't know how to spell a word, choose another. Readers are not supposed to grade your spelling, but poor spelling can cast a shadow on the rest of your essay.
- Watch your time. Spending too much time on the first essay could mean running out of time on the last essay.
- Think before you write. In fact, do more than think—make notes, jot ideas, create an outline. The more work you do before you write, the neater and more organized your essay will be.

Part IV
Drills

Chapter 3
Period 1
Technological and Environmental Transformations c. 8000 B.C.E. to 600 B.C.E.
Drills

DRILL 1

1. Myths are useful to historians for all of the following reasons EXCEPT

   (A) they may include reflections of real events
   (B) they illustrate the values and traditions of their societies
   (C) they preserve and explain ancient technology for modern adaptation
   (D) they sometimes reveal commonalities among early societies

2. Which of the following is a key characteristic of all early civilizations?

   (A) Basic written communication
   (B) Some economic specialization
   (C) Some military organization
   (D) Complex astronomical knowledge

3. Each of the following civilizations sprang up around major river complexes EXCEPT

   (A) Sumer
   (B) Harappa
   (C) Olmec
   (D) Xia

4. All of the following faiths are polytheistic EXCEPT

   (A) Shinto
   (B) Hinduism
   (C) Sikhism
   (D) Taoism

5. Which of the following is NOT a technological innovation that led to major change and improvement in the lives of Neolithic peoples?

   (A) Plows, which were used to till agricultural land
   (B) Seaworthy craft, which allowed long-distance travel by water
   (C) Wheeled vehicles, which facilitated overland travel and trade
   (D) Pottery, which improved cooking, food storage, and thus nutrition

6. Which of the following directly contributed to the increase in permanent and semi-permanent settlements around the Nile Valley around 5000 B.C.E.?

   (A) The decline in cattle populations forced people to adopt agriculture.
   (B) The warming of the climate drying out the Sahara drove people east.
   (C) The introduction of ironwork facilitated building larger settlements.
   (D) The end of the Ice Ages created a more hospitable climate for settlement.

7. The Code of Hammurabi codified which of the following principles?

   (A) *Primae noctis*, first rights to maidens' virginity in feudal society
   (B) *Status quo antebellum*, re-establishment of prewar conditions
   (C) *Quid pro quo*, the exchange of one favor for another
   (D) *Lex talionis*, scaled retributive justice

8. "To bring about the rule of righteousness in the land, so that the strong should not harm the weak."

The quote above comes from the Babylonian law code, better known as

(A) the Code of Hammurabi
(B) the Law of the Twelve Tables
(C) the Tang Code
(D) the Napoleonic Code

9. Women in Egypt in 1300 B.C.E. could do all of the following EXCEPT

(A) own property
(B) appear in court
(C) dissolve their marriages
(D) serve in government positions

From the grave of Menna, the agricultural scribe of the Pharaoh. Scene: Threshing of grain. c. 1422-1411 B.C.E. until 1600

Source: Original illustration by The Yorck Project Gesellschaft für Bildarchivierung GmbH. Uploaded by Jan van der Crabben, published on 26 April 2012 under the GNU Free Documentation License.

10. The image above is an illustration of what activity essential to the development of ancient civilizations?

(A) Agriculture
(B) Hunting
(C) Animal husbandry
(D) Trade

Check your answers on page 113.

DRILL 2

1. The decline of the three classical civilizations by 600 C.E. were all characterized by

   (A) centralized government
   (B) outside invasions
   (C) the rise of Islam
   (D) famine

2. The rise of agricultural societies saw the rise of all of the following EXCEPT

   (A) the development of democratic societies
   (B) the general deterioration of the status of women
   (C) the creation of bureaucracy
   (D) the development of systems of law

3. Early civilizations contributed all of the following achievements EXCEPT

   (A) alphabets
   (B) animal husbandry
   (C) mathematics
   (D) divisions of time

4. Each of the following became centers of civilization in the ancient world EXCEPT

   (A) the Middle East
   (B) India
   (C) South America
   (D) Egypt

5. The civilization most responsible for the modern English alphabet is

   (A) The Phoenicians
   (B) The Hebrews
   (C) The Sumerians
   (D) The Egyptians

6. The use of which of the following metals had the greatest influence on the development of weapons and warfare during ancient times?

   (A) Bronze
   (B) Steel
   (C) Copper
   (D) Iron

7. By around 3500 B.C.E., Sumerians developed all of the following EXCEPT

   (A) an alphabet
   (B) the wheel
   (C) astronomy
   (D) complex religious systems

8. In comparison to its Mesopotamian neighbors, Egyptian society showed a higher level of sophistication in

   (A) its development of science
   (B) its alphabet
   (C) defense against invaders
   (D) mathematics

9. During the Neolithic Revolution, which of the following advancements was key to the transition of nomadic societies into fixed communities and the start of civilizations?

   (A) Written language
   (B) Domestication of animals
   (C) Cultivation of plants
   (D) Development of simple tools

10. Ziggurats were pyramid-like temples that were formed to worship deities in which of the following early civilizations?

    (A) Indus Valley
    (B) Egyptian
    (C) Greek
    (D) Sumerian

Check your answers on page 114.

DRILL 3

1. The development of coined money for trade as an alternative to the barter system is attributed as a chief contribution from which of the following societies?

   (A) Lydian
   (B) Phoenician
   (C) Akkadian
   (D) Hebrew

2. All of the following describe elements of ancient Egyptian society EXCEPT

   (A) use of hieroglyphs for written communication
   (B) mummification for preservation in the afterlife
   (C) monotheistic religion
   (D) hierarchical social structure

3. Which of the Egyptian Kingdoms encompassed the peak of Egyptian civilization including its largest geographic size?

   (A) Old Kingdom
   (B) Nubian Kingdom
   (C) Middle Kingdom
   (D) New Kingdom

4. The Phoenicians developed a simplified 22 letter alphabet that is the origin of many current written alphabets today. Which of the following best explains why this alphabet was able to spread so efficiently to societies throughout the region?

   (A) The Phoenician spoken language associated with the alphabet was similar to most of the other languages of the Mediterranean.
   (B) The Phoenicians established naval city-states across the Mediterranean and were actively involved in maritime trade with many different societies.
   (C) The Phoenicians conquered many of their neighboring civilizations and the alphabet was spread through assimilation of culture.
   (D) The Phoenicians were rapidly conquered by the Egyptians, which spread the written system by extensive trade routes to the east.

5. The Code of Hammurabi was associated with which of the following early civilizations?

   (A) Persian
   (B) Hittite
   (C) Babylonian
   (D) Egyptian

6. The picture above depicts Egyptian peasants harvesting papyrus reeds. For what purpose was this plant likely harvested?

   (A) To be broken down for consumption
   (B) To be used to generate scrolls as a writing surface
   (C) To be burned during a religious ceremony
   (D) To be used to mummify the recently deceased

Check your answers on page 116.

Chapter 4
Period 1
Technological and Environmental Transformations
c. 8000 B.C.E. to 600 B.C.E.
Answers and Explanations

ANSWER KEY

Drill 1
1. C
2. B
3. C
4. C
5. B
6. B
7. D
8. A
9. D
10. A

Drill 2
1. B
2. A
3. B
4. C
5. A
6. D
7. B
8. D
9. C
10. D

Drill 3
1. A
2. C
3. D
4. B
5. C
6. B

EXPLANATIONS

Drill 1

1. **C** Remember that you're looking for the one that *isn't* true. Myths have not preserved and explained ancient technology for modern adaptation on anything like a large enough scale to make them useful to historians in that capacity. They have, however, shed light on real events, even without detailing them perfectly, illustrated the values and traditions of their societies, and revealed commonalities among early societies, such as flood-related episodes in key origins stories, so cross off (A), (B), and (D).

2. **B** When a population's farmers achieved agricultural surplus, allowing some people freedom from the need to farm, those non-farmers' activities diversified the economy and helped create civilizations from what were previously subsistence groups. Basic written communication, military organization, and complex astronomical knowledge were not necessary preconditions for the development of civilization, so cross off (A), (C), and (D).

3. **C** This is a tough question because all of these societies sprang up around rivers. However, the Olmecs' river system is comparatively minor and played less of an integral role in their society than in the other three. Sumer was located between the Tigris and Euphrates Rivers, a major river complex, so cross off (A). Harappan civilization sprang up in the Indus River valley, and the Harappans maintained trade with societies on the Indian subcontinent (such as Mohenjo-Daro) and beyond (such as Sumer), thanks to river access—so cross off (B). The Xia were the first dynasty built on the Huang He, or Yellow, River, the largest river in modern-day China, so cross off (D).

4. **C** Sikhism, founded in the fifteenth century in India, is the only monotheistic religion on this list.

5. **B** While some Neolithic peoples developed boats, not all did, and significant sea travel did not occur until the last few millennia before the common era. Plows, the wheel, and pottery were major inventions occurring much earlier that were crucial in the development of Neolithic civilizations, so cross off (A), (C), and (D).

6. **B** After the Ice Ages ended around 10,000 B.C.E.—cross off (D)—the area we now know as the Sahara Desert was actually a fertile, green valley. But around 5000 B.C.E., the climate dried out and became increasingly harsh. This drove people east to settle in greater concentrations around the Second Cataract of the Nile River Valley. The increase in agricultural production was not a result of a decline in cattle population—cattle-raising preceded the development of agriculture, but agriculture developed independently of changes in the cattle population, so cross off (A). Finally, ironwork did not develop in Africa until approximately 1000 B.C.E., so cross off (C).

7. **D** *Lex talionis* is the Latin term for the principle often expressed as it is in the Code of Hammurabi, "an eye for an eye." This justice is retributive, but it is also scaled—an eye merits no more than an eye, and under the Code of Hammurabi, different levels of the realm's subjects with different levels of rights had different levels of responsibility under the law. Cross off (A) because this principle is associated with feudal Europe, several millennia after the Code of Hammurabi was laid down in Babylon in approximately 1772 B.C.E. *Status quo* antebellum means "the way things were before the war" and generally operates on an international scale, whereas the Code of Hammurabi dealt with domestic law, so cross off (B). And *quid pro quo* is not a purely legal principle and does not appear in the Code of Hammurabi, so cross off (C).

8. **A** Even if you don't have these different documents memorized, use the reference to a Babylonian law code as a hint. Hammurabi's Code (A) was written by Hammurabi, the Babylonian king. The Law of the Twelve Tables (B) was at the cornerstone of ancient Roman law. You should associate the Tang Code (C) with the Tang dynasty in China, and the Napoleonic Code (D) with post-Revolution France, at the turn of the nineteenth century.

9. **D** Ancient Egyptian society did not see men and women as equals, but as complements. Women were seen as equal to men under the law. They could own land (A), represent themselves in court cases, sit on juries and testify in trials. Women could divorce (C) and sue their husbands in court for property.

10. **A** The oxen and the rake should give away that this is agriculture. The animals aren't being killed (B), they're not being selected for specialized breeding (C), and they're not being exchanged for money or goods (D).

Drill 2

1. **B** The three classical civilizations—India, China, and Rome—all faced outside invasions which caused weak states to fall. It was weak governments who could not protect themselves against these invasions that caused the fall (A). The rise of Islam did not cause the Fall of Rome (C).

2. **A** As civilization moved forward, women became more tied to the home. Agriculture and farming was the first step in removing women from the public sphere (B). Bureaucracies (read: governments) were built to help organize societies (C), and laws to help govern them (D).

3. **B** Ask yourself which of these seems out of context; which one would be the first handful of things new civilizations would need in order to organize themselves. Early civilizations created their own alphabets (A), studied mathematics (C), and first introduced concepts such as the day and other divisions of time (D). Animal husbandry was not the first part of domestication, though, and it wouldn't be until the eighteenth century that the practice became a science.

4. **C** Civilization began in Africa and spread from there, so it would take longer for individuals to reach the Americas. Egypt (D), the Middle East (A), and India became centers for great civilizations.

5.   **A**   The Phoenicians had the greatest effect on the later Greek and Roman alphabets. The Sumerians had cuneiform (C), the Egyptians had hieroglyphics (D), and the Hebrews had an alphabet unique to themselves (B).

6.   **D**   The Iron Age changed warfare, making weapons stronger. In many places, iron and steel (B) were developed at the same time, but iron was more prevalent, so the era was called the Iron Age. Copper isn't really used for weapons (C). Bronze was used in ancient times to maybe cover things, as decoration, but not to make weapons (A).

7.   **B**   By about 3500 B.C.E., the Sumerians had developed the first known human writing, cuneiform (A). They also were characterized by the development of astronomical sciences (C), intense religious beliefs (D), and tightly organized city-states. The Sumerians, along with other civilizations, seemed to invent the wheel a bit later, by 2500 B.C.E.

8.   **D**   The Mesopotamian societies include the Sumerians and the Babylonians. The cuneiform alphabet of the Sumerians and the scientific developments of these groups proved more sophisticated than Egyptian hieroglyphics and the scientific endeavors of this society. Egypt was relatively remote and therefore less open to invasion. However, Egypt was the ancient powerhouse of mathematics. In the ancient world, the mathematician priests of the Nile Valley had no peers. Four mathematical papyri still survive. They show that the priests had mastered all the processes of arithmetic, including the theory, but they began to develop algebra and trigonometry as well.

9.   **C**   The development of agriculture and cultivation of plants permitted early societies to remain localized to specific areas. As crop yield increased, these communities were able to grow and expand into the earliest civilizations. Written language (A) did not emerge until after the formation of fixed agricultural societies. Domestication of animals (B) and development of simple tools (D) were critical advancements within the hunter-gather clans and pastoral societies, which precede the Neolithic Revolution.

10.   **D**   Ziggurats are directly associated with the civilizations of Mesopotamia (Sumerians, Persians, and Babylonians). Egyptians (B) did build pyramids; however, these structures are not considered ziggurats, nor were they typically used for religious worship (burial). There is no evidence of great temples associated with the Indus Valley civilization (A) and the Greeks did not build pyramid-like temples (C).

Drill 3

1. **A** Coined money first emerged in the seventh century B.C.E. in Lydia. The Phoenicians (B) provided a simplified alphabet for written communication. The Akkadians (C) contributed the earliest known codes of laws. The Hebrews (D) developed the religious beliefs commonly called Judaism.

2. **C** Ancient Egyptians, similar to most other early civilizations, were polytheistic worshipping many deities. Hieroglyphs (A) and mummies (B) have been found in numerous pyramids and temples from the three kingdoms and Egyptian society exhibited a clear hierarchy (D) of social status including in order the pharaoh, priests, nobles, artisants, peasants, and lastly slaves.

3. **D** The New Kingdom (around approximately 1400 B.C.E.) encompassed the peak of Egyptian power and control with the civilization stretching from Asia-Minor to Nubia. The Nubian Kingdom (B) is not considered one of the three great Egyptian kingdoms. Egypt during the Old (A) and Middle Kingdoms (C) was largely isolated to the Nile River valley.

4. **B** The Phoenicians are known for their extensive trade within the Mediterranean and the development of their phonetic alphabet. The spread of the Phoenician alphabet was greatly enhanced by the their widespread trade throughout the region. There were many different languages (A) spoken throughout the Mediterranean, which would have likely hindered spread rather than facilitated it. The Phoenicians were not known for conquering many different civilizations (C) nor did the Egyptians (D) conquer the Phoenicians.

5. **C** Hammurabi was a Babylonian king and established the code as an early system of law, which outlined justices for infractions.

6. **B** Egyptians primarily used papyrus for the development of writing scrolls. Although parts of the papyrus plant are edible, the plant was not specifically harvested for consumption (A). There is no direct use of papyrus for religious ceremonies (C) or mummification (D).

Chapter 5
Period 2
Organization and Reorganization of Human Societies c. 600 B.C.E. to 600 C.E.
Drills

DRILL 1

1. The Roman and Han Empires traded via which of the following?

   (A) The Strait of Gibraltar
   (B) The Triangular Trade Route
   (C) The Silk Roads
   (D) The Suez Canal

2. Lao-Tzu argued that

   (A) obligations of filial piety included extended family
   (B) ambition and activism lead to chaos
   (C) order was achievable through strong, centralized government
   (D) all life is suffering

3. Monotheistic Zoroastrianism shares its origins as a belief system with

   (A) Sufism
   (B) Islam
   (C) Judaism
   (D) Hinduism

4. The Vedic religions

   (A) featured monotheism, as did Judaism
   (B) contributed to the development of India's caste system
   (C) were practiced predominantly within the Roman Empire
   (D) considered reincarnation incompatible with a focus on hard work

5. The Han and Gupta Empires both

   (A) fell in part because of economic issues stemming from a concentration of wealth in the hands of a few
   (B) were more successful than the Roman Empire at defending themselves from invasion
   (C) were more successful than the Persian Empire at using the environment to further their goals
   (D) fell in part because they concentrated military troops within their cities

6. Which of the following belief systems was notably changed between 600 B.C.E. and 600 C.E. due to the growth of trade and communication networks throughout its region?

   (A) Judaism, which began to incorporate monotheistic ideas at this point
   (B) Christianity, which adapted as it spread through the efforts of missionaries
   (C) Buddhism, which began to consider the idea of predestination during this time
   (D) Confucianism, which spread along the Silk Road and began incorporating elements of Hinduism

7. The Peloponnesian War in the late fifth century B.C.E. was fought primarily between

   (A) the Persians and the Cretans, for control over Mediterranean trade routes
   (B) the Macedonians and the Peloponnesians, as part of Philip II of Macedon's bid to control Greece
   (C) the Delian League and the Peloponnesian League, for dominance of Greece
   (D) the Minoans and Mycenaens, for control over islands in the Aegean Sea

8. By the early fourth century C.E., the Empire of Axum on the Red Sea had

   (A) adopted Christianity as its state religion
   (B) risen to become the chief trading power in Africa
   (C) converted to Islam thanks to the efforts of missionaries
   (D) slipped into economic decline

9. From the first century B.C.E. through the third century C.E., all of the following were true about Korea EXCEPT

   (A) its capital was located in Nanglang, now called Pyongyang
   (B) it was known as Gojoseon and was a major trade area
   (C) it was controlled in part by Chinese commanderies
   (D) it was home to the Protectorate General to Pacify the East

10. Qin China and the African Nok culture were both noted for their creation of

   (A) graves for horses alongside their masters
   (B) life-size terra cotta figures
   (C) major walled defenses for the realm
   (D) legalist bureaucracies

Check your answers on page 133.

DRILL 2

1. The bulk of Alexander the Great's territorial gains came through conquering

   (A) India
   (B) the Arabian Peninsula
   (C) the Persian Empire
   (D) north Africa

2. Which of the following is true of Octavius Caesar, Marcus Lepidus, and Marc Antony?

   (A) They formed the First Triumvirate, ruling the Roman Republic by unofficial arrangement until the death of one of the triumvirs.
   (B) They formed the Second Triumvirate, ruling the Roman Republic until ambition and rivalry sent them to war against each other.
   (C) They served together as consuls of Rome, advising the emperor on military matters and governance of the empire.
   (D) They conspired together to assassinate Julius Caesar in order to position themselves as the military commanders of the empire.

3. One major difference between China during the Tang Dynasty, as compared to China at the fall of the Han Dynasty, four centuries earlier, is that until the reign of Emperor Wuzong, China under the Tang

   (A) systematically crushed religions the ruling elite found threatening
   (B) grappled with foreign invaders challenging territorial borders
   (C) had an economy backed by a centralized system of hard currency
   (D) was more receptive to Buddhism's influence on Confucianism

"Beloved-of-the-Gods, King Piyadasi, conquered the Kalingas eight years after his coronation. One hundred and fifty thousand were deported, one hundred thousand were killed and many more died (from other causes). After the Kalingas had been conquered, Beloved-of-the-Gods came to feel a strong inclination towards the Dhamma, a love for the Dhamma and for instruction in Dhamma. Now Beloved-of-the-Gods feels deep remorse for having conquered the Kalingas."

4. The excerpt above from the Rock and Pillar Edicts of Ashoka Maurya explain his decision to convert to which of the following religions?

   (A) Hinduism
   (B) Buddhism
   (C) Judaism
   (D) Daoism

5. In contrast to classical Indian society, classical Roman society boasted greater

   (A) social mobility
   (B) commitment to the development of science
   (C) reliance on an agricultural economy
   (D) diversity of faith systems

6. One of the most significant factors in China's development into one of the first elaborate classical societies was

   (A) its comparatively open society, which allowed for social mobility and freedom of religion
   (B) its stable political leadership
   (C) its access to gold and other precious metals
   (D) its ability to remain isolated and avoid outside invasion

7. All of the following were characteristics of both the Qin and Han dynasties EXCEPT

   (A) strong centralized governments
   (B) an expansion of China's territory
   (C) extreme brutality
   (D) a reliance on the political and social philosophies of Confucius

8. The Great Wall of China, pictured above, was built during which Chinese dynasty?

   (A) Zhou
   (B) Qin
   (C) Han
   (D) Mauryan

9. One of the greatest differences between Hinduism and Buddhism is the former's emphasis on

   (A) reincarnation
   (B) one central being
   (C) personal development
   (D) the caste system

10. What do Confucianism, Hinduism, and Judaism have in common?

    (A) Each created guidelines and moral authority for the cultures to which they belonged.
    (B) Each demanded that the cultures to which they belonged evangelize and spread the philosophies of the culture.
    (C) Each is a polytheistic faith.
    (D) Each was developed in the Indus River Valley.

Check your answers on page 134.

DRILL 3

Map of World Religion, c. 600 C.E.

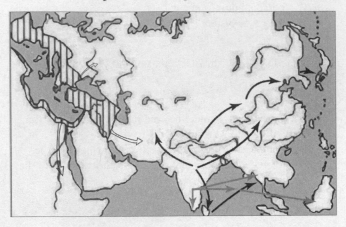

1. The striped gray and white arrows represent the spread of which major religion?

   (A) Buddhism
   (B) Hinduism
   (C) Christianity
   (D) Islam

2. The three classical civilizations of China, India, and the Mediterranean (Greece and Rome) are similar in that

   (A) each relied primarily on an agricultural economy
   (B) each supported the development of science
   (C) each emphasized clear social strata
   (D) all of the above are true

3. Daoism promotes a belief that one should

   (A) advocate for what one believes is moral
   (B) seek harmony with nature
   (C) concentrate on spreading the beliefs of Daoism
   (D) all of the above are true

4. All of the following spread along trade routes in the Classical period EXCEPT

   (A) art
   (B) disease
   (C) agriculture
   (D) all of the answers are true

5. The Mayan of Mesoamerica were similar to the Egyptians in that the Mayan

   (A) built pyramids
   (B) saw warfare was a religious ritual
   (C) used large animals in their agricultural projects
   (D) mummified their dead

6. Which two Classical civilizations would face attacks from Huns and end by 600 C.E.?

   (A) Rome and India
   (B) Rome and China
   (C) China and India
   (D) Greece and India

7. Women experienced the greatest freedoms under which Classical civilization?

   (A) Greece
   (B) China
   (C) India
   (D) Rome

8. One significant change that differentiated Classical civilizations from the earlier river-valley societies was that the Classical civilizations

    (A) warred less with their neighbors
    (B) created larger political structures, making them capable of controlling more territories
    (C) had societies with more social equality
    (D) were more agricultural

9. All of the following correctly match the belief system with the corresponding geographic location in which the system thrived by 600 C.E. EXCEPT

    (A) Christianity in West Europe
    (B) Buddhism in Korea
    (C) Buddhism in China
    (D) Christianity in East Europe

10. In Classical India, an individual's occupation was dictated by that person's

    (A) education
    (B) financial strength
    (C) caste
    (D) gender

Check your answers on page 136.

DRILL 4

1. Though vastly different belief systems, Christianity, Hinduism, and Buddhism all support the concept of

   (A) disapproval of other belief systems
   (B) a strong priesthood
   (C) clear church hierarchy
   (D) life after death

2. Greeks, Romans, the Chinese, and other groups of "civilized" peoples drew distinctions between themselves and "barbarian" peoples by differentiating between themselves and the other person's

   (A) culture
   (B) race
   (C) ethnicity
   (D) level of education

3. During the Gupta Empire of India, women's rights deteriorated and

   (A) girls as young as six or seven were married to guarantee their purity
   (B) lost the right to own or inherit property
   (C) could not participate in sacred rituals or study religion
   (D) all of the above

4. Though most early civilizations were polytheistic, the Greek faith was unique in that its gods

   (A) were all-powerful
   (B) had human emotions
   (C) were considered branches of one great being
   (D) interfered directly in everyday life

5. The greatest difference between Greek society and the later Roman society, which was largely based on the Greeks, was the Greeks'

   (A) democratic system of government
   (B) reliance on slave labor
   (C) polytheistic faith system of gods
   (D) considered women were inferior to men

6. Which of the following was a feat of Roman engineering?

   (A) A large road system
   (B) A system of aqueducts
   (C) Large and lasting bridges
   (D) All of the above

7. The above portrait within its mummy wrappings, from the first century C.E., shows the influence of which other contemporary civilization?

   (A) Chinese
   (B) Indian
   (C) Greek
   (D) Persian

8. By 600 B.C.E., which of the following world regions had experienced the most extensive decline?

   (A) Western Europe
   (B) India
   (C) China
   (D) Japan

   > There is a thing confusedly formed,
   > Born before heaven and earth.
   > Silent and void
   > It stands alone and does not change,
   > Goes round and does not weary.
   > It is capable of being the mother of
   > the world.
   > I know not its name,
   > So I style it "the way."

9. The passage above is quoted from the *Tao Te Ching* by Lao Tzu and is the essential text for followers of which faith?

   (A) Hinduism
   (B) Judaism
   (C) Islam
   (D) Daoism

10. The concept of zero, an essential mathematical development, was invented independently in which two civilizations?

    (A) The Chinese and the Indian
    (B) The Indian and the Mayan
    (C) The Mayan and the Chinese
    (D) The Chinese and the Egyptians

Check your answers on page 137.

DRILL 5

1. Confucianism, Hinduism, and Judaism are all similar in that

    (A) they preach evangelism to convert others to the cause
    (B) they are all religions
    (C) they believe non-believers were condemned to hell in the afterlife
    (D) they all provide guidelines for living and define a moral authority

2. The trade and agricultural development which drove the classical Indian, Chinese, and Greek economies led to the rise and spread of all of the following EXCEPT

    (A) coinage
    (B) gaps among the social classes, often defined by land
    (C) warfare
    (D) cultural ideas

3. Compared to Western Europe, classical China was more technically advanced due to all of the following inventions EXCEPT

    (A) irrigated fields
    (B) ox-drawn plows
    (C) water-powered mills
    (D) paper

4. Which of the following civilizations developed in isolation?

    (A) The Olmecs of Central America
    (B) The Polynesian of Fiji and Samoa
    (C) The Polynesian of Hawai'i
    (D) All of the above

5. The "Constantinian shift" refers to Roman Emperor Constantine the Great's conversion to

    (A) Judaism
    (B) Christianity
    (C) Legalism
    (D) Mercantilism

6. All of the following are philosophers who lived before 100 B.C.E. EXCEPT

    (A) Buddha
    (B) Confucius
    (C) Muhammed
    (D) Socrates

7. The first civilizations to emerge in sub-Saharan Africa were influenced by

    (A) Indian merchants and religions
    (B) Egypt and Hellenism
    (C) Rome and Sumer
    (D) Jewish peoples fleeing from Israel

8. All of the following early civilizations emerged within large river valleys or systems EXCEPT

    (A) Egyptian
    (B) Mesopotamian
    (C) Indus
    (D) Olmec

9. The Zhou Dynasty developed the concept of Mandate of Heaven which

    (A) provided justification for patriarchal society in China
    (B) justified the overthrow of leaders that were unjust or unwise
    (C) established feudalism
    (D) rationalized the demand for tribute to rulers

10. Which of the dynasties of China is most closely associated with the formation of the Great Wall?

    (A) Zhou
    (B) Qin
    (C) Han
    (D) Ming

Check your answers on page 140.

DRILL 6

1. The Han dynasty lasted from approximately 200 B.C.E. to 460 C.E. Which of the following represents a significant development originating from Han China?

   (A) Paper
   (B) Mathematical Concept of Pi
   (C) Calendar
   (D) Coined Money

2. Before the Athenians embraced a democratic form of government, the civilization was ruled by an aristocracy. Which of the following aristocrats was fundamental in the eventual transition of Athens to a democracy?

   (A) Alexander the Great
   (B) Solon
   (C) Aristotle
   (D) Plato

3. The Golden Age of Pericles saw many advancements in Athens among these were all of the following EXCEPT

   (A) democracy for all adult males
   (B) rebuilding after the Persian wars
   (C) establishment of the Delian league
   (D) the writings of the *Iliad* and *Odyssey* by Homer

4. The Greek social class of free people with no political rights was most similar to what class of the early Roman republic?

   (A) Patricians
   (B) Plebeians
   (C) Prisoners
   (D) Slaves

5. All of the following contributed to the spread of Hellenism in the classical world EXCEPT

   (A) the conquests of Alexander the Great
   (B) incorporation of Greek culture and philosophy in the Roman Empire
   (C) extensive trading between Greeks and the Chinese
   (D) wars with the Persian Empire

6. The Roman victories during the Punic wars were significant because

   (A) they gave Rome control over the Greeks and the Aegean sea.
   (B) they granted Rome control over the northern European territories of Gaul and Britain.
   (C) they gave Rome control of the western Mediterranean.
   (D) they gave Rome control of the Germanic territories.

7. Of the following, which was not a member of the First Triumvirate of Rome?

   (A) Crassus
   (B) Pompey
   (C) Julius Caesar
   (D) Octavian

8. The cause of the collapse of the Mayan empire remains an ongoing mystery. Which of the following is NOT a potential reason for the fall of the Mayan empire?

   (A) Disease
   (B) Spanish conquest
   (C) Drought
   (D) Social revolution

9. The emergence of Christianity coincided with persecution under Roman control. Which of the following Roman emperors was instrumental in the ending of violence towards Christians?

   (A) Julius Caesar
   (B) Augustus
   (C) Nero
   (D) Constantine

10. Which of the following was a primary reason for the eventual fall of the Roman and Gupta empires in the fifth and sixth centuries C.E.?

    (A) Disease and famine
    (B) Religious uprisings
    (C) Insecure borders prompting invasions
    (D) Political instability

Check your answers on page 141.

DRILL 7

1. Classical Greek, Roman, and Chinese civilizations were similar in that they

   (A) shared the same religious beliefs
   (B) used the same trade routes
   (C) were predominately patriarchal
   (D) were directly conquered by the Huns

2. Confucianism and Legalism differ in that

   (A) Confucianism focuses on generating an orderly society based on the principle of individual goodness whereas Legalism uses law to eliminate the role of human nature and maintain absolute authority.
   (B) Legalism focuses on generating an orderly society based on the principle of individual goodness whereas Confucianism uses law to eliminate the role of human nature and maintain absolute authority.
   (C) Confucianism is a religion, whereas Legalism is not.
   (D) Legalism is a religion, whereas Confucianism is not.

3. Which of the following religions had the least impact on social order prior to the fall of the Roman Empire?

   (A) Judaism
   (B) Christianity
   (C) Paganism
   (D) Islam

4. The reigns of the Roman emperors Diocletian and Constantine in the fourth century c.e. set the stage for what major change in the geopolitical landscape of Europe?

   (A) The power of the Roman empire was shifted from Rome to Constantinople in the east.
   (B) Roman control of Britain was lost during the Norman invasion.
   (C) Christianity was established as the official state religion of the Roman Empire.
   (D) The power of Rome was consolidated to the western reaches of the empire.

5. The Twelve Tables of Rome are most similar to which of the following?

   (A) Edict of Milan
   (B) Code of Hammurabi
   (C) *Pax Romana*
   (D) *Analects* of Confucius

6. The Delian League and the Peloponnesian League, respectively, were alliances associated with the cities of

   (A) Sparta and Rome
   (B) Athens and Corinth
   (C) Athens and Sparta
   (D) Athens and Rome

7. One major advantage aiding the rise of the Roman Empire was the geographical position of Rome. Which of the following was NOT an advantage afforded by Rome's geography?

   (A) It was protected from Northern invasion by the Alps.
   (B) It is located on a peninsula that would require an invasion by sea.
   (C) It is located centrally within the Mediterranean.
   (D) It is easily accessible by land for trade with neighboring regions.

La Morte di Cesare, 1804–1805 by Vicenzo Camuccini

8. The above image depicts the assassination of Julius Caesar. Which of the following resulted directly from the death of Julius Caesar?

(A) Caesar's power was returned to the Senate and the Roman Republic was restored.
(B) The Second Triumvirate defeats the assassins of Caesar and breaks up the Roman Republic.
(C) The absence of Caesar causes unrest leading to the Punic Wars.
(D) The First Triumvirate is formed to stabilize the Roman Republic.

10. The image above depicts the Temple of Hatshepsut, the first known female ruler in history. All of the following were rights of women during the Egyptian New Kingdom EXCEPT

(A) inherit property
(B) buy and sell property
(C) dissolve marriages
(D) all of these were rights of women

Check your answers on page 143.

9. The Temple of Herculus Victor was built close to the Tiber in Rome in the late second century B.C.E. Which of the following civilizations had the greatest impact on its architectural design?

(A) Persian
(B) Mesopotamian
(C) Egyptian
(D) Greek

Chapter 6
Period 2
Organization and Reorganization of Human Societies c. 600 B.C.E. to 600 C.E.
Answers and Explanations

ANSWER KEY

Drill 1
1. C
2. B
3. D
4. B
5. A
6. B
7. C
8. A
9. D
10. B

Drill 2
1. C
2. B
3. D
4. B
5. A
6. D
7. C
8. B
9. D
10. A

Drill 3
1. C
2. D
3. B
4. D
5. A
6. A
7. D
8. B
9. C
10. C

Drill 4
1. D
2. A
3. D
4. B
5. A
6. D
7. C
8. A
9. D
10. B

Drill 5
1. D
2. C
3. A
4. D
5. B
6. C
7. B
8. D
9. B
10. B

Drill 6
1. A
2. B
3. D
4. B
5. C
6. C
7. D
8. B
9. D
10. C

Drill 7
1. C
2. A
3. D
4. A
5. B
6. C
7. D
8. B
9. D
10. D

EXPLANATIONS

Drill 1

1. **C** The Silk Roads connected Asia to the Mediterranean, through what we now call the Middle East—the Roman and Han Empires represented two poles of this trade route, along which not only goods but also knowledge, culture, and religion spread. The Strait of Gibraltar, the Triangular Trade Route, and the Suez Canal all involve maritime trade, which was not significant between the Romans and the Han. So cross off (A), (B), and (D). The Triangular Trade Route was the transatlantic trade that carried African slaves to the Americas, and the Suez Canal did not exist until the 1860s, approximately two millennia after the Roman and Han Empires.

2. **B** Lao-Tzu argued that the Tao is passive and yielding, and humans should accomplish everything by doing nothing, as the Tao does(n't). Confucianism advocated ambition and activism, but Lao-Tzu warned this would lead to chaos. (A) is a Confucian belief, so cross that off. (C) describes Legalism, also not what we need. Finally, (D) is one of Buddhism's Four Noble Truths, so that isn't it either.

3. **D** This is tricky, because Hinduism is polytheistic. Zoroastrianism believes in one god, Ahura Mazda, incorporating the duality of body and mind. This inclusion of dual elements in a single entity, as well as Zoroastrianism's belief in a self-creating universe, gives the faith common elements with Brahminic Hinduism. Sufism is a form of Islam, but neither connects with Zoroastrianism, so cross off (A) and (B). Nor are Zoroastrianism's origins related to Judaism, so cross off (C).

4. **B** The Vedas are seminal texts in Hinduism, which is polytheistic, nothing to do with the Roman Empire, and believes in reincarnation without any conflict regarding hard work—so cross off (A), (C), and (D).

5. **A** The corruption of the oligarchy in the Han and Gupta Empires contributed to the empires' fall in each case. Class-based resentment led to uprisings and conflicts of power. The Huns were also an exacerbating factor in the decline of the Gupta Empire. The Han dealt with invasion by the Xiongnu, but these invasions did not contribute substantively to their empire's decline. Cross off (B), as you can't make this statement about both empires. There's no support for (C), so cross that off. Troop concentration wasn't a problem, so cross off (D).

6. **B** Christianity developed in slightly different ways in different communities, as missionaries adapted teachings to new contexts. Judaism had always been monotheistic, so cross off (A). Predestination runs counter to the Buddhist ideas of karma and dharma, so cross off (C). And Confucianism and Hinduism did not blend, despite Silk Road contacts, so cross off (D).

7. **C** Athens headed the Delian League, a confederation of Greek kingdoms who found themselves at war with the Peloponnesian League, led by Sparta, in the fifth century. This was actually the second such war between these two groups, but this time, the Spartans were backed by the Persians and succeeded in defeating the Delian League, bringing all of Greece under Spartan hegemony. Philip II's bid to control Greece would happen a century later, so cross off (B). Crete wasn't involved, so cross off (A). The Mycenaeans and Minoans (who were Cretans, by the way) were societies that interacted in the second and third millennia B.C.E., long before the Peloponnesian War, so cross off (D).

8. **A** The Empire of Axum, which corresponds roughly with modern-day Ethiopia, was introduced to Christianity in approximately 322 C.E., when King Ezanawas baptized as a Christian and adopted it as the state religion. For that same reason, cross off (C)—Islam also generally didn't have missionaries. While Axum was a trading power, it was not the foremost trading power in Africa, so cross off (B). Furthermore, there was no marked economic decline at this time, either, so cross off (D).

9. **D** Remember that you're looking for the one that *isn't* true. The Protectorate General to Pacify the East was established in Pyongyang by China's Tang Dynasty in 668 C.E., long after the time period mentioned in the question. Pyongyang was the capital of Korea, or Gojoseon (as it was called then), but at the time it was known as Nanglang, so cross off (A) and (B). Parts of Korea were also under the control of the Chinese, divided into units known as commanderies, so cross off (C).

10. **B** Emperor Qin Shi Huang's Terra Cotta Army and the life-size terra cotta figures of the Nok culture are two rare examples of life-size terra cotta work. The Qin emperor had the figures produced for his tomb, and the Nok culture seems to have used them for a variety of ceremonial purposes. (A), (C), and (D) are all true of China but not of the Nok culture, so cross them off.

Drill 2

1. **C** Conquering the Persian Empire brought Alexander large swaths of the Middle East and Asia. While his conquered territories did include Egypt (where you'll recall he founded the city of Alexandria, a great center of culture and knowledge), he did not conquer the rest of North Africa, so cross off (D). He was rebuffed from India, so cross off (A), and he died planning his conquest of the Arabian Peninsula, so cross off (B).

2. **B** Octavius, Marcus Lepidus, and Marc Antony formed the Second Triumvirate, ruling Rome together until Marcus Lepidus was driven into exile and Octavius, who would take the name Augustus, defeated Marc Antony at the Battle of Actium in 31 B.C.E. The First Triumvirate was made up of Julius Caesar, Crassus, and Pompey, lasting until Crassus's death in 53 B.C.E., so cross off (A). Antony, Lepidus, and Octavius did not serve together as consuls, so cross off (C), and they in fact defeated the assassins of Julius Caesar in order to establish themselves as the Second Triumvirate, so cross off (D).

3. **D**   Emperor Wuzong of Tang *hated* Buddhism, as well as other 'non-native' faiths such as Zoroastrianism and Manicheanism, but before his reign, the Tang were generally supportive of Confucianism's adoption of Buddhist ideas (which created neo-Confucianism). The Han, though, had been critical of Buddhism, and Buddhists faced persecution during that period. Cross off (A) because that's what Wuzong did. Cross off (B) as that was true of both dynasties. Cross off (C) because this was established during the Han.

4. **B**   There are a few hints in the excerpt itself to help you POE out some answers. Whoever the passage refers to, he is the "beloved-of-the-**gods**," which means it's a polytheistic faith. So get rid of (C), since Judaism is monotheistic. It keeps referring to the "Dhamma," which is a Buddhist concept.

5. **A**   The most significant difference between Indian society and Roman society was the strict adherence to social strata in India, which affects the society even today. Both pursued science (B), both were agricultural societies (which is a main factor in filing them members of the "classical society" group) (C), and both tolerated many faith systems in their empires (D).

6. **D**   This is a common sense question – which of these answer choices either was the reason why societies began to develop (agriculture, language, that sort of thing) or which one mentions avoiding something that brought societies down (outside invasion, internal corruption, and weakness). In China's case, they built a big ole wall to keep people out. China, like most societies back then, did not have any real societal mobility (A). It had a cycle of different dynasties (B), but didn't have significant access to silver or gold (C).

7. **C**   Though the Qin dynasty lasted for only a very short time (221–206 B.C.E.), they did some amazing things. Most famously, they built the Great Wall. They accomplished this, though, through extreme brutality and enslavement. Otherwise, the Qin and Han dynasties were very similar.

8. **B**   Though the Qin dynasty was very short (221–206 B.C.E.), it gets a mention in the history books due to the first Emperor of China, Qin Shi Huang's work on the Great Wall. Several walls had been built in order to deter invaders as far back as the seventh century B.C.E. However, during the Qin dynasty, Emperor Qin Shi Huang built and unified several parts of the wall. When we refer to The Great Wall of China, we refer to the giant public works project that this Emperor accomplished.

9. **D**   Buddhism was founded by a Hindu, but Hinduism is a religion and a social system. It's tied to India's caste system, that you belong to in the caste you are born into because of what you did in a past life. Buddhism is a much more spiritual philosophy, which did not address India's caste system.

10. **A**   All three gave guidelines of how to live. Each of these belief systems are tied to the cultures from which they arose, so none are particularly evangelic (B). Judaism is not polytheistic, and Confucianism is more a philosophy (C). Judaism did not develop in the Indus River Valley (D).

Drill 3

1. **C** Christianity came from the Mediterranean region. Jesus taught in Jerusalem, on the far east edge of the Mediterranean. Islam didn't exist until a little later, so it's out of era and you should eliminate it (D). The black arrows show the spread of Buddhism (A) and the light gray show Hinduism (B). But those clearly are religions that didn't start in the Middle East, so you should POE them out anyway.

2. **D** All three characteristics helped form the stability and structure necessary for civilization to flourish.

3. **B** The Dao is defined as the way of nature or the cosmos. Adherents are encouraged to become one with the world, to yield and flow with it.

4. **D** Trade routes were paths for for art, disease, and agriculture. They were where all the world interacted.

5. **A** The Mayan built their own pyramids. We've even found some new ones recently. They did not use large animals (C) or mummify their dead (D). They did see war as a religious ritual, but the Egyptians did not (B).

6. **A** Rome and India were attacked by the Huns. The Greeks were already gone (D) and the Chinese had built a big wall (B) and (C).

7. **D** In Rome, women enjoyed slightly better rights than they had in Greece (A). In Greece, women could not be citizens, but they had the right in Rome. They could also own property. In India (C) and China (B), women were clearly subservient to men. They couldn't inherit property. In India, they weren't even allowed to read the sacred texts.

8. **B** Early civilization is characterized by its development of agriculture (D). They warred just as much as any societies (A), and women were subservient in those societies, as well (C). The early civilizations, however, were very simplistic. It's the development of larger political structures that made Classical civilizations stronger.

9. **C** Buddhism in China is the correct answer because the question asks for the geographic location that matches the belief system in 600 C.E. and in that era, Confucianism was completely tied to the Chinese way of life.

10. **C** Your caste—your social class you were born into—in India dictated everything about your life. Hindus believed you were born into a caste based on your closeness to Brahma, the creator. The lower your caste, the worse you'd been in a past life, and the more spiritual work you should do on yourself. You could not change your caste until you died and were reborn into a new one.

Drill 4

1. **D**   Though Christianity doesn't believe in reincarnation, Hinduism and Buddhism believe you have a very clear life after death—another life. Christians have a strong priesthood (B) and clear church hierarchy (C), and tend to be intolerant of other faith systems (A). Hinduism is as much a social system as it is a belief system, so there's no real priesthood. Buddhism strives to be tolerant of the nature of the world, so it has little to say on other belief systems, so much so that it was eventually reabsorbed back into Hinduism in India.

2. **A**   Most classical civilizations—the Greeks, Romans, Chinese, and even Aztecs—defined "barbarians" as those who didn't come from their culture. The world civilization is derived from the Latin word civilis, which means "of the citizens." The term was coined by the Romans who used it to distinguish between themselves as citizens of a cosmopolitan, urban-based civilization and the "inferior" peoples who lived in the forests and deserts on the fringes of their empire. The Greeks, centuries earlier, also distinguished between themselves and outsiders in similar ways. The boundaries between civilized and barbarian for these societies were strictly cultural. It was possible for free people to become members of any of these groups by adopting the customs and languages of their "civilized" counterparts.

3. **D**   Though the Guptas brought a period of peace, prosperity, and artistic endeavors, women's position in society deteriorated. An emphasis on an urban culture increased the desire for land and women lost the right to own or inherit land. Girls were married off at a tender age of six to seven years. The early marriage of girls guaranteed that they were chaste. Widow re-marriage was permitted at times. However, by and large the concept of widow re-marriage was not very well received by the Gupta people. If a woman opposed to throw herself in the funeral pyre of her husband (a practice called sati), she was eschewed by the society members. Women were also restricted from studying sacred texts or even participating in any rituals.

4. **B**   The Greeks did believe their gods to be all-powerful, and to interfere directly with everyday life (A and D), but so did most polytheistic faiths at the time. What was unique about the Greeks was that they saw their gods as flawed and imperfect, capable of jealousy and spite, just like their worshippers.

5. **A**   Slavery was an important element in both Greek and Roman society as a large labor pool. At one point, slaves comprised one-third of the Roman population (B). The Romans absorbed most of the Greek gods into their faith system (C) and so had a very similar set of gods. Roman women could own property, just as Spartan women could (D). The great difference between the two societies was their systems of government—a democracy in Greece compared to a republic in Rome (A). In Greece, citizens were expected to participate in debates and decision-making processes. In Rome, a representative republic formed. The main governing body was made up of two distinct bodies: the Senate, which comprised patrician families, and the Assembly, which was initially made up of patricians, but later was opened to plebeians. Two consuls were annually elected by the Assembly. The consuls had veto power over decisions made by the Assembly.

6. **D** What have the Romans ever done for us? A lot, actually. The Romans built a huge road network (at its largest, around 53,000 miles) throughout the empire, mostly for easy transport of military troops. The roads were constructed using stones and concrete, another helpful Roman invention (A). The Romans also constructed numerous aqueducts to supply water. The city of Rome alone was supplied with eleven limestone aqueducts that provided the city with over 1 million cubic metres of water each day (enough for 3.5 million people by today's standards) (B). Roman bridges were among the first large and lasting bridges built. They were built with stone and had the arch as their basic structure. Most utilized concrete, as well. Built in 142 B.C.E., the Pons Aemilius, later named Ponte Rotto (broken bridge) is the oldest Roman stone bridge in Rome, Italy. The biggest Roman bridge was Trajan's bridge over the lower Danube, constructed by Apollodorus of Damascus, which remained for over a millennium the longest bridge to have been built both in terms of overall and span length. They were most of the time at least 60 feet above the body of water (C). The Romans also built dams and indoor plumbing.

7. **C** The mummy wrapping should have clued you in to the Egyptians. This portrait is one of a series found on mummies called the Fayum portraits unearthed throughout Egypt dating from the Roman period, from the late first century B.C.E.. or the early first century C.E. onwards. Under Greco-Roman rule, Egypt hosted several Greek settlements, mostly concentrated in Alexandria, where Greek settlers lived alongside several million Egyptians. The Fayum portraits show a synthesis of the predominantly Egyptian culture of the area and that of the Greek minority in the area. Researchers tell us the people inside these mummies are much more likely to be of Egyptian than Roman descent. That aside, you should be able to pick out the naturalistic depiction of the individual and the wreath (which symbolizes status) as typifying Greek art.

8. **A**   From 200 to 600 c.e., all three classical civilizations collapsed entirely or in part, and all three were invaded by outside groups from central Asia. The central Asian nomadic Huns attacked all three classical civilizations. About 100 c.e., the Han dynasty (C) began serious decline. Weakened central government, social unrest led by overtaxed peasants, and epidemics were the most prominent sources of decline. These combined to make the government unable to stop invading nomads. However, by 600, China revived, first with the brief Sui dynasty and later (and more gloriously) with the Tang. Confucianism and bureaucracy revived. Unlike those in Rome, the cultural and political structures in China were too strong to be fully and permanently overturned. The decline in India was not as drastic as in China. By 600, Huns destroyed the Gupta Empire (B). For several centuries, no native Indian led a large state there. Hinduism gained ground as Buddhism, unappealing to the warrior caste, declined in its native land. After 600, Islam entered India and Arab traders took control of Indian Ocean trade routes. What survived was Hinduism (Islam never gained adherence from a majority of the population) and the caste system.

Decline in Rome (A) was multifactorial. Population declined, leadership faltered, the economy flagged, tax collection became more difficult, and, as a result and perhaps most significantly, despondency pervaded much of the citizenry. The decline in Rome was more disruptive than in China or India and was more pronounced in the Western portion of the empire than in the eastern. In Italy, Spain, and points north, the fall of Rome shattered unities and reduced the level of civilization itself. Emperors Diocletian and Constantine slowed the spiral of decay but only temporarily; the latter moved the capital to Constantinople and allowed Christianity. When Germanic tribes invaded in the 400s, there was little power or will to resist. In the eastern half, a remnant of the empire survived as the Byzantine Empire. In earlier days of the Roman Empire, two Middle Eastern civilizations, the Parthian and then the Sassanid, attempted to revive the Persian Empire.

9. **D**   The Dao (also spelled Tao) is defined as the way of nature, the way of the cosmos. Founded by Lao Tzu, a legendary Chinese philosopher, this belief system is based on an elusive concept regarding an eternal principle governing all the workings of the world. The Dao is passive and yielding; it accomplishes everything yet does nothing. The overly poetic language and the reference to "the way" should be cues for you that this may refer to Daosim.

10. **B**   Though all civilizations had relatively accurate calendars, only the Mayan had a 365-day calendar. Both the Maya and the Gupta separately invented the concept of zero.

Drill 5

1. **D** Each of these belief systems is tied to the culture in which it was practiced and therefore is not particularly evangelical (A). Confucianism is not a religion (B), and for this reason does not consider what happens in the afterlife (C). As systems used to sustain the culture to which they belong, they provide guidelines on how to live (as any belief system does) and define moral authorities.

2. **C** The rise of trade routes spread philosophies and religions along trade routes; not only merchants, but also teachers and philosophers traveled the Silk Road (D). With trade came a desire to trade easily for goods, thus the rise of currency (coinage). Each civilization had its own, usually made of metal (A). Agricultural societies seem to naturally create a division between those groups that own the land and those that do not, and usually farm it (B).

3. **A** The Chinese worked hard to advance technologically. Ox-drawn plows were introduced to farms around 300 B.C.E. (B) Under the Han, the first water-powered mills were introduced (C). It was also during this time that paper was invented (D). Though there is record that early China used terrace irrigation, this was not unique to China, so your answer is (A).

4. **D** In Central America, the Olmecs (A) developed and spread throughout Central America. Though they didn't seem to have a written language, they cultivated corn, domesticated animals, and produced massive, pyramid-shaped religious monuments. They disappeared by 400 B.C.E. Though it is not entirely clear how the Polynesian people came to settle many islands of the Pacific, most theories state that the people came in canoes from the Taiwan (southeast China) region. The Samoan and Fiji islands (B) were some of the first islands settled, and the cultures developed in isolation from mainland Asia. The Hawai'ian archipelago was initially settled by Polynesian long-distance navigators sometime between 300 and 800 B.C.E.

5. **B** Sometime referred to the Triumph of the Church, the Peace of the Church, or the Constantinian shift, the Emperor Constantine's conversion to Christianity (B) is a small mystery to historians. In 313 B.C.E., Constantine issued the Edict of Milan legalizing Christian worship. The Emperor was exposed to the faith through his mother, Helena, but was 42 when he publicly declared himself a Christian. Remember that Legalism (C) is a philosophy you should associate with China.

6. **C** Siddhartha Gautama Buddha (A) was a sage you should associate with classical India whose teachings are the foundation of Buddhism. He lived around 563 B.C.E.. to around 483 B.C.E. Confucius (B), another scholar whose teachings are the basis of Confucianism, is a figure you should associate with classical China. He lived 551 B.C.E. to 479 B.C.E. Socrates (D) was a classical Greek Athenian philosopher and is seen as one of the founders of Western philosophy. He lived around 469 B.C.E. to 399 B.C.E. Muhammed, the father of Islam, lived from 570 C.E. to 632 B.C.E., much later than the other men in these answer choices.

7. **B** The Saharan Desert created a great barrier between sub-Saharan Africa and Eurasia. The spread of agriculture, writing, and the wheel, for example, took longer to make it through this natural obstacle. Sub-Saharan African culture began in Nubia, the region around the section of the Nile River that lies in modern-day northern Sudan and the southernmost part of Egypt, and so the Nile provided a connection to the ancient Egyptian civilization. The Nubians united with the Kush, who were eventually destroyed by the Ethiopians (also called the Aksum). This detail is not necessarily essential to know, but make sure you know that the Nile provided a highway for culture and technology to travel down, and could break through the natural impediment of the Saharan Desert.

8. **D** The Olmec (and later Chavin) civilizations emerged within dense terrain, which lacked large river valleys and systems. Egyptian civilization (A) emerged in the Nile River valley. The Mesopotamian (B) civilizations emerged in the Tigris and Euphrates river valleys and the Indus civilization (C) was named for its river valley system.

9. **B** The Zhou dynasty established the principle of Mandate of Heaven, which granted rulers the power to rule from heaven provided that they governed wisely and justly. In other words, the Zhou would continue to rule only with the blessing from heaven. Patriarchal society (A) remained in the Zhou dynasty, however the mandate specifically related to rule of Zhou China. Both feudalism (C) and tribute (D), which also arose during the Zhou dynasty, refer to social hierarchy rather than absolute Zhou rule.

10. **B** Qin Shi Huang rejoined much of China and connected the various wall fortifications that had been previously assembled for protection to form the Great Wall of China.

Drill 6

1. **A** The Han dynasty is credited with the invention of paper. The concept of Pi (B) emerged in the Gupta dynasty of India and the first calendar (C) and coined money (D) were developed hundreds of years before the Han dynasty.

2. **B** Solon attempted to transform Athenian society to provide more fairness and equality. His efforts are recognized for their push towards the acceptance of democracy. Alexander the Great (A) was not an Athenian (he was Macedonian) and the philosophers Aristotle (C) and Plato (D) lived after the transition to democracy.

3. **D** Homer's epics were written approximately 800 years prior to the Golden Age and recounted sacking of Troy. At the time of Pericles, all of the east (where Troy would have been located) was under Persian control. Pericles established democracy for adult males (A), oversaw the rebuilding of Athens after the Persian wars (B) and the formation of the Delian league (C) to protect Greece in the event of a future invasion.

4. **B** In Roman society, free people with limited or no political rights were referred to as plebeians. In later years, plebeians would take part in the Roman Assembly. However, most political power and decisions were reserved for the patricians (A). Prisoners (C) and slaves (D) were neither free nor did they have any political power.

5. **C** The spread of classic Greek culture and society (Hellenism) did not penetrate into the far east as trading with China would not occur readily for hundreds of years. The conquests of Alexander the Great (A) played a major role in the Hellenization of the classical world. The adoption of many elements of Greek culture and society and the future expansion of the Roman empire (B) also led to the spread throughout the classical world. Lastly, wars between the Greeks and the Persians (D) led to exchange of culture and ideas as well as joined the various city-states of Greece against a common enemy.

6. **C** During the three Punic wars, the Romans defeated and destroyed the Carthaginians eliminating the only major naval power in the western Mediterranean. After seizing control of the western Mediterranean, later conquests would result in the captures of Greece (A), Gaul and Britain (B) and some of the Germanic territories (D) expanding the Roman empire.

7. **D** The First Triumvirate of Rome consisted of Pompey, Crassus, and Julius Caesar. Octavian (D) along with Marc Antony and Lepidus formed the Second Triumvirate after Caesar's assassination.

8. **B** The Spanish would not arrive in the New World until the late fifteenth century at least 800 years after the start of the decline of the Mayan empire. All of the other potential explanations are feasible as diseases (A) were known to circulate, droughts occurred often (C; which prompted sacrificial worship to deities), and internal unrest (D) has led to the collapse of many other great societies.

9. **D** With the issuance of the Edict of Milan, Constantine ended Christian persecution in 313 C.E. Christianity had not emerged during the rules of Caesar (A; ended in 44 B.C.E.) and Augustus (B; 14 C.E.) and although Christianity had emerged by the rule of Nero (C), Christians were greatly persecuted (including shows in the Coliseum) under his rule.

10. **C** Both Rome and Gupta were eventually conquered by invasion due in large part to insecure borders. Although, disease (A), religion (B) and political instability (D) were present at times in both civilizations, the inability of the two empires to maintain their vast land claims made them susceptible to invasion.

Drill 7

1. **C** All three civilizations shared a common male-dominated social system. The three civilizations differed substantially in religion (A), their use of trade routes (B; China was largely isolated from Europe until late during the Roman empire) and the Huns (D) did not directly cause the end of any of the civilizations (although you may argue that they had a role in several of their eventual demises).

2. **A** Confucianism is a social philosophy focusing on the good in inter-relationships to build an ordered society. Legalism utilizes tough laws and harsh punishments to eliminate individual opposition and create a strong centralized government. Both Confucianism and Legalism are philosophies, not religions (C and D).

3. **D** Islam did not emerge until the seventh century C.E., well after the fall of the Roman Empire. Judaism (A), Christianity (B), and Paganism (C) were all active and involved in society during the peak of the Roman Empire.

4. **A** Diocletian split the Roman empire in to Western and Eastern regions. This divide was further delineated with the formation of Constantinople during the reign of Constantine, which created a new seat of power. Although Constantine consolidated the two regions of the empire into one, his death led once again to the split of the empire. The Norman invasion (B) did not occur until the eleventh century. Christianity (C), although becoming dominant during the reigns of Diocletian and Constantine, was not declared the official state religion until 391 C.E. (with the reign of Theodosius I) and this change had a minimal impact on the geopolitical landscape of Europe. With the formation of Constantinople, the power of Rome never returned and the power of the Western Roman Empire (D) continued to decline into the fifth century.

5. **B** The Twelve Tables of Rome were the codified law of the Roman Empire. Only the Code of Hammurabi represents a legal system for society. The Edict of Milan (A) ended Christian persecution at the hands of the Roman empire. The *Pax Romana* (C) was a long period of peace and stability. The *Analects* of Confucius (D) were the sayings and ideas of Confucius, which establish much of the philosophy of Confucianism.

6. **C** The Delian League involved alliances dominated by the power and authority of Athens. The Peloponnesian League was alliance centered on the powerful army of Sparta. The differences between these alliances ultimately led to the Peloponnesian war.

7. **D** The location of Rome on a peninsula sheltered by the Alps made invasion difficult for foreign armies. However, trade routes by land were greatly limited and often required maritime transport.

8. **B** Following Caesar's murder, the Second Triumvirate is formed (consisting of Marc Antony, Octavian, and Lepidus) which defeats the conspirators of the assassination (Brutus and Cassius) and split up the Republic. Julius Caesar was originally part of the First Triumvirate (D) and the Punic Wars (C) occurred hundreds of years before the rise and fall of Caesar.

9. **D** Roman architecture (similar to other facets of society) was heavily influenced by the Greeks. The columnar design of the temple is highly reminiscent of the religious temples found in Athens and other regions of Greece.

10. **D** By law, essentially men and women had equal rights. Women could buy and sell property, inherit property, will their property, and had the ability to dissolve marriages.

Chapter 7
Period 3
Regional and Transregional Interactions
c. 600 C.E. to c. 1450
Drills

DRILL 1

1. The T'ang Dynasty achieved which of the following?

   (A) Wrote the Code of Bushido, codifying a code of chivalry similar to that of Europe
   (B) Successfully fended off invasion by Genghis Khan
   (C) Wrote extensive collections of encyclopedias and histories, thanks to their development of printing processes
   (D) Expanded Chinese territory to include parts of Manchuria, Mongolia, Tibet, and Korea, organized into a tribute system

2. The Fujiwara Shogunate was characterized by all of the following EXCEPT

   (A) an emperor with only nominal power
   (B) emphasis on education as a path to advancement
   (C) a noble warrior class of powerful landowners
   (D) strict social constraints on the role and duties of women

3. Magyars and Vikings in the ninth century C.E. shared which of the following characteristics?

   (A) Raiding by tribal bands for resources and political power
   (B) Catholic faith and strong allegiance to the pope
   (C) Naval strength and navigational skill
   (D) The abolition of slavery

4. The spread of Islam influenced medieval Europe in which of the following ways?

   (A) Proclamation of religious tolerance in England
   (B) Widespread use of Arabic in French and Italian market towns
   (C) Religious reform within the Catholic Church
   (D) New interest in Greek and Arab writings and technology

5. From the early thirteenth century onward, the English king shared power with the people as a result of

   (A) an arrangement between Norman conquerors and the Saxon population they conquered
   (B) a compromise ending a century-long bloody war of succession
   (C) a nobles' rebellion securing the rights of both nobles and commoners
   (D) a break with the Catholic Church that established the king as the head of the Church of England

6. The Roman and Abbasid Empires each declined largely as a result of

   (A) extended famine
   (B) the spread of Islam
   (C) invasions by borderland Mongols
   (D) increasing reliance on mercenary armies

7. Which of the following statements about the development of Buddhism and Christianity is accurate?

   (A) Neither founder presented himself as divine during his life.
   (B) Both grew from other religions and developed monastic orders.
   (C) Neither faith's followers faced persecution for their beliefs.
   (D) Both faiths relied heavily on texts written by their founders.

8. The Incan and Aztec Empires were similar in all of the following ways EXCEPT

   (A) innovative use of agricultural techniques to increase production
   (B) the practice of ritualized human sacrifice
   (C) a regularized monetary system
   (D) an upper class of priests and royalty

9. Western European and West African leaders between 1000 and 1450 C.E. were similar in which of the following ways?

   (A) Both adopted scholarship from Muslim civilizations.
   (B) Neither allowed forced labor in their realms.
   (C) Both made use of new sailing techniques to visit other continents.
   (D) Neither engaged in territorial warfare to gain power and resources.

10. Between the tenth and mid-fifteenth century, sub-Saharan Africa's economy was primarily driven by

    (A) the export of gold to the Middle East and Europe
    (B) the import of cowrie shells from other coastal regions
    (C) the wealth of Muslim traders on the Mali-Great Zimbabwe trade route
    (D) the transatlantic trade sending slaves to the Americas

Check your answers on page 167.

DRILL 2

1. The Ottoman and Holy Roman Empires' treatment of non-believers in the dominant faith was similar in which of the following ways?

   (A) Non-Muslims and non-Christians, were openly persecuted by the imperial governments.
   (B) Non-Muslims and Jews, were allowed some degree of religious freedom but faced higher taxes and local instances of persecution.
   (C) Each tolerated the presence of Jewish populations better than the presence of Christian or Muslim populations.
   (D) Each engaged in forced conversions of conquered populations.

2. Buddhism spread from China to Japan and Korea by which of the following means?

   (A) Trade on the Silk Road
   (B) Imperial campaigns against Shinto believers
   (C) Missionary efforts and tribute relations
   (D) Military conquest followed by missionary efforts

3. Which of the following statements about Osman Bey is the most accurate?

   (A) He unified Anatolia and built the Muslim Ottoman Empire to challenge the Byzantine Empire.
   (B) His reign inaugurated a golden age of arts and military greatness, and he led the conquest of Hungary.
   (C) His Cossacks expanded Russian territories beginning in the sixteenth century, ensuring access to the Caspian Sea.
   (D) He led a Moorish rebellion against the Reconquista in Spain at the beginning of the sixteenth century.

4. In thirteenth century Japan, the daimyo were

   (A) leaders of Buddhist monasteries
   (B) large landowners similar to lords in feudal Europe
   (C) warrior-peasants serving in the shogun's army
   (D) the shogun's inner circle of military advisers

5. Under the rule of the Delhi Sultanate, Hindus in India

   (A) experienced a renaissance and constructed many grand temples
   (B) were no longer subjected to the constraints of the caste system
   (C) were taxed and faced a certain measure of persecution
   (D) could not own property or participate in public life

6. All of the following are accurate statements about the Yuan Dynasty EXCEPT that

   (A) its social structure was highly stratified with little upward mobility
   (B) it was the first occurrence of Muslim rule in China
   (C) it was founded after Mongols overran the Song Dynasty
   (D) its last ruling members escaped to northern territories and disputed the legitimacy of their Ming successors

7. After the death of Genghis Khan, all of the following were true EXCEPT

   (A) his empire was divided among his three sons and two grandsons
   (B) mongols expanded their control of European and Asian territory
   (C) internal dissention caused the collapse of the empire within a generation
   (D) trade continued to flourish thanks in part of Mongol control of the Silk Road

8. Chinese influence in Japan abated in the ninth century largely because

   (A) the Code of Bushido called for an isolationist stance in Japanese foreign policy
   (B) the ruling shogunate deliberately sought out western innovations and technology
   (C) Shinto declined in popularity compared to Buddhism as the primary religion in Japan
   (D) of a conscious effort to promote Japanese cultural identity under the Fujiwara family

9. Which of the following empires beat back both the Crusaders and the Mongols?

(A) The Mughal Empire
(B) The Dehli Sultanate
(C) The Abbasid Empire
(D) The Mamluk Sultanate

10. Which of the following is an example of Islamic influence in Spain?

(A) The Royal Chapel of Granada
(B) The Royal Palace of Madrid
(C) The Hagia Sofia
(D) The Alhambra

Check your answers on page 168.

DRILL 3

1. The Bantu-speaking peoples' migration into sub-Saharan Africa helped facilitate the spread of

   (A) tribal religions that had previously been unknown in the region
   (B) maritime advances similar to those previously seen in the Roman Empire
   (C) domesticated animals who transformed the region's economy
   (D) ironwork technology that made creation of tools and farming implements easier

2. The Dehli Sultanates, Muslim Iberia, and Abbasids are all examples of

   (A) feudalistic governments that developed concurrently
   (B) Islamic states that developed concurrently
   (C) city-states that developed concurrently
   (D) military alliances that developed concurrently

3. West African and Mongol women between the seventh and mid-fifteenth centuries

   (A) were not allowed to own property or sign their names to legal documents
   (B) were the undisputed leaders of their societies
   (C) had more power and influence than women in Europe's patriarchal societies
   (D) had less power and influence than European women because of cultural restrictions on behavior

4. The Little Ice Age contributed to

   (A) the rise of commerce, since the dry weather made travel easier
   (B) a decline in invasion-based warfare, allowing a resurgence of cities
   (C) the growth of agricultural technology to adapt to the changes in climate
   (D) the decline of large cities that had previously been centers of power

5. Which Portuguese innovation produced increased travel and trade with West Africa?

   (A) The practice of allowing locals to serve as officers on trade ships
   (B) The development of a school for navigation
   (C) Better cataloging of West African climate and geography
   (D) New ship designs better suited for waterways in the area

6. The Islamic Golden Age began with

   (A) the Mongol conquest of Baghdad, bringing the collected wisdom of Genghis Khan to the Arab World
   (B) the rise of the Abbasid Caliphate, when the capital relocated from Damascus to Baghdad
   (C) the extension of the Silk Road into China under the Han Dynasty
   (D) the rise of the Ottoman Empire as the Mongol Khanates began to fall apart in the fourteenth century

7. Both of the images above depict

   (A) statues of Shinto deities prior to Buddhism's arrival in Japan in the sixth century C.E.
   (B) idols created by polytheistic Middle Eastern cultures before the spread of Islam
   (C) representation of African deities carved in stone centuries before European contact
   (D) statues created by southern hemisphere cultures in the early second millennium C.E.

8. From the seventh through the ninth centuries C.E., India experienced

   (A) resurgent interest in Hinduism and development of most modern Indian languages
   (B) a period of decline in elaborate temples as Buddhist ascetism gained wider popularity
   (C) the import of cultural and political systems from other countries in southeast Asia
   (D) a period of isolation from outside cultural influences in order to purify Indian culture

9. Pope Urban II called for the First Crusade in order to

   (A) open European access to African trade routes
   (B) gain political power during the Great Schism
   (C) restore Christian access to the Holy Land
   (D) destroy Jewish populations in Europe

10. Yaroslav the Wise inaugurated the Golden Age of Kievan Rus by

   (A) uniting the principalities of Novgorod and Kiev and codifying legal traditions in the Russkaya Pravda
   (B) initiating state sponsorship of literary and artistic endeavors, as well as widespread industrialization
   (C) conquering much of present-day Russia and maintaining control through liberal policies of limited autonomy
   (D) endowing the Eastern Orthodox Church with state sponsorship for developing great works of devotional art

Check your answers on page 170.

DRILL 4

1. All of the following are true about the Black Death EXCEPT

    (A) it caused greater mortality among the affected populations than any other epidemic in world history
    (B) it likely began in Asia and traveled via the Silk Road to the Mediterranean and into Europe
    (C) it produced a range of religious, economic, and social disturbances that changed the nature of European societies
    (D) its effects were worsened by chronic malnutrition in Europe as a result of reduced harvests after the Little Ice Age

2. Between the seventh and eleventh centuries C.E. in Madagascar,

    (A) cultivation of staples such as potatoes and corn allowed for substantial population growth and social development
    (B) settlers arriving from Borneo in outrigger canoes developed the island through slash-and-burn agriculture
    (C) arab and Bantu-speaking newcomers brought new ideas, technologies, and livestock to the island
    (D) irrigated rice paddies were the primary sites of agricultural cultivation on the island

3. Portugal's development of the carrack in the fifteenth century was significant because

    (A) these three- and four-masted ships became the main vehicle of European exploration in the Atlantic and beyond
    (B) this design was exported to China and adapted as the junk, which would form the basis of China's first navy
    (C) the deep hulls of these ships were primarily adapted for the purpose of carrying slaves from Africa to the Americas
    (D) it improved upon a Viking design with the use of a fixed rudder rather than the more unstable steering oar

4. Mali emperor Mansa Musa and Yuan emperor Kublai Khan had which of the following in common?

    (A) Each was a devout Muslim who undertook a hajj.
    (B) Each expanded the imperial territory he inherited.
    (C) Each introduced his empire's first coinage system.
    (D) Each was of a different ethnicity from his subjects.

5. In the early Middle Ages, in comparison to the educated classes of the Arab world, the educated classes of Europe were more

    (A) worldly
    (B) religious
    (C) provincial
    (D) secular

6. All of the following contributed to the impact of the Black Plague in the fourteenth century EXCEPT

    (A) crowded conditions in European cities
    (B) a lack of sanitation
    (C) trade with China
    (D) trade with Africa

7. Who of the following was a literary figure during the Abbasid period?

    (A) Saladin
    (B) Omar Khayyam
    (C) Muhammad ibn Qasim
    (D) Mira Bai

8. Which of the following is true about the Islamic and Hindu cultures?

   (A) Islamic culture highlighted the egalitarianism of all believers, compared to the strict social structure of the Hindus
   (B) Hindu culture highlighted the egalitarianism of all believers, compared to the strict social structure of the Islamic conquerors
   (C) The Hindu were more evangelical than the Islamic culture
   (D) The Islamic culture was more open and tolerant of a variety of faiths

9. Until 1450 C.E., the greatest contact with the rest of the world for sub-Saharan Africa in the post-classical era was provided by

   (A) Christians
   (B) the Huns
   (C) Muslims
   (D) the Mongols

10. All of the following are true about the development of civilization in sub-Saharan Africa before the introduction of Islam EXCEPT

   (A) African communities shared language and beliefs similarities
   (B) Africa, unlike Europe, did not develop a universal system of governance
   (C) the center of cultural life was found in Timbuktu
   (D) stateless and secret societies flourished in this period

Check your answers on page 172.

DRILL 5

1. Which of the following sects of Islam was a response to cultural interactions outside Arabia?

   (A) Shi'a
   (B) Sunni
   (C) Sufism
   (D) All of the above

2. After the introduction of Christianity to Africa,

   (A) converted Africans gave up their animist faith
   (B) the Kush forcibly converted the rest of the continent
   (C) Christian missionaries began a Crusade in east Africa in search of the Ark of the Covenant
   (D) ancestor worship was absorbed into Christian practices

3. The Ethiopian building from twelfth century above is

   (A) a church
   (B) a grain mill
   (C) a mosque
   (D) a shrine

4. Which of the following is true of Mansa Musa's *hajj* in 1324 C.E.?

   (A) Due to his giving to the poor, gold became devalued in Cairo, Mecca, and Medina.
   (B) The wealth of Mali was displayed to the world.
   (C) His caravan included 60,000 men, 12,000 slaves, and 80 camels.
   (D) All of the above are true.

5. The mosque pictured above is an example of Islam's spread to

   (A) southeast Asia
   (B) Africa
   (C) China
   (D) western Europe

6. Which of the following is true about Islam's effect on the Sudanic empires of Western Africa?

   (A) Women began to veil themselves.
   (B) Several massacres occurred in regions which refused to convert.
   (C) Demand for slaves increased significantly.
   (D) The arrival of Islam marked the introduction of another authority figure, causing kingdoms to splinter.

7. What is the name of the family of languages to which most African languages belong?

    (A) Swahili
    (B) Amharic
    (C) Ethiopian
    (D) Bantu

8. Compared to their European counterparts, women in postclassical Africa

    (A) practiced polyandry, taking more than one husband
    (B) were often sold into slavery if they displeased their husbands
    (C) died significantly younger on average
    (D) enjoyed more rights and better status in civil society

9. Which of the following is true about the religious makeup of Africa?

    (A) Though no universal religion existed, both Christianity and Islam found adherents.
    (B) Powerful indigenous animist religions made it difficult for either Islam or Christianity to convert Africans.
    (C) Islam swept the continent around 1200 c.e. and created a universal cultural foundation.
    (D) Crusaders invaded the continent and took complete control of civil life.

10. Which of the following is an accurate characterization of trade with the Swahili coast in postcolonial Africa?

African goods	Traded for
(A) Ivory and gold	Pottery and slaves
(B) Slaves and gold	Pottery and beads
(C) Pottery and slaves	Ivory and beads
(D) Beads and slaves	Pottery and gold

Check your answers on page 174.

DRILL 6

1. Which of the following statements regarding the split of the Christian church in 1054 is NOT accurate?

   (A) Different rituals grew from Greek and Latin versions of the Bible.
   (B) Emperors in the East resisted papal attempts to interfere in religious issues.
   (C) Deep disagreements over the celibacy of priests and the type of bread to use in communion could not be rectified.
   (D) The sects could not decide on the exact site in Jerusalem of Jesus' crucifixion and, therefore, site for the Church of the Holy Sepulcher.

2. The Medieval Byzantine political system was similar to the earlier Chinese system in all of the following ways EXCEPT

   (A) the emperor was seen as ordained by god
   (B) an elaborate bureaucracy existed which supported imperial authority
   (C) women could not rule
   (D) bureaucratic officials tended to be from aristocratic classes

3. Hagia Sophia was

   (A) a huge church built during Justinian's reconstruction of Constantinople
   (B) a prayer recited by Orthodox Christians, which contributed to the Schism within the church
   (C) a relic of Saint Sophia stolen by Muslim invaders of Constantinople
   (D) burned and looted, destroying the library within, when Mongols sacked Constantinople

4. Civilizations in the Middle Ages were marked almost globally by all of the following EXCEPT

   (A) population growth
   (B) technological innovation
   (C) intolerance towards other faith systems
   (D) growth of economies beyond subsistence farming

5. Examples of agricultural technologies introduced in Medieval Europe included

   (A) horse collars, soil supplements, and domesticated oxen
   (B) the plow, the three-field system, and horse collars
   (C) the three-field system and irrigation
   (D) the plow and irrigation

6. Which of the following contributed to the growing cultural distance between Russia and Western Europe in the Middle Ages?

   (A) Parts of Russia used the Cyrillic alphabet.
   (B) Roman churches refused to interact with Eastern Orthodox clergy.
   (C) The Mongol invasion created a rift between east and west.
   (D) All of the above were contributing factors.

7. The Middle Ages introduced which of the following unique governing systems to western Europe?

   (A) Manors
   (B) Guilds
   (C) Kingdoms
   (D) Parliaments

8. What effects did the Crusades have on Western Europe?

   (A) Crusaders converted to Islam and brought the faith with them to Europe.
   (B) Europeans were exposed to ancient Greek philosophy.
   (C) Crusaders brought great wealth back, starting a migration east.
   (D) Europeans were disgusted by eastern society and became more insular.

9. Which of the following was NOT true of European women's experience in the Middle Ages?

(A) Women led religious services.
(B) Women's monastic groups provided an alternative to marriage.
(C) A growing literature stressed women's roles as assistants to and comforters of men.
(D) Women played an important role in local commerce in some economies.

10. Which of the following is true of both Aztec and postclassical Chinese women?

(A) Technology greatly affected their lives.
(B) Both societies were egalitarian.
(C) Marriages were arranged and female virginity was important.
(D) Both societies practiced foot binding.

Check your answers on page 176.

DRILL 7

1. The city above, in the Andes Mountains, was built by which Native American group?

    (A) Aztecs
    (B) Mayans
    (C) Incas
    (D) Cherokee

2. The Inca shared similarities with which other world civilization?

    (A) The classical Egyptian, who mummified their dead
    (B) The classical Chinese, who created and educated a class of bureaucrats
    (C) The Romans, who were masters of engineering
    (D) All of the above are aspects of Inca civilization

3. Which of the following was common to both the Aztec and Inca empires?

    (A) A writing system
    (B) A tribute system
    (C) Extensive use of colonization
    (D) None of the answers are correct

4. The economies of the Tang and Song dynasties of postclassical China relied on

    (A) the Silk Road and canal system
    (B) the Silk Road and an extensive roads system
    (C) the canal system and an extensive roads system
    (D) an extensive roads system and railroads

5. The Korean *hwacha* pictured above is utilizing which technological innovation of Song China?

    (A) Archery
    (B) Gunpowder
    (C) Metalwork
    (D) Military organization

6. Expanding global trade patterns greatly altered which language after 1000 C.E.?

    (A) Arabic
    (B) Sanskrit
    (C) Latin
    (D) Swahili

7. Judaism, Christianity, and Islam all share which of the following?

    (A) They are polytheistic faiths.
    (B) They revere Jerusalem and Rome as pilgrimage sites.
    (C) They recognize Moses and Abraham as prophets.
    (D) They share the Gospels and the Quran as holy books.

8. Which of the following is true about urbanization in the postclassical world?

    (A) Centralized governments tended to form by universal suffrage.
    (B) Farmers became idealized images of the Ideal Man.
    (C) Rulers tended to wield complete control over civil life.
    (D) Women tended to lose rights.

9. Which of the following is NOT an accurate statement concerning the Viking and Mongol civilizations?

   (A) Both groups used local governments to help govern their conquered lands.
   (B) Both groups travelled as far as Russia.
   (C) Both were very mobile groups and excelled at quick attacks.
   (D) Both groups raided mainly for resources.

10. One of the major reasons the Chinese failed to completely assimilate the Vietnamese into postclassical Chinese culture was

   (A) failure to create a common tongue
   (B) the lack of impact Chinese cultural imports made on the Vietnamese peasantry.
   (C) the absence of Buddhism in Vietnam
   (D) the widespread cultural impact of Japanese culture in Southeast Asia

Check your answers on page 178.

DRILL 8

1. Which of the following statements concerning the nomadic society of the Mongols prior to the construction of their empire is NOT accurate?

   (A) The basic social unit of the Mongols was the tribe.
   (B) The Mongols were primarily herders of cattle and horses.
   (C) Mongol leaders were selected by all free males for as long as they could hold power.
   (D) The Mongols created tribal confederations in times of war.

2. During the time of the Mongol invasions, Russia

   (A) was launching a series of successful assaults on Islamic territories of the Abbasid dynasty
   (B) was united under the kings of Kiev
   (C) was part of the Byzantine Empire
   (D) was divided into numerous petty kingdoms centered on trading cities

3. In addition to the destruction of the Abbasid political capital at Baghdad, what significant impact did the Mongol conquest have on the Islamic heartland?

   (A) Much of the population in the Islamic heartland was converted to the animist religion common among the Mongols.
   (B) The Mongol nomads embraced Islam and most converted.
   (C) Shi'ism was eliminated as a major sub-sect within Islam.
   (D) The destruction of Islamic cities from central Asia to the Mediterranean destroyed the centers of Islamic civilization.

4. All of the following are associated with the Renaissance EXCEPT

   (A) Gothic architecture
   (B) interest in Greco-Roman styles
   (C) greater interest in nature and things of this world
   (D) interest in classical models

5. Why did the West begin to explore new trade routes around 1400?

   (A) Islamic armies closed off all trade routes to the east.
   (B) Almost constant warfare with the Mongols in the east made trade difficult.
   (C) Technological barriers that limited previous explorations were overcome.
   (D) African pirates made it difficult to utilize previous routes.

6. After the expansion of Islam into Africa, a vibrant Christian community remained

   (A) along the Salt Road
   (B) in Algeria
   (C) on the Swahili coast
   (D) in Egypt and Ethiopia

7. Which of the following characterized Middle Eastern trade practices between 1000 and 1450?

   (A) A unified Islamic Empire imposed protective tariffs to stimulate manufacturing.
   (B) Merchants traded regularly with China, India, and sub-Saharan Africa.
   (C) The area ceased trading with Europe, but initiated trade with sub-Saharan Africa.
   (D) The Ottoman Empire controlled the trade routes and imposed significant taxes on travelling merchants.

8. Which of the following is NOT characteristic of the Polynesians before 1400?

   (A) Polynesians in Hawaii created a thriving culture and imported from the Society Islands.
   (B) Polynesians created a complex writing system in order to stay connected to the monarchy in the Society Islands.
   (C) Polynesians travelled as far as New Zealand.
   (D) Polynesian communities did not have access to metal tools.

9. The beginning of Islam was associated with the passage of words from Allah (God) to Mohammad in which of the following centuries?

   (A) Twelfth century B.C.E.
   (B) Sixth century B.C.E.
   (C) First century C.E.
   (D) Seventh century C.E.

10. All of the following are pillars of the Islamic faith EXCEPT

   (A) confession of faith
   (B) prayer five times a day
   (C) pilgrimage to Mecca once during a lifetime
   (D) confession of sins

Check your answers on page 180.

DRILL 9

1. The Islamic Empire, which coincided with the beginnings of Islam was ruled by which form of government?

   (A) Theocracy
   (B) Oligarchy
   (C) Monarchy
   (D) Democracy

2. All of the following constitute major changes during the Umayyad Dynasty of the Islamic Empire EXCEPT

   (A) Zoroastrianism briefly became the official religion during the Umayyad reign
   (B) the capital moved from the religious site of Mecca to Damascus
   (C) Muslims advance into Europe by way of the Iberian peninsula
   (D) the two main sects of the Islamic faith (Shia and Sunnis) emerge

3. The fall of the Umayyad Dynasty was most closely associated with which of the following?

   (A) Internal conflicts due to the emergence of a religious divide between Shiite and Sunni Muslims
   (B) Widespread outbreaks of disease carried by way of the Silk Road
   (C) Inability to defend its borders from attack by Mongols
   (D) None of the above

4. Baghdad became a world cultural center and the seat of major advancements in the arts and sciences during a golden age in the early to mid-ninth century C.E. in which of the following dynasties?

   (A) T'ang Dynasty
   (B) Umayyad Dynasty
   (C) Abbasid Dynasty
   (D) Merovingian Dynasty

5. The Qu'ran was established in the mid-seventh century C.E. and had a major effect on the treatment of women in Islamic society. All of the following represent changes in women's rights EXCEPT

   (A) women were considered equal before Allah.
   (B) infanticide was strictly forbidden in Islamic society.
   (C) men could no longer keep dowries if they divorced their wives.
   (D) men could have only one wife.

6. Under the reign of Justinian, the Byzantine Empire flourished. Which of the following Byzantine cities competed with the Islamic city of Baghdad for cultural supremacy of trade and the arts?

   (A) Jerusalem
   (B) Constantinople
   (C) Rome
   (D) Athens

7. Following the collapse of the Roman Empire, Western Europe was largely in disarray until the rise of the early Frankish kingdoms. The founding of the Carolingian Dynasty represented a significant event for European politics because

   (A) it maintained a common culture and unified state against conquest from Muslim invasions in the Iberian and Italian (Apennine) peninsulas
   (B) led to the legitimacy of the Roman Catholic Church's approval in political rule
   (C) established the basis of what would eventually become the Holy Roman Empire
   (D) all of the above

8. Compared to the sizes of the Byzantine, Islamic, and Persian Empires at the peaks of their powers, the Holy Roman Empire was

   (A) substantially smaller
   (B) substantially larger
   (C) approximately the same size
   (D) larger than the Persian Empire, but smaller than the Islamic and Byzantine Empires

Check your answers on page 181.

Chapter 8
Period 3
Regional and Transregional Interactions
c. 600 C.E. to
c. 1450
Answers
and Explanations

ANSWER KEY

Drill 1
1. D
2. B
3. A
4. D
5. C
6. D
7. B
8. C
9. A
10. A

Drill 2
1. B
2. C
3. A
4. B
5. C
6. B
7. C
8. D
9. D
10. D

Drill 3
1. D
2. B
3. C
4. D
5. B
6. B
7. D
8. A
9. C
10. A

Drill 4
1. A
2. C
3. A
4. B
5. C
6. D
7. B
8. A
9. C
10. B

Drill 5
1. C
2. D
3. A
4. D
5. B
6. C
7. D
8. D
9. A
10. B

Drill 6
1. D
2. C
3. A
4. C
5. B
6. C
7. D
8. B
9. A
10. C

Drill 7
1. C
2. D
3. B
4. A
5. B
6. D
7. C
8. D
9. A
10. B

Drill 8
1. B
2. D
3. D
4. A
5. C
6. D
7. B
8. B
9. D
10. D

Drill 9
1. A
2. A
3. A
4. C
5. D
6. B
7. D
8. A

EXPLANATIONS

Drill 1

1. **D** The T'ang Dynasty (618–907 C.E.) did expand Chinese holdings to include parts of Manchuria, Mongolia, Tibet, and Korea, but the T'ang rulers overextended themselves and lost control of their territory to warlords, leading to the fall of the dynasty. These areas were organized under a tribute system during the T'ang and would again be under the Ming a few centuries later. Cross off (B) because the T'ang Dynasty preceded Genghis Khan by a half a millennium. Cross off (C), because this describes the Song Dynasty, which followed the T'ang.

2. **B** While education was valued in many Chinese societies of this era, the Fujiwara Shogunate of Japan valued noble birth much more highly. The Shogunate was, however, characterized by an emperor who officially named the shogun, or military leader, but held no real power in government; a land-owning samurai class known as the daimyo; and particularly repressive treatment of women, so cross off (A), (C), and (D).

3. **A** Both the Magyars and Vikings were known at this time for their fearsome raids, whether for food and wealth, or for political reasons. While both groups would eventually convert to Catholicism, this did not happen until at least the tenth century for each group, so cross off (B). The Vikings were known for their naval strength and navigational skill, but the Magyars were land-based raiders, so cross off (C). And slavery was very much a part of both cultures at this time, so cross off (D).

4. **D** The spread of Islam brought with it a spreading of classical knowledge, some of it new to Europe, some of it merely long forgotten. This led to the rebirth of European creativity and artistic expression known as the Renaissance. It did not, however, result in either widespread use of Arabic in French and Italian market towns (even if some traders learned to speak Arabic) or religious reform within the Catholic Church, so cross of (B) and (C). Nor did it lead to proclamation of religious tolerance in England—that would come later as a result of conflict between Catholics and Protestants under the Tudors—so cross off (A).

5. **C** A successful rebellion by English nobles against King John produced the Magna Carta in 1215, a document that guaranteed the rights of feudal lords but also extended the rule of law to commoners and laid the groundwork for Parliament, which was established shortly thereafter. The Norman conquest of England occurred in 1066, so (A) is much too early—cross it off. The Hundred Years War (which actually lasted 116 years) took place in the fourteenth and fifteenth centuries, and while it was a bloody war of succession, its end had nothing to do with the people's power-sharing with the king, so cross off (B). Similarly, the English king's break with the Catholic Church came well after the early thirteenth century and was not the cause of the king's losing sole power in the kingdom, so cross off (D).

6. **D** Power slipped away from the Romans and the Abbasids as they found themselves paying others' armies for their loyalty and service, which caused significant military breakdowns over time. It wasn't extended famine, the spread of Islam (the Abbasids were Muslim!), or the Mongols that did them in, so cross off (A), (B), and (C).

7. **B**   Buddhism developed out of the Hindu tradition, much as Christianity developed out of the Judaic tradition, and both formed orders of monks. Cross off (A) because, according to Biblical tradition, Jesus Christ did present himself as the son of God during his lifetime. (The Buddha, however, considered the existence of gods to be unimportant.) Cross off (C) because this was true of both faiths in many points in history. Finally, cross off (D) because both Buddhism and Christianity were originally taught and spread orally, and their founders' lessons were usually recorded much later by others.

8. **C**   Remember that you're looking for the answer that *isn't* true of both. Choice (C), a regularized monetary system, was true of the Aztecs but not the Incas. Both civilizations, however, used innovative agricultural techniques to boost production, practiced ritual human sacrifice, and had an upper class comprising priests and royalty, so cross off (A), (B), (D).

9. **A**   Muslim scholarship was transmitted to both western European and West African realms via trade. Both also allowed forced labor, as well as engaging in territorial warfare to gain power and resources, so cross off (B) and (D). Only Western Europeans made significant use of new sailing techniques to visit another continent (Africa). Even scholars who argue that African explorers may have reached South America before the Europeans believe they used the same basic technology and techniques with which they navigated the African coast. So cross off (C).

10. **A**   Gold was the major export and economic driver for sub-Saharan Africa at this time. The import of cowrie shells was no significant factor, nor was the transatlantic slave trade (which did not start in earnest until the sixteenth century), so cross off (B) and (D). Also, while Muslim traders were important players in trade along these routes, it was the gold sub-Saharan Africans pulled from the ground that formed the basis of the economy, so cross off (C).

Drill 2

1. **B**   Choice (B), Non-Muslims and Jews were allowed some religious freedom but higher taxes and local instances of persecution, is the best description of the dominant religions' relationship with non-believers at the imperial level in the Ottoman and Holy Roman Empires. The Ottoman rulers were happy enough to collect taxes from non-believers living in their midst in exchange for leaving well enough alone, and there was very little conflict. The rulers of the Holy Roman Empire did take a harder stance, sometimes taxing Jewish populations to the point of driving them from their homes, but Holy Roman Emperors considered the Jewish populations within their borders their possessions and protected them enough to sustain them as a source of revenue. For all of these same reasons, cross off (A). While (C) is arguably true of the Holy Roman Empire, it isn't really an accurate statement about the Ottoman Empire, so cross it off. And (D) is not an accurate characterization of either on the imperial level, so cross it off.

2. **C** Buddhism spread from China to Japan and Korea in different ways. Missionaries carried Chinese culture to Japan in 522 C.E., where all things Chinese, including Buddhism, caught on quickly. Seon, or Zen, Buddhism was slowly transmitted to Korea in the seventh through ninth centuries C.E., when Korea was a vassal-state of China's T'ang Dynasty. Cross off (A) because this is how Buddhism came to China, not how it traveled to Korea or (the island of) Japan. Cross off (B) because these simply didn't happen—in Japan, many people practiced Buddhism and Shinto simultaneously. And cross off (D) because military conquest wasn't part of the equation—Korea was a vassal-state by choice, and Japan was entirely independent of China at this time.

3. **A** Choice (A) is a correct description of Osman Bey's rule over the Ottoman Turks. Cross off (B), as it describes one of his successors, Suleiman I. The Cossacks were peasant soldiers in Russia under Ivan III and Ivan IV, so cross off (C). Cross off (D), as Osman Bey had nothing to do with Spain or the Moors.

4. **B** The daimyo were major landholders who owed allegiance to the shogun but divided their land among lesser samurai (for whom peasants, in turn, worked the land), much like lords in feudal Europe. They were warriors, not peasants, so cross off (C). While some daimyo may indeed have been advisers to the shogun, that isn't what made them daimyo, so cross off (D). Also, this isn't about Buddhism, so cross off (A).

5. **C** This is an accurate description of non-Muslims' status under most Muslim regimes, even if non-Muslim faiths were *technically* tolerated under Muslim law. This was no condition to support a renaissance, though, so cross off (A), and the caste system was very much in effect, so cross off (B), but if they paid their higher taxes, Hindus were entitled to own property and be full participants in society, so cross off (D).

6. **B** Remember that you're looking for the one that *isn't* true. While Islam did reach China during the Yuan Dynasty, the Yuan rulers were not Muslim. They were, however, Mongols who overran the Song Dynasty and whose last members escaped a popular uprising to form the Northern Yuan, a dynasty-in-exile that remained at loggerheads with the Ming for several generations—so cross off (C) and (D). Yuan society was highly stratified, too, with little upward mobility, so cross off (A).

7. **C** Shortly before Genghis Khan's death, he split his empire among his four sons (one of whom died shortly before he did, resulting in his territory being divided between that son's two sons), so after his death, there were four Khanates, and Genghis Khan's successors expanded his empire for another century as trade continued to flourish along the Silk Road—so cross off (A), (B), and (D).

8. **D** During the Heian period, beginning in 794 C.E., Japan deliberately turned inward to focus on domestic cultural development. The aristocratic Fujiwara family, which had intermarried with the imperial family, was largely responsible for this rejection of external cultural influences. The shoguns and the Code of Bushido belong to the following period of Japanese history, so cross off (A) and (B). Cross off (C) because Shinto was a native Japanese faith, so this answer goes against the nature of the question. It also isn't true.

9. **D**   The Mamluks beat the Mongols in 1260 at the Battle of Ain Jalut and drove the Crusaders from the Levant by 1291. The Abbasids lost power in 1258—so, close but no cigar. Cross off (C). The Delhi Sultanate is the right time, but Delhi should make you think India, which isn't where the Crusades were happening, so cross off (B). Finally, the Mughals didn't build their empire until the 1500s, long after the Crusades, so cross off (A).

10. **D**   The Alhambra was built by the Moorish Nasrid kings in Andalucia's capital city of Granada. The Hagia Sofia, while a former mosque, is not located in Spain, so cross off (C). Both Madrid and Granada are in Spain, but Madrid was not in Moorish territory, and the fact that (A) is a chapel while not a definitive indicator of a lack of Muslim influence, does reflect its Catholic origins—so cross off (A) and (B).

DRILL 3

1. **D**   While the Bantu both learned and spread the practice of animal husbandry, this did not have the effect of transforming the region's economy, so cross off (C). They were not a maritime people, so cross off (B). Some Bantu peoples did participate in the spread of Islam, but not all, and not tribal religions in any significant way, so cross off (A). The ability to make iron tools, though, was tremendously important for the societies the Bantu encountered.

2. **B**   Each of these names should suggest something Muslim or Arabic, because they were. The sultanates were Islamic governments—so, too, was that of Muslim Iberia. And the Abbasid Caliphate was a Muslim dynasty headquartered in Baghdad that ruled Persia and much of the Middle East. All arose in the late first millennium C.E. While the other answers have some applicability to one or two regimes in this group, only (B) correctly and completely describes all three.

3. **C**   While these weren't exactly egalitarian societies, these women were not entirely powerless in public terms as European women were—good reason to like (C), cross off (A), and cross off (D). They were not, however, undisputed leaders, so cross off (B).

4. **D**   The key here is food. As the climate changed for the colder, there were significant agricultural failures. Famine devastated cities, so cross off (B), as well as (C), because agricultural technology just couldn't keep up. Commerce was developing in some quarters, but it had nothing to do with the Little Ice Age and in fact sometimes occurred *in spite of it*, so cross off (A).

5. **B**   Prince Henry of Portugal was not himself a navigator but took great pride in allowing his palace to become a place for navigators to meet and trade knowledge and discoveries. There was better cataloguing of West African climate and geography, but that was the result, not the cause so cross off (C). New ship designs alone were not the key factor, so cross off (D). And locals serving as officers was not any coordinated phenomenon with larger results, so cross off (A).

6. **B**   The Abbasid Caliphate inaugurated a resurgence of interest in classical knowledge, as well as new developments in literature, art, architecture, and other aspects of culture. The Mongol conquest of Baghdad, the Abbasid capital, effectively ended the Islamic Golden Age, so cross (A) off. The Silk Road reached into China well before the spread of Islam, so cross off (C). And while the Ottoman Empire did rise from some remnants of the Mongol Khanates, this was well after the founding of the Abbasid Caliphate in 1258, so cross off (D).

7. **D**   These images are from Easter Island and San Agustin, Colombia, respectively. Statues from each culture would have been created sometime between the mid-thirteenth century and the end of the sixteenth century. This timing puts them well after (A) or (B), so cross those off. They are not African, though, so cross off (C).

8. **A**   During this period Tamil, Hindi, and other modern Indian tongues largely achieved their current form. The development of Tamil devotional hymns spread as a cultural phenomenon, driving a resurgence of interest in Hindu culture. Rather than a period of decline in elaborate temples, these centuries saw the development of more temple towns consistent with the resurgence in interest in Hinduism, so cross off (B). Cultural and political systems were not imported at this time, but rather *exported* to other countries in southeast Asia, so cross off (C). This cultural export, while it was more about what went out than came in, didn't mean India isolated itself from other influences, so cross off (D).

9. **C**   The pope exhorted his Crusaders to free the Holy Land from Muslim occupation to restore Christian pilgrims' access to sacred sites. This had no bearing on African trade routes, so cross off (A). The Great Schism, in the late fourteenth and early fifteenth centuries, was significantly later than the First Crusade (1096–1099 C.E.), so cross off (B). And while several communities of European and Middle Eastern Jews fell victim to the advances of the Crusaders, this was not the explicit purpose with which Urban II set the Crusaders off, so cross off (D).

10. **A**   Yaroslav the Wise was Grand Prince of Kiev and vice-regent of Novgorod when his older brother Svyatopolk went on a power-hungry murderous rampage, killing three other brothers. The Novgorodians supported Yaroslav's successful move against his brother. By uniting the principalities of Novgorod and Kiev, Yaroslav streamlined governance and laid down the Russkaya Pravda, codifying legal customs into formal law. There was no large-scale institutionalized support for arts, literature, and technology, despite a few isolated cases; nor was any collaboration between the Prince and the Eastern Orthodox Church a significant factor in inaugurating the Golden Age—so cross off (B) and (D). Kievan Rus also did not expand past the principalities of Novgorod and Kiev at this time, so cross off (C).

DRILL 4

1. **A**   Remember that you're looking for the one that *isn't* true. While the Black Death killed off 30 to 60 percent of the populations of Europe and Asia, European diseases brought to the Americas by explorers killed off approximately 90 percent of the native population. It did, however, begin in Asia, in all likelihood, and spread west via fleas on rats and other animals carried along the Silk Road, so cross off (B). The death of so many people from across so many segments of society did change the economic and social landscape, and religious upheavals occurred as people questioned why the priests of the Church could not save them from such devastation and death so cross off (C). And its effects were indeed made worse by the chronic malnutrition that had plagued Europe for a century as climate change caused by the Little Ice Age devastated grain harvests, so cross off (D). This latter problem was improved by the arrival of the potato as a crop from the Americas after Columbus's transatlantic voyages.

2. **C**   Arab people arrived from the seventh through ninth centuries, bringing with them the burgeoning knowledge and technology of the Arab world, and in approximately 1000 C.E., Bantu-speaking peoples brought with them the zebu, a long-horned cattle domesticated in herds. (A) refers to crops that came to Africa from the Americas after Columbian contact, centuries later, so cross that off. (B) describes the initial settling of Madagascar between the fourth century B.C.E. and the sixth century C.E., so cross that off. Finally, irrigated rice paddies in Madagascar date only to about 1600 C.E., so cross off (D), too.

3. **A**   Portugal, as well as other nations, used the Portuguese-designed carrack to do most of their exploration of the Atlantic and Indian oceans in the years after the mid-second millennium C.E. The Chinese junk did form the basis of China's first navy, but that was a couple centuries before the Portuguese developed the carrack, so cross off (B). While these ships did have deep hulls, and while some of these ships were used to carry slaves between Africa and the Americas, that was not the purpose behind their development, so cross off (C). The carrack was also not the first ship to employ a fixed rudder as an improvement over the unstable steering oar, so cross off (D).

4. **B**   Kublai Khan was the only Mongol khan to expand his holdings after 1260, the first non-Chinese emperor to bring all of China under his control. Mansa Musa, or Musa I, expanded his holdings to include major salt-producing regions north of Timbuktu. Only Mansa Musa, though, was a Muslim, so cross off (A). Neither introduced his empire's first coinage system, so cross off (C). And while Kublai Khan was a non-Chinese ruler of China, Mansa Musa was Malian, so cross off (D).

5. **C**   While the Islamic Empire under the Abbasids developed an economy reliant on merchants and trade, the Europe of the early Middle Ages instituted the feudal system. This farming-centric economy led to a more individual, less worldly general population. Remember, however, that as surplus food is produced, those from the lower classes began to learn skills and create materials for trading. As this progressed, the economy of the Middle Ages changed, until cities and towns developed.

6. **D** The Black Plague, or the Black Death, originated in China, where it killed an estimated 35 million people. Spread through Europe through trade routes (like most diseases, ideas, and religions, historically), the Plague killed a third of Europe's population within 50 years. Crowded conditions in Europe's cities and the lack of adequate sanitation and medical knowledge all contributed to its rapid spread.

7. **B** Omar Khayyam (B) wrote the *Rubaiyat of Omar Khayyam*. Saladin (A) you should remember for retaking large parts of the Levant (modern-day Lebanon, Israel, the Palestinian Territories, Jordan) back from Crusader invaders. Muhammad ibn Qasim (C) conquered the Sindh and Punjab regions, opening the East up to Muslim invaders. Mira Bai (D), along with Kabir, is responsible for the bhaktic movement, which stemmed conversion to Islam. Mira Bai is also out of context; she won't show up until the end of the fifteenth century.

8. **A** In the seventh century, Muslim conquerors invaded India. The open, tolerant, and inclusive Hindu religion was based on a social system dominated by castes; whereas Islam was doctrinaire, monotheistic, evangelical, and egalitarian. In the earlier period of contact, conflict predominated, but as time passed, although tensions persisted, peaceful commercial and religious exchange occurred in a society where Muslim rulers governed Hindu subjects.

9. **C** The spread of Islam across the northern third of the African continent produced significant effects on the continent. From the mid-seventh century, Muslim armies pushed westward from Egypt across the regions called Ifriqiya by the Romans and the Maghrib (the West) by the Arabs. By 711 they crossed into Spain. These conquerors linked the African continent more closely to the outside world through trade, religion, and politics. Trade and long-distance commerce were carried out in many parts of the continent and linked regions beyond the Muslim world. Though the northern region of the continent was well integrated into the world economy, until about 1450, with the arrival of the Portuguese, Islam provided the major external contact between sub-Saharan Africa and the world.

10. **B** Due to its size, the African continent boasted diverse societies. Differences in geography, language, religion, politics, and other aspects of life contributed to Africa's lack of political unity over long periods of time. Unlike in many parts of Asia, Europe, and north Africa, neither universal states nor universal religions characterized the history of sub-Saharan Africa. Stateless societies, organized around kinship or age sets—people of a certain age—did not need rulers or bureaucracies and existed side by side with states. Among peoples of the west African forest, secret societies of men and women controlled customs and beliefs and were able to limit the authority of rulers.

DRILL 5

1. **C** Shi'a and Sunni Islam developed out of disagreements over the proper mode of succession after the death of Muhammad. Sufism is a mystic and ascetic movement which begun in the ninth century after the wide geographical spread of Islam, and the absorption of mystic traditions from outside Arabia, especially Greater Persia. Sufism became a more formalized movement in the twelfth century and has adherents mostly in non-Arab parts of the world.

2. **D** In another example of worlds colliding, many converted African groups who began to follow Christianity held to former beliefs of ancestor worship. Interestingly, Christians began to see Jesus as an ancestor, a unifying of local custom and tenets of a foreign faith. As to the Ark of the Covenant—the chest described in the Bible which, according to Jewish and Christian tradition, carries the tablets of stone on which God wrote the Ten Commandments—some biblical archaeologists (those studying things related to the time the Bible refers to) believe that, at some point, the Ark made it down to present-day Ethiopia, and may still be there today. A modern-day Indiana Jones adventure!

3. **A** The Church of St. George (Bete Giyorgis) is one of eleven monolithic (made from stone) churches in Lalibela, an ancient city in Ethiopia. Christianity was spread to Ethiopia and Kush by the Egyptian Christians (Copts), way back in the first century C.E. These great stone churches built by King Lalibela. You don't need to know about King Lalibela. What's important to remember is, as Islam encroaches into the African continent, Ethiopia will stay largely Christian.

4. **D** Mali king Mansa Musa's trip to Mecca to make his *hajj* was the stuff that legends are made of. Musa was a devout Muslim and his pilgrimage made him well-known across northern Africa and the Middle East. To Musa, Islam was the foundation of the "cultured world of the Eastern Mediterranean." He worked to grow of Islam in his empire. Musa made his pilgrimage in 1324, with a procession reported to include 60,000 men, 12,000 slaves who each carried 4-lb. gold bars, heralds dressed in Persian silks who bore gold staffs, organized horses, and handled bags. Also in the train were 80 camels, which varying reports claim carried between 50 and 300 pounds of gold dust each. He gave the gold to the poor he met along his route (remember alms-giving is another of the Five Pillars of Islam). Musa not only gave to the cities he passed on the way to Mecca, including Cairo and Medina, but also traded gold for souvenirs. Musa's generous actions, however, inadvertently devastated the economy of the region. In the cities of Cairo, Medina, and Mecca, the sudden influx of gold devalued the metal for the next decade. Prices on goods and wares super inflated in an attempt to adjust to the newfound wealth that was spreading throughout local populations. To rectify the gold market, Musa borrowed all the gold he could carry from money-lenders in Cairo, at high interest. This is the only time recorded in history that one man directly controlled the price of gold in the Mediterranean.

5. **B** Though Muslim invaders conquered parts of all these regions, associate this mud brick building with Sudanic architecture in Africa, something said to have been perfected under the famous Mali king, Mansa Musa. Mali architects used the materials available to them, so since Islam needed a mosque (notice the two minarets at the front of the building), stone wasn't available, and wood was hard to come by, this one is built of beaten earth reinforced by wood or reeds, which create bristles on the outside of the building.

6. **C** Even though most of the population in the Sudanic states (Mali and Songhay are the most famous) did not convert to Islam, the introduction of the faith in the tenth century reinforced, not undermined, ruling power. Not all Islamic traditions took hold, however. Men and women mixed freely; women went unveiled and young girls at Jenne in Songhay were naked. However, although slavery had existed in Africa prior to the coming of Islam, Muslim demand for slaves and the commercialization of the region intensified the practice.

7. **D** The Bantu languages are a family of languages which spread throughout sub-Saharan Africa as early as 3000 B.C.E. This expansion into modern-day central, east, and south Africa led to over 250 languages, of which Swahili (A) is the most popular. Amharic (B) is the Semitic language spoken in Ethiopia (Ethiopia is a country, not a language).

8. **D** Women in the African continent lived in more egalitarian societies than did European women. Many Sudanic societies were matrilineal and did not seclude women. Slavery and a slave trade to the Islamic world lasting more than 700 years had a major effect on women and children. All individuals might become slaves, but the demand for concubines and eunuchs increased demand for women and children. Men did not have the power over their wives to sell them into slavery, however. Life expectancy was not markedly different between African and European populations.

9. **A** Remember that as Muslim armies swept across the northern stretch of the African continent, they brought their religion along with them, just as they had in Asia. Before Islam, though, Egyptian Christians, known as Copts, had spread their influence to Kush (also called Nubia, but we find the name Kush in the Bible) and Ethiopia. These civilizations will have a rich Christian tradition they'll adhere to, even after the arrival of Islam. Before all this, though, an animist religion—a belief in natural forces personified as gods—was common in Africa, and affected the way this continent developed its faith systems. Africa's religious makeup, then, was very diverse, just like the cultural and economic makeup of the continent. Keep that in mind as you answer all your questions about the beginning of Africa's history.

10. **B** The east coast of Africa is known as the Swahili Coast. The word comes from the Arabic word for "coasters," or traders. Trade with the Muslims began in the early tenth century as Swahili traders brought gold, slaves, ivory, and other exotic products to the coast. Chinese pottery and Arabian beads have been found in the ruins of Great Zimbabwe.

DRILL 6

1. **D** There is a laundry list of reasons why the church split in 1054 C.E., the date that the pope excommunicated the patriarch of Constantinople, who did the same to the pope. This date became known as the East-West Schism and from then on Orthodoxy influenced the East and Roman Catholicism influenced the West. Things had been bad for a while. The two camps disagreed over the sacrament of communion, whether priests should be allowed to marry, and the use of local languages in church. The East read the Bible in Greek and translated it from this language, while the West in Latin. Subtleties in translations led to different traditions. They even were at odds regarding the nature of God, specifically God as a trinity, and they disagreed over the placement of icons during worship.

2. **C** Like the Chinese, the Byzantines educated their bureaucrats. Technically, anyone could study and become a cog in the government machine, but because the lower classes tended to need to farm to survive, most of those who made it through the process were from the higher classes. Both painted the emperor as semi-divine, appointed by god to rule. Emperors were surrounded by elaborate court ritual and headed both the church and the state. Women occasionally ruled, the Byzantine Theodora likely the most famous woman to rule and the Empress Wu Zetian on the Chinese side.

3. **A** Hagia Sophia began life as a church, first for the Eastern Orthodox, then Roman Catholics. After the area (present-day Istanbul, Turkey) was taken over by the Turks, it was converted to a mosque. Today, it's a museum. The current building was originally constructed as a church between 532 and 537 on the orders of the Byzantine Emperor Justinian and was the third Church of the Holy Wisdom to occupy the site, the previous two having both been destroyed by rioters.

4. **C** Population growth was made possible by better farming, which allowed civilizations to feed their populations. Once these groups developed beyond subsistence farming, with the help of new farming technologies, into surplus farming, people were freed up to pursue other interests. People became craft- and tradesmen, creating markets and interactions with other communities. Though some civilizations were very intolerant of other faith systems, others (most significantly Indian Hindus and some African groups) were able to absorb evangelical beliefs, such as Islam and Christianity. So, postclassical civilizations weren't universally intolerant.

5. **B** The moldboard plow (which helped to turn the soil), the three-field system (in which three fields, one fallow to rest), and horse collars were all introduced to Medieval Europe and created surpluses of crops, which allowed for population growth and freed individuals so they could take on other trades. Irrigation is just about as old as farming, so Medieval Europe had forms of it. Oxen were domesticated already, likely during the Neolithic era, so that answer choice is out of context.

6. **C** The Eastern Orthodox Christians in eastern Europe and Russia spent much time and effort defending themselves from the colonization of various western invaders. It wasn't until 1242 that Russia succumbed to the Tatars (a group of Mongols from the east) under Genghis Khan. The Tatars ruled a large chunk of Russia for two centuries, leading to a cultural rift that further split eastern and western Europe. The Roman Catholic church worked in the eleventh century to reform the Church and will, most significantly, work against the Protestant Reformation in the sixteenth century. The Eastern Orthodox church will not go through any reforming movements, so these reforms will more significantly distance the churches from one another.

7. **D** Parliaments were representative bodies, the beginning of a distinctive political process not present in other civilizations. Manors were self-sufficient agricultural estates, where serfs worked the land and gave parts of what they grew to the lords of the estate. Guilds grouped people in similar occupations, regulated apprenticeships, maintained good workmanship, and discouraged innovations. They played an important political and social role in cities, as they in one sense controlled commerce. Though these three were developed in the Middle Ages, kingdoms had been around for a while.

8. **B** The Crusades, though many were unsuccessful in conquering land in the east, prove that even the efforts of conquest and expansion that fail to reach their goals still have a major impact on world history: They lead to interaction between cultures that might not otherwise interact. The Crusades put Europe back into the sphere of the Eastern Mediterranean for centuries. That interaction fueled trade and an exchange of ideas. It also led to western Europe's rediscovery of its ancient past, which was being preserved by the Byzantine and Islamic Empires. That rediscovery fueled huge changes in Europe (the Renaissance, for one).

9. **A** Remember that as urbanization happens, women will lose grounds as to their rights. With women's history, hunter-gatherers were the most egalitarian. Once the world moves onto farms, women begin to lose power, and their power is eroded until the twentieth century. Women in western Europe were not as restricted as their counterparts in the Islamic world, but they definitely lost ground. They were increasingly restricted by patriarchal structures. They could help with the family business. Christian emphasis on spiritual equality remained important, while female monastic groups offered a limited alternative to marriage. Veneration of the Virgin Mary and other female religious figures provided positive role models for women. They could not run services, though.

10. **C** Aztecs were relatively equal, though think of the Aztecs in this way—the civilization's lack of technology holds it back (for example, the absence of milling technology meant that women spent many hours daily in grinding maize by hand for household needs, which kept them busy a lot). Remember that patterns of urbanization tend to take power away from women. In Mesoamerica, women inherited and passed on property, but in political and social life they were subordinate to men. Though women's rights actually progressed in the Tang and early Song dynasties, by the end of the Song, foot binding became vogue and women found it harder and harder to find educational opportunities. In communities in which women don't have many rights, keep in mind that ideas such as women's purity become important, so female virginity before marriage was important in both societies.

DRILL 7

1. **C**   The city is Machu Picchu, the Lost City of the Incas. The Andes should be a red flag that you're talking about the Inca, one of the great Native American tribes of the New World, and the only group centered there. The Cherokee are out of context. Before the arrival of Europeans, the most important American civilizations to know are the Mayan (who disappear before the arrival of Europeans), the Aztecs (more north, in what is modern-day southern Mexico), and the Inca (obviously, in the Andes Mountains, in modern-day Peru). Though the Aztec built roads, the Inca were the most impressive engineers of the new world, with almost 2,500 miles of road, complicated agricultural terraces, and impressive stonecutting.

2. **D**   Remember that the Egyptians mummified their dead and built tombs (such as the pyramids) to house their famous, wealthy dead. The Inca venerated their royals and mummified them, as well. The Chinese, since the Han dynasty (206 b.c.e.–220 c.e.), formed schools specifically to educate a bureaucratic class. The Incas developed a state bureaucracy in which almost all nobles played a role. The Incas' real genius was best displayed, though, in their land and water management, extensive road system, statecraft, and architecture and public buildings. They developed ingenious agricultural terraces on the steep slopes of the Andes (which can be seen in the remains of the famous city Machu Picchu). The empire was linked together by almost 2,500 miles of roads, many of which included rope suspension bridges over mountain gorges and rivers. They were also awesome stonecutters, and were able to build huge buildings.

3. **B**   Both the Aztecs and Incas required tribute (with the Aztecs, this included humans for sacrifice) from their conquered and allied neighbors. This is how the cities fed themselves. Though both had bureaucracies, the Incas did not have a distinct merchant class. Both conquered, but did not colonize. Neither had a writing system.

4. **A**   In the postclassical era, China will rely more heavily on the agricultural riches of the south. The Grand Canal, which Yangdi (Tang dynasty) risked his throne to have built, was designed to link the original centers of Chinese civilization on the north China plain with the Yangtze River basin more than 500 miles to the south. Because of this impressive engineering success, the Tang were able to reopen the Silk Roads to Persia. All this led to an explosion of trade, which eventually led to impressive urbanization, with the Tang capital and its suburbs boasting a population of 2 million.

   Railroads are WAY out of era. Get rid of (D). Though roads were important, associate the Tang and Song with the canal system; it's what changes everything for this population.

5. **B**   The Korean *hwacha* was a multiple rocket launcher developed and used in Korea in the late fourteenth century. It was highlighted in a MythBusters show in 2008 and it was confirmed that it can shoot as far as 500 yards. Archery is a technology out of era, so get rid of it, as is metalwork. Military organization is also as old as civilization.

   The Tang and Song are famous for their accomplishments in science, technology, literature, and the fine arts. Technological and scientific discoveries—new tools, production methods, weapons—passed to other civilizations. The arts and literature passed to neighboring regions. Engineering feats, such as the Grand Canal, dikes and dams, irrigation systems, and bridges, were especially noteworthy. New agricultural implements and innovations—such as banks and paper money stimulated prosperity. Explosive powder was invented. On the domestic side, chairs, tea drinking, the use of coal for fuel, and kites were introduced. Compasses were applied to ocean navigation, and the abacus helped numerical figuring. In the eleventh century, the artisan Bi Sheng devised printing with movable type. Combined with the Chinese invention of paper, printing allowed a literacy level higher than that in any other preindustrial civilization.

6. **D** Remember that Arabic traders will have the most contact with the Swahili people (Arabic for "coasters," or traders) of east Africa. Though the Swahili may have had a Bantu language specific to their group, the language, to be elevated to a trading language, absorbed a multitude of Arabic words, since many of the goods and techniques for trade weren't needed before contact with traders. Arabic, Latin, and Sanskrit may have changed as they came in contact with other cultures, but the languages' developments were not driven by trade the way Swahili was.

7. **C** Remember that these are your three great monotheistic faiths. If a person mentioned is someone before Jesus (Moses, Abraham, Adam; i.e. important to Judaism), then the faiths likely share the person as a prophet. The Jewish people worship from the Tanakh (or Jewish Bible) and the Talmud (the commentary on the Bible). Christians pray from books containing the Old and New Testament, which includes the Gospels. Muslims pray from the Quran. Everyone cares about Jerusalem, but Jews don't have an interest in other cities. Catholics care about Rome, but Copts don't. Muslims care about Mecca and Medina, as well.

8. **D** One of the common themes throughout postclassical civilizations, as surplus farming led to further urbanization and the creation or growth of cities, was that women more and more had their rights compromised. Remember that upper-class women, in the Islamic world and western Europe and China, all go through some process of losing rights, whether it's foot binding in China or veiling in Arabia, for example. The feudal system in western Europe and Japan usually put more power in the hands of local nobles. In most places, rulers were chosen by a battle of power politics; in very few places in the world, and not to a large extent, did anyone vote for a ruler or government official. It happened, but it just wasn't common.

9. **A** Remember that both Vikings and Mongols were militaristic peoples who raided due to the poor resources they could access in their home regions. What was unique about the Mongols, and contributed to why they were so successful at keeping their empire together, was that, in conquered lands, Mongols usually set up governments populated by the former local government. Both groups were open to conquered communities keeping their former traditions, and spread rather far and wide—the Vikings to the New World and the Mongols to all of Asia. The Mongols were horsed and the Vikings used the fastest ship in European waters.

10. **B** Keep in mind that Buddhism will be the great driving force adopted and adapted by all the civilizations China affects—the Japanese, Korean, and Vietnamese. The Vietnamese belong to the Southeast Asian culture, though—they had a language which developed separate from the Chinese. Since Japan is being affected by China, Japan wasn't affecting Vietnam. China's great failure with the Vietnamese, why Vietnam failed to assimilate when Korea and Japan did, was that peasants did not absorb the Chinese culture. Buddhists were more deeply entrenched.

DRILL 8

1. **B** The Mongols were nomadic herders of goats and sheep who lived off the products of their animals. Boys and girls learned to ride as soon as they could walk. The basic unit of social organization, the tribe, was divided into kin-related clans. Confederations were organized for defensive and offensive operations. Men held dominant leadership positions; women held influence within the family. Leaders were elected by free men. They gained their positions through displays of courage and diplomatic skills and maintained power as long as they were successful.

2. **D** Genghis Khan started his conquering in 1207. During this time, Rus' was actually a Medieval polity of Europe and had begun to break up into separate elements in the twelfth century, into three separate nations and the Grand Duchy of Moscow, with no real centralized power. This division helped Genghis Khan take over the area piece by piece.

3. **D** Think about this one logically. Rarely does a conquered area ever completely convert to the conqueror's religion. It also wasn't the case with the introduction of the Mongols and their animist faith to Islamic lands. Remember that Islam was founded in a region that had enjoyed an animist faith prior to Muhammad. Also, conquerors are even less likely to take on religious practices from the groups they conquer. Though it's possible to destroy a whole population, this wasn't the case with the Mongol invasions and Shi'ism, especially since the Mongols practiced a "live-and-let-live" governing policy, for the most part, in the places they took over. Mongols were very destructive, though, and tended to decimate cities. If that happens, it destroys a center of culture, which was the case with the attacks on Islamic cities.

4. **A** The Renaissance represented the first great surge of curiosity, really, that helped launch Western Europe into a world power. It initially was a movement native to southern Italy which concentrated on literature and art. It introduced techniques such as chiaroscuro and perspective to European art, and renewed interest in the literature of the great Greek philosophers. It's important to keep in mind none of this would have been possible without Islam's preservation of these works, and then the Mongol invasions to create a bridge between east and west. Choice (A) is correct because Gothic architecture emerged during the Middle Ages (prior to the Renaissance).

5. **C** Associate the Mongols with openness of trade and exchange of culture. The Islamic armies were being pushed back at this time throughout Europe. African civilizations were traders, but did not boast pirate armies. Europeans could not go too far into the oceans due to lack of technological tools. Europeans solved problems through building better ships and learning from the Arabs the use of the Chinese compass and astrolabe. European mapmaking also steadily improved. These improvements allowed Europeans to go farther afield.

6. **D** Islam comes to Africa through the Swahili coast. Remember that you'll have a great Egyptian Copt (Orthodox Christian) community, which will spread the faith down the Nile to Ethiopia, where it'll take hold and stay even after Islam sweeps the continent.

7. **B** The Ottoman Empire's out of era; get rid of that answer choice. The Islamic Empire is known for its trade, especially with sub-Saharan Africa. Merchants were a significant part of the Empire's economy, so associate merchants, and not manufacturing with the Islamic Empire.

8. **B** The Polynesians were the last group of humans who had developed in isolation. Before their introduction to the "civilized" world, they traveled from the Society Islands (Tahiti, Samoa, Fiji) to Hawaii, New Zealand, and surrounding areas. They lacked metallurgy and a writing system, relying heavily on oral traditions.

9. **D** The religion of Islam is often quoted as having started around the year 622 C.E. which coincides with the migration of Mohammad and his followers from the city of Mecca to Medina (called the hijra). This also marks the first year of the Muslim calendar.

10. **D** The Five Pillars of Islam are confession of faith (A), prayer five times per day (B), charity to the needy, fasting during Ramadan, and a pilgrimage to Mecca once during a lifetime (C). Confession of sins is a practice associated with Christianity and is not a pillar of the Islamic faith.

DRILL 9

1. **A** The Islamic empire was ruled by a caliph, whose role consisted of ruling by religious doctrine. The caliphs of the Islamic empire were both head of state and served as chief religious leader.

2. **A** Zoroastrianism remained most closely associated with people of the Persian Empire and never became a dominant religion of the Islamic Empire. The capital of the Umayyad Dynasty did move to Damascus (although Mecca remained a key religious center). Muslims advanced on the Iberian peninsula during 732 C.E. and Shia and Sunni sects developed due to issues related to succession within the empire.

3. **A** The emergence of the Shia and Sunni sects was due to issues related to succession. As the two religious camps fought for control the Islamic state eventually declined and was replaced by the Abbasid Dynasty around 750 C.E. Although disease did spread throughout Asia and the Middle East, it was not directly tied to the demise of the Umayyad Dynasty. Mongol attacks would not result in a transference of power until the thirteenth century (far after the fall of the Umayyad Dynasty).

4. **C** The height of the Abbasid dynasty occurred during the early to mid-ninth century C.E. which coincided with the rise of Baghdad as a key cultural center. The Umayyad Dynasty (B) fell and gave way to the Abbasid Dynasty in the mid-eighth century C.E. about the same time as the fall of the Merovingian Dynasty (D) in France. Although the T'ang Dynasty (A) coincided with the rise of Baghdad, the Chinese did not control the city.

5. **D** The Qu'ran established many rights for women; however, Islamic society remained largely patriarchal and men could have many wives providing that they would be able to support them equally.

6. **B** Constantinople was the heart of the Byzantine Empire and during the reign of Justinian, was associated with great advancements in the arts and sciences (including the building of the Hagia Sophia). Although the Byzantines controlled Rome, Athens and Jerusalem during Justinian's rule, the seat of power remained in Constantinople.

7. **D** During the early Middle Ages, no true empire emerged until the unification of much of Western Europe under the Holy Roman Empire. Charles Martel was instrumental in forming the Carolingian dynasty and uniting the Franks to resist the spread of Islam by Muslim invasions (A). His son's (Pepin the Short) succession was legitimized by the pope (B) and later his grandson Charlemagne established what became known as the Holy Roman Empire (C).

8. **A** At the peak of the Holy Roman Empire, it encompassed northern Italy, Germany, France, and Belgium. This area was markedly smaller than the peaks of the Byzantine, Islamic, and Persian Empires. However, the unification of a large region of Western Europe was significant as it began to restore stability to the region and would lay much of the groundwork which would carry Europe into the next millennium.

Chapter 9
Period 4
Global
Interactions
c. 1450 to
c. 1750
Drills

DRILL 1

1. All of the following reflect American British colonists' adherence to British civilization EXCEPT

   (A) British colonies formed government assemblies based on broad male participation
   (B) a comparatively high percentage of colonists were literate
   (C) colonists were exposed to African slaves who were employed in the colonies
   (D) colonists rebelled against European control in the eighteenth century, citing political ideas and economic goals first debated in western Europe

2. During the Age of Exploration beginning in the fifteenth century, which region was especially drawn to Christianity?

   (A) The Philippines
   (B) Indonesia
   (C) Taiwan
   (D) India

3. After 1450, international trade was increasingly controlled by

   (A) China
   (B) The West
   (C) Japan
   (D) The Ottomans

4. Which of the following concerning the relationship between Asian civilizations and the rise of the world commercial trade in the sixteenth and seventeenth centuries is NOT accurate?

   (A) Asian civilizations had enough political and economic strength to avoid dependence on European trade.
   (B) China was able, in large part due to its strong navy, to prevent the creation of European ports.
   (C) Chinese exports were in such high demand, more American silver could be found in China than any other country.
   (D) Japan's initial interest in Western advances in gunnery and shipping mostly ceased after the successful creation of a local gun-making industry.

5. Which of the following was the first worldwide war?

   (A) Hundred Years' War
   (B) War of Roses
   (C) Seven Years' War
   (D) The Crusades

6. The mercantilism that arose in sixteenth-century Europe

   (A) did not affect empires and populations outside Europe
   (B) encouraged importation of foreign goods
   (C) slowed European colonial pursuits
   (D) sparked further rivalries among European nations

7. Which civilization boasted a political system in which citizens enjoyed the greatest amount of self-rule in the early eighteenth century?

   (A) England
   (B) Japan
   (C) France
   (D) The Ottoman Empire

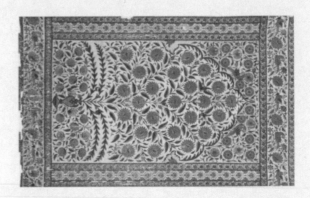

8. The eighteenth-century tent depicted above from Mughal India shows the influence of which other civilization?

   (A) Islamic
   (B) European
   (C) Chinese
   (D) Southeast Asian

9. Which of the following regions' trade patterns remained similar to its pre–eighteenth century economy?

(A) China
(B) Japan
(C) Russia
(D) The Philippines

10. Which of the following accurately portrays the exchange through the Columbian Exchange?

From the New World	From Europe
(A) Smallpox and beans	Sweet potatoes and rice
(B) Sweet potatoes and beans	Rice and smallpox
(C) Sweet potatoes and smallpox	Rice and beans
(D) Beans and rice	Sweet potatoes and smallpox

Check your answers on page 205.

DRILL 2

1. Peter the Great of seventeenth-century Russia and Africa's Mansa Musa had which of the following characteristics in common?

    (A) Both leaders turned to foreign societies to modernize their societies.
    (B) Both leaders passed laws concerning the appearance of state officials.
    (C) Both leaders were devout Muslims.
    (D) Both leaders influenced the countries they travelled to more than these countries influenced the leader's home country.

2. Which of the following was an effect of Mongol control of Russia?

    (A) Increased significance of Roman Catholicism
    (B) Urbanization
    (C) Closer ties to the West
    (D) Lowered cultural and educational levels

3. By the end of the early modern era and Catherine the Great's reign, the Russian government

    (A) mimicked the governments of Western Europe, especially England's and its Parliamentary system
    (B) had freed its serf community
    (C) was unable to function due to uncontrollable peasant revolts
    (D) was strongly centralized, but ceded control of the serfs to the nobility

4. African kingdoms between 1450 and 1750

    (A) were uninterested in European trade goods, like the Chinese
    (B) engaged in the slave trade before the European system increased demand
    (C) enslaved their own people
    (D) took slaves from populations in the coastal region

5. Which of the following is true about the trans-Atlantic slave trade?

    (A) The primary destination for ships were sugar plantations.
    (B) More men than women made the journey west.
    (C) Mortality rates averaged around 20 percent.
    (D) All of the above are true.

6. All of the following were contributions by African slaves to the Americas EXCEPT

    (A) skill at growing African crops
    (B) African forms of worship and folklore
    (C) African social structures
    (D) African cuisine

7. Which of the following was a contributing factor to the difference between British colonies in the southern part of North America and Latin American colonies?

    (A) The British colonies did not need to rely as heavily on imported Africans as did the Latin American colonies.
    (B) Manumission was significantly more commonplace in the British colonies, creating a cheap workforce.
    (C) Latin American colonies outlawed slavery by the end of the eighteenth century.
    (D) The British colonies had to abandon agricultural endeavors in the southern region due to poor soil, and therefore no demand for slaves existed.

8. Which of the following is an accurate list of the Gunpowder Empires?

    (A) Safavid Persia, Ottoman Turkey, Tokugawa Shogunate
    (B) Safavid Persia, Ottoman Turkey, Mughal India
    (C) Ottoman Turkey, Mughal India, Tokugawa Shogunate
    (D) Mughal India, Tokugawa Shogunate, Seljuk Turks

9. Spanish and French colonization efforts in the Americas differed in that

   (A) the Spanish were exclusively interested in resource extraction from American colonies
   (B) the Spanish were less interested in converting Native Americans to Christianity than were the French
   (C) the French were less interested in permanent settlements in the Americas than the Spanish
   (D) the French limited exploration to North America

10. Which of the following characterizes the new global trade system that arose in 1450?

   (A) The entire globe became linked by numerous trade routes.
   (B) The work of Polynesian weavers found new markets.
   (C) China came to dominate world markets.
   (D) European wealth and commercial dominance increased.

Check your answers on page 206.

DRILL 3

1. The Netherlands fostered commercial relationships or established colonial interests in all of the following areas EXCEPT

   (A) Japan
   (B) North America
   (C) Southern Africa
   (D) Western Africa

2. The Enlightenment and Scientific Revolution contributed all the following innovations to the European world EXCEPT

   (A) the concept of the Social Contract
   (B) heliocentrism
   (C) movable type
   (D) Diderot's Encyclopedia

3. Which two groups are depicted in the map above, circa 1560?

   (A) Roman Catholic and Orthodox Christian groups, after the Great Schism
   (B) Roman Catholic and Protestant groups, during the Protestant Reformation
   (C) The Holy Roman Empire and Napoleonic France, after the French Revolution
   (D) The Holy Roman Empire and France, after the signing of the Peace of Westphalia

4. Japanese feudalism and European feudalism shared all of the following characteristics EXCEPT

   (A) both systems ended by the sixteenth century
   (B) both systems rely on peasants to farm the land in exchange for protection and a portion of their harvests
   (C) in both systems, class was hereditary with little room for social mobility
   (D) in both systems, constant warfare lent importance to the warrior class

5. Why did Spain not initially participate in the Renaissance?

   (A) Islamic influence in Spain caused disinterest in Renaissance art and philosophy.
   (B) Renaissance humanistic ideas and writers were severely censored by the Spanish government.
   (C) Renaissance philosophy tracts could not be translated into Spanish, due to the limitations of the language.
   (D) A Spanish revival of Catholicism led to disinterest in humanistic philosophies.

6. All of the following were part of the makeup of Spanish American colonial society EXCEPT

   (A) mestizos
   (B) peninsulares
   (C) encomiendas
   (D) criollos

7. What aspect of the 1688 Glorious Revolution in England was unique?

   (A) It began as a popular uprising among the peasant and farmer class.
   (B) At the end, universal male suffrage was ensured by the signing of the Bill of Rights.
   (C) It reinstated an oppressive regime, turning the clock back on reforms.
   (D) It involved very little violence.

8. What European nation established the largest land-based empire by the mid-eighteenth century?

   (A) Russia
   (B) Great Britain
   (C) France
   (D) India

9. Which of the following is a unique characteristic of Spanish and British colonization of the Americas?

   (A) European colonizers succeeded in supplanting their cultures into the New World.
   (B) Contact with Native Americans introduced Europe to a new form of writing.
   (C) Crops from the Americas changed commerce and European economies.
   (D) Europeans benefited more from contact with the Americas than the Americas benefited from contact with Europeans.

10. What were the major trading products produced by fifteenth-century China?

   (A) Tea, paper, and porcelain
   (B) Paper, porcelain, and silk
   (C) Porcelain, silk, and tea
   (D) Tea, porcelain, and silk

Check your answers on page 208.

DRILL 4

1. Which of the following is a characteristic shared by the Russian Empire and Ming China?

   (A) They improved the position of women in the period 1450–1750.
   (B) They imposed new religions on their respective empires.
   (C) They established policies in response to the Mongol presence in central Asia.
   (D) They successfully expelled the Mongols from their lands.

2. All of the following were characteristic of European colonization in both Africa and the Americas EXCEPT

   (A) these communities lacked centralized power, and so could not fend off European aggression
   (B) these communities lacked military sophistication, and so could not fend off European aggression
   (C) Europeans were responsible for the deaths of great numbers of people from both these civilizations
   (D) European desire for resources on these continents drove them to take over each civilization quickly

"You know well or ought to know, that whereas we have been informed that in these our kingdoms there were some wicked Christians who Judaized and apostatized from our holy Catholic faith… we ordered the separation of the said Jews in all the cities, towns and villages of our kingdoms and lordships and [commanded] that they be given Jewish quarters and separated places where they should live, hoping that by their separation the situation would remedy itself."

3. The "we" in the document above refers to

   (A) William and Mary of England
   (B) Ferdinand and Isabella of Spain
   (C) Pope Julius II
   (D) Catherine the Great of Russia

4. The Jewish population of Spain fled to which regions during the Spanish Inquisition?

   (A) The Americas
   (B) The Netherlands
   (C) The Ottoman Empire
   (D) All of the above

5. Which of the following was a contributing factor of the rise of the nation-state in Europe?

   (A) Roving nomadic bands caused principalities to unify into larger governing bodies to exploit the military power of many.
   (B) Shockingly bloody wars and the rise of Ming China encouraged Europe to unify in order to compete economically.
   (C) A diverse group of culturally distinctive individuals living close together created natural divisions among different states.
   (D) The Black Plague left so few people alive that those who survived lived far apart, with no easy access to one another.

6. The greatest difference between the philosophies of Divine Right of Kings in Europe and Mandate of Heaven in Zhou China is

   (A) the Mandate of Heaven stated a ruler would only be given the authority to rule as long as he pleased heaven
   (B) Divine Right of Kings stated that a ruler was chosen by the divine
   (C) the Mandate of Heaven stated that a ruler was chosen by the divine
   (D) Divine Right of Kings stated that a ruler would be given the authority to rule only as long as he pleased heaven

7. Which of the following correctly matches the seventeenth-century Enlightenment philosopher with the literature he authored?

   (A) Jean-Jacques Rousseau—*Book of the Courtier*
   (B) John Locke—*Two Treatises on Government*
   (C) Diderot—*Leviathan*
   (D) Voltaire—*The Social Contract*

8. What do the Jesuits, the Sufis, and the followers of Kabbalah all have in common?

   (A) They all began in the Middle East.
   (B) They all profess a belief in Jesus.
   (C) They are all mysticism movements within their respective faiths.
   (D) They all encourage evangelism.

9. Which of the following is true about the effects of the rise of global trade on the world's civilizations between 1450 and 1750?

   (A) Populations and demographics throughout the world were significantly changed.
   (B) Access to new crops created population growth.
   (C) New philosophies painted Europeans as the world's protectors and superior civilization.
   (D) All of the above are true.

10. In contrast to the European Renaissance, the rise of interest in art in Japan during the Tokugawa Shogunate

   (A) was mostly a literary movement
   (B) was meant to cater exclusively to domestic audiences
   (C) used new art techniques to make art more personal to the viewer
   (D) was meant to cater exclusively to international audiences

Check your answers on page 210.

DRILL 5

1. Which of the following is a shared characteristic of the Protestant and Catholic Reformations?

   (A) Both emphasized education as an essential element of their philosophies.
   (B) Both abandoned church traditions.
   (C) Both sought the Eastern Orthodox church as an ally.
   (D) Both defined a strict hierarchy within the Church.

2. Which of the following concepts associated with the period between 1450 and 1750 does NOT rely on natural laws?

   (A) Deism
   (B) Predestination
   (C) The social contract
   (D) The scientific method

3. Why did the Tokugawa shogunate close Japan's borders from 1603 to 1853?

   (A) To keep Japanese culture unique, and not allow it to spread to the rest of the world
   (B) To prepare Japanese peasants for modernization
   (C) To keep European influence out of everyday life
   (D) To institute sweeping government reforms

4. Which of the following is NOT an accurate representation of Russian expansion between 1450 and 1800?

   (A) The Ottoman Empire's weakness facilitated Russia's successful expansion.
   (B) Russia succeeded in taking control of a warm water port.
   (C) Russian territory spread as far as northern California.
   (D) Mongol hordes kept Russia engaged on its southern border, slowing expansion in that direction.

5. Which of the following shows an accurate ranking of isolationism of civilizations in the period 1450 to 1750, from least to greatest?

   (A) China, Japan, Africa, Europe
   (B) China, Japan, Europe, Africa
   (C) Japan, China, Africa, Europe
   (D) Japan, China, Europe, Africa

6. Which of the following was the most important new technology to contribute to the Protestant Reformation?

   (A) The spinning jenny
   (B) The printing press
   (C) Paper
   (D) Cement

7. All of the following describe the Scientific Revolution EXCEPT

   (A) it emphasized the importance of empirical research
   (B) it strove to describe the nature of the universe
   (C) it was violently suppressed in England
   (D) it believed in the overall goodness of humanity

8. During a global period of remarkable new transoceanic maritime reconnaissance, what happened in Oceania and Polynesia?

   (A) The Portuguese developed a network of foreign trading posts.
   (B) Frequent voyages established China as the early dominant power in the region.
   (C) Mariners from that region became regarded as the most skilled in the world.
   (D) The region's exchange and communication networks were largely unaffected.

9. European merchants in Asia prior to the mid-eighteenth century

   (A) were rare and of little significance
   (B) developed new routes for the transport of laborers
   (C) mostly transported goods between Asian markets
   (D) introduced new products and techniques to European colonists

10. Fruit trees, grains, and sugar were all examples of

   (A) agricultural products introduced by Europeans to the Americas
   (B) American foods introduced as staple crops in Europe and Asia
   (C) crops native to the Middle East that spread to Europe
   (D) African staple crops brought to the Americas by slaves

Check your answers on page 212.

DRILL 6

1. Which of the following was NOT a land empire?

   (A) Manchu
   (B) Ottoman
   (C) Dutch
   (D) Russian

2. In The Social Contract, Jean-Jacques Rousseau argued all of the following EXCEPT

   (A) all men are inherently equal
   (B) in a rational society, individuals subject themselves to the rule of law
   (C) living according to religious principles is the essence of freedom
   (D) legislative power belongs to the people

3. The greatest number of deaths during the Spanish conquest of the Aztec and Incan Empires can be attributed to

   (A) firearms used by conquistadors
   (B) human sacrifices performed to appease conquistadors
   (C) diseases such as smallpox which coincided with Spanish arrival
   (D) the overwhelming numerical superiority of Spanish forces in battle

4. Martin Luther's *95 Theses*, posted in 1517, were arguments pertaining to

   (A) his frustrations with church institutions and practices
   (B) issues of taxation plaguing the German government
   (C) criticisms of Albrecht Dürer and the naturalist movement in art
   (D) the heliocentric model of the solar system advanced by Galileo

5. Which of the following is NOT an example of the isolationist policies of both Japan and China in the seventeenth and eighteenth century?

   (A) Prohibiting trade with any European nation
   (B) Banning of Christianity and persecution of Christians
   (C) Restricting exploration for territorial and commercial purposes
   (D) Limiting travel to and from the country

6. Between the sixteenth and mid-eighteenth centuries, the Americas had established economic links to all of the following EXCEPT

   (A) Europe
   (B) India
   (C) South East Asia
   (D) Africa

7. Which of the following most accurately describes the role of the aristocracy in European absolute monarchies in the seventeenth and eighteenth centuries?

   (A) They exercised absolute control over peasant populations through feudal obligations.
   (B) Like the monarch, they believed their status and power had been divinely ordained.
   (C) They used traditional powers to exert influence over politics and the monarchy.
   (D) They funded colonization attempts so the monarch would not have to.

8. Introduction of new crops from the Americas to China in the seventeenth and eighteenth centuries caused

   (A) the Chinese to abandon traditional foods
   (B) large-scale immigration from regions where food sources were less available
   (C) widespread adoption of the European three-field system
   (D) a rapid increase in population due to better nutrition

"According to this foundation of reciprocal Amity, and a general Amnesty, all and every one of the Electors of the sacred Roman Empire, the Princes and States (therein comprehending the Nobility, which depend immediately on the Empire) their Vassals, Subjects, Citizens, Inhabitants (to whom on the account of the Bohemian or German Troubles or Alliances, contracted here and there, might have been done by the one Party or the other, any Prejudice or Damage in any manner, or under what pretence soever, as well in their Lordships, their fiefs, Underfiefs, Allodations, as in their Dignitys, Immunitys, Rights and Privileges) shall be fully re-establish'd on the one side and the other, in the Ecclesiastick or Laick State, which they enjoy'd, or could lawfully enjoy, notwithstanding any Alterations, which have been made in the mean time to the contrary."

9. This quotation from the *Peace of Westphalia* in 1648 establishes

(A) the right of leaders in the Holy Roman Empire to promote nobles within the Church without fear of papal recrimination
(B) the right of German princes to control their lands and follow the Christian denomination of their choosing
(C) France's right to German territories, as supported by the feudal structure of the Catholic Church
(D) that peace will only be temporary while social problems in Bohemia and Germany are worked out with the help of the Church

10. Mughal India, Safavid Persia, and Ottoman Turkey were collectively known as

(A) the Balkan States
(B) the Gunpowder Empires
(C) the Golden Horde
(D) the Great Khanates

Check your answers on page 214.

DRILL 7

1. Which of the following correctly pairs the first successful French settlement in the Americas with the explorer who settled it?

   (A) Charlesfort on Parris Island, Jacques Cartier
   (B) Saint-Domingue, Henri de Feynes
   (C) Quebec City, Samuel de Champlain
   (D) Nova Gallia, Giovanni da Veranzano

2. England's Interregnum ended when

   (A) the House of Tudor defeated the House of York, with Henry VII ascending to the throne
   (B) Oliver Cromwell executed Charles I and declared himself Lord Protector of the realm
   (C) a mostly bloodless revolution resulted in William and Mary's installation as joint monarchs
   (D) Charles II was restored to the throne after living in exile France and the Netherlands

3. One significant effect of the Black Death was

   (A) the rise of feudalism in western Europe as a means of imposing order on the chaos caused by the plague
   (B) the development of humanist thought in response to the suffering and staggering death toll
   (C) an oversupply of material goods in western Europe left unused by the large percent of the population who died
   (D) a population increase in China, where the effects of the disease were less severe than in Europe

4. The Council of Trent was convened primarily in order to

   (A) codify Catholic orthodoxy, repudiate Protestant heresies, and reform Church practices
   (B) revise a prior ban on the veneration of icons in the Eastern Orthodox Church
   (C) end the Great Western Schism by deposing one of two competing popes but eventually electing a third
   (D) disband and denounce the Knights Templar

5. All of the following statements about the Taj Mahal are true EXCEPT

   (A) it was built as a memorial for a shah's late wife.
   (B) it was built by a Muslim ruler in a historically Hindu country.
   (C) it is a site of considerable significance to the Buddhist faith.
   (D) it was looted by the British in the nineteenth century and repaired a half-century later.

6. Which of the following became staple crops in parts of Africa and Asia due to the impact of the Columbian Exchange?

   (A) Sugar and tobacco
   (B) Mint and bananas
   (C) Maize and manioc
   (D) Okra and rice

7. Which of the following countries did NOT establish a maritime empire in the Americas?

   (A) Russia
   (B) Portugal
   (C) The Netherlands
   (D) Spain

8. Global circulation of what metal from the Americas spurred commercialization and the creation of a global economy?

   (A) Nickel
   (B) Copper
   (C) Silver
   (D) Gold

9. Which of the following was NOT an example of major developments in transportation and communication during the nineteenth and twentieth centuries?

   (A) Steamships
   (B) Telegraphs
   (C) Canals
   (D) Tollways

10. What led to the contraction of the Ottoman Empire?

   (A) Anti-imperial resistance
   (B) New patterns of migration
   (C) The impact of generations of intermarriage
   (D) Changes in European and American demand for exports

Check your answers on page 215.

DRILL 8

1. Explorers from which country discovered Australia in 1606?

   (A) The Netherlands
   (B) Great Britain
   (C) China
   (D) India

2. The inauguration of Constantine XI in 1449 marked the last

   (A) period of Ottoman control over Constantinople
   (B) Mongol invader to rule Byzantium
   (C) pagan regime in the Roman empire
   (D) reign of a Byzantine emperor

3. Commercial and cultural interaction between Japan and the West was instigated in

   (A) the sixteenth century by Jesuit missionaries from Portugal
   (B) the thirteenth century by Italian explorer Marco Polo
   (C) the nineteenth century by American sailors headed west from California
   (D) the fifteenth century by Spanish explorers dispatched by Ferdinand and Isabella

4. Rather than rely on the bonds of Islamic identity or tribal identification, the Mughal Empire established imperial unity through

   (A) violent persecution of minority groups, who fled or died
   (B) common Persian-based culture and a powerful emperor
   (C) economically liberal policies with minimal taxation
   (D) promotion of Mughal nationalism through bold military displays

5. The Ottoman conquest of which city formally established the Ottoman Empire?

   (A) Ankara
   (B) Constantinople
   (C) Baghdad
   (D) Alexandria

6. Immediately before the arrival of Hernan Cortes in Central America, all of the following were true of the Aztecs EXCEPT that

   (A) they had defeated the Zapotecs and Mixtecs for control of Mesoamerica's Pacific coast
   (B) their trained horsemen struck fear in the hearts of other Central American tribes, leading to widespread conquest
   (C) they had undertaken a major rebuilding of Tenochtitlan, including expanding the Great Pyramid
   (D) their Triple Alliance for military control over Mesoamerica engaged in so-called "flower wars" involving human sacrifice

7. English maritime exploration was largely privately financed at first because

   (A) the Church of England would not permit the monarchy to undertake exploration
   (B) the English monarchy did not want to appear to be in conflict with the French
   (C) explorers sought to make claims for themselves without informing the Crown
   (D) the monarchy lacked comparable resources to Spain's or Portugal's

8. The Spanish Inquisition, as established by Ferdinand of Aragon and Isabella of Castile in 1481, was primarily intended to

   (A) identify and destroy anyone practicing witchcraft in Spanish territories
   (B) guarantee Catholic orthodoxy among converts from Judaism and Islam
   (C) control the population at large using surprise and fear as its chief weapons
   (D) investigate possible avenues of exploration to increase the wealth of the Church

9. Which of the following statements about Portuguese colonization of the New World is accurate?

   (A) The Portuguese traded their New World colonies to the Dutch for rights to Africa.
   (B) Armed conflict with Spanish settlers drove the Portuguese out of South America.
   (C) The Treaty of Tordesillas limited Portuguese settlement of South America to Brazil.
   (D) Portuguese explorers first reached the South American coast by sailing around Africa.

10. Which of the following is the correct chronological order from earliest to most recent of the start of the following European movements: the Age of Enlightenment, Protestant Reformation, the Renaissance and the Scientific Revolution?

   (A) Renaissance, Protestant Reformation, Scientific Revolution, Enlightenment
   (B) Renaissance, Enlightenment, Protestant Reformation, Scientific Revolution
   (C) Scientific Revolution, Enlightenment, Protestant Reformation, Renaissance
   (D) Enlightenment, Renaissance, Protestant Reformation, Scientific Revolution

Check your answers on page 216.

DRILL 9

1. All of the following are differences between medieval art and Renaissance art EXCEPT

    (A) medieval art was mostly isolated to cathedrals whereas Renaissance art could be found in both religious and public places
    (B) medieval art displayed humans as very flat or stiff in appearance, whereas Renaissance art made humans more realistic and softer in appearance
    (C) religious leaders mostly commissioned medieval art, whereas religious and secular leaders commissioned Renaissance art
    (D) medieval art was almost entirely religious in subject, whereas Renaissance was almost all secular in subject

2. The development of the Gutenberg press in the mid-fifteenth century was significant for all of the following reasons EXCEPT

    (A) it constituted the first printing press in the world
    (B) it made books more easy to produce and more afford-able to the general European public
    (C) it promoted the printing of texts in languages other than Latin and thus more accessible to the reading public
    (D) it led to increased higher education and literacy across Europe

3. Martin Luther's list of *95 Theses* was largely written for which of the following reasons?

    (A) Luther sought to organize the Germanic states into one unified political state.
    (B) Luther protested the use of Catholic indulgences as a means of controlling salvation and availability of the word of God to non–Latin speaking peoples.
    (C) Luther attempted to undermine the power of the Roman Catholic church and that of the pope.
    (D) Luther aimed to consolidate the power of religion and state into a single Saxon state.

4. Which of the following best explains the motivation of English king Henry VIII in establishing the Anglican Church (or Church of England) as a separate entity from the Roman Catholic Church in 1534?

    (A) The pope refused to grant Henry an annulment of his marriage to Catherine of Aragon.
    (B) Henry embraced the Protestant movements sweeping across the English isles.
    (C) Henry sought to separate England and its religion from the rival Catholic states of France and Spain.
    (D) Henry refused to permit the Roman Catholic Church from holding English land without paying taxes.

5. The Catholic counter-reformation during the sixteenth century was effective in reestablishing control over many regions and peoples that had embraced Protestant beliefs. All of the following were largely Catholic by 1600 C.E. EXCEPT

    (A) Spain
    (B) Italy
    (C) Scotland
    (D) France

6. Copernicus' *On the Revolutions of the Heavenly Spheres* and Galileo's *Dialogue Concerning the Two Chief Systems of the World* were ultimately accepted because

    (A) the Ptolemaic model of celestial motion became more established.
    (B) the Roman Catholic Church embraced the geocentric model.
    (C) Galileo was able to justify the perceived motion of the planets and stars using his telescope.
    (D) the Roman Catholic Church did not ban Galileo's work as heretical and it was widely read and accepted.

7. Which of the following scientists invented calculus, which validated many of the scientific theories proposed at that time and it remains regularly used today?

   (A) Francis Bacon
   (B) Tycho Brahe
   (C) Galileo
   (D) Isaac Newton

8. The development and application of the scientific method was a critical step during the Scientific Revolution because

   (A) it validated previous approaches by using pure reason
   (B) it required experimental or mathematical proof, rather than just reason, for validation and acceptance
   (C) it allowed European scientists to follow a common approach or convention with scientists in China and Middle East
   (D) of none of the above

9. In the late fifteenth century, European nations began sailing to new regions of the globe including the Americas and the Orient. Which of the following best explains the rationale for the earliest expeditions?

   (A) To find gold and riches to finance their respective nations
   (B) To establish new trading routes with the Orient
   (C) To conquer new lands and expand their respective domains
   (D) To convert and offer salvation to non-Christians in other regions of the world

10. Spain and Portugal were in direct competition for exploration and claiming of lands in the newly discovered Americas during the late fifteenth century. Which of the following treaties was signed to delineate territorial possessions in the new world at this time?

    (A) Treaty of Guadeloupe Hidalgo
    (B) Treaty of Tordesillas
    (C) Treaty of Utrecht
    (D) Treaty of Madrid

Check your answers on page 218.

Chapter 10
Period 4
Global
Interactions
c. 1450 to
c. 1750
Answers
and Explanations

ANSWER KEY

Drill 1
1. C
2. A
3. B
4. B
5. C
6. D
7. A
8. A
9. B
10. B

Drill 2
1. A
2. D
3. D
4. B
5. D
6. C
7. A
8. B
9. C
10. D

Drill 3
1. D
2. C
3. B
4. A
5. B
6. C
7. D
8. A
9. A
10. B

Drill 4
1. C
2. D
3. B
4. D
5. C
6. A
7. B
8. C
9. D
10. B

Drill 5
1. A
2. B
3. C
4. D
5. C
6. B
7. C
8. D
9. C
10. A

Drill 6
1. C
2. C
3. C
4. A
5. A
6. B
7. C
8. D
9. B
10. B

Drill 7
1. C
2. D
3. B
4. A
5. C
6. C
7. A
8. C
9. D
10. A

Drill 8
1. A
2. D
3. A
4. B
5. B
6. B
7. D
8. B
9. C
10. A

Drill 9
1. D
2. A
3. B
4. A
5. C
6. C
7. D
8. B
9. B
10. B

EXPLANATIONS

Drill 1

1. **C** The colonists referred to are the ones who will found the United States, so really these colonies are populated by British ex-pats. The only main difference between these countries will be the use of the slave trade, that slaves are brought to mainland North America. During the American Revolution, American colonists complained about their representation in British Parliament and their desire to control their own economies.

2. **A** The Dutch East India Company was mostly interested in Taiwan and Indonesia, so these places were not really where you'd find proselytes, missionaries attempting to convert the populate. That was really the role of Spain—spreading Christianity all over. The Philippines had the most contact with Spain, and thus the rise of Christianity there. India also garnered the attention of France and Britain mostly as a market for those countries' goods, so India didn't get much from Christian missionaries either.

3. **B** In the closing years of the fifteenth century, remember that the Portuguese and Spanish are going to take to the seas. With technological innovations which help them bypass land routes to Asia, they take control of the seas. China and Japan will not engage significantly in this development of a more strongly integrated world economy, though they contribute to it. The Ottoman empire was the bridge between East and West and won't get involved with the move to the New World, or the rise of mercantilism.

4. **B** Remember that Japan will initially welcome Western Christianity and technologies, but the Japanese ruling elite will quickly worry about a dependence on Western ideas and trade, and minimize contact as soon as the civilization duplicates some of the technology Japan admires. The civilizations couldn't be colonized the way the New World could, in part because they could push back invaders. There were European ports, however, most famously in Macao, controlled by the Portuguese.

5. **C** The Seven Years' War, fought between Great Britain and its allies against France and its allies, was a world war (fought in Europe, North America, South America, Africa, India, and the Philippine Islands) driven by desires for colonial empires. Think "global" or "worldwide" only post-1450. All the other wars mentioned in the answer choices are out of era, so eliminate them, even if you don't remember what the Seven Years' War was about.

6. **D** Mercantilism, the philosophy that the economy is a zero-sum game and it is better to export goods than import them, created even more significant rivalries in Europe, since the philosophy states there can be only one winner. Empires, then, needed more markets, which pushed European colonization of the world. Any place Europeans colonized, or attempted to, was affected by European ambition and ways of life.

7. A   Parliament already held a great amount of control in 1700s England, allowing for comparatively greater autonomy for citizens, especially compared to the absolute monarchies that ruled Russia and France. The Ottoman Empire was under the control of the sultan.

8. A   The Mughal Empire ruled over an Islamic state on the Indian subcontinent. Mughal art and architecture reflected Persian and Indian architectural structures. The Mughals controlled the northern and central portions of India. Their rule ended in the return of traditional regional government in India. This motive, with vivid colors and complicated design, was indicative of an Islamic art.

9. B   Russian trade remained local and regional throughout the beginning and growth of an international trade system. Japan and China both encouraged regional trade, but engaged in limited long-distance trade. The Philippines were controlled by Spain, who used the islands as a market for goods, and a source for resources.

10. B   The New World gave Europe sweet potatoes, potatoes, tomatoes, corn, tobacco, beans, vanilla, peanuts, and a handful of other foods Europe quickly grew attached to. Europe gifted a number of diseases, livestock (including the horse), grains, sugar cane, bananas, coffee beans, and alcohol to inhabitants in the other hemisphere.

Drill 2

1. A   Mansa Musa of Mali is the famous African king who performed his *hajj* in 1324, spreading gold throughout Egypt and Arabia. He believed the Muslims had a more advanced culture and worked to bring Islam and its culture back to Mali. Peter the Great travelled to Europe in 1697 to bring European culture back to Russia. Peter imposed a tax on beards and long robes. Mansa Musa was Muslim, but Peter the Great was Orthodox Christian.

2. D   The Mongols didn't set up strong governance wherever they took control, so Russia didn't develop during the Mongol period. The Mongols were animist, so they didn't try to take the area back over for Roman Catholicism (remember the Schism?). Even though the Mongols created a bridge between east and west, Russia did not benefit from the Mongol's access to Western markets.

3. D   Though Catherine felt it necessary to continue the cultural reforms begun by Peter the Great, she doesn't extend this interest to Western philosophy (A). Though she appreciated the French Enlightenment, she banned all political writings from the same era, so she certainly didn't free the serf community (B). She faced peasant revolts, but never anything that brought the government down (C). She centralized the government, but decided to give power to the nobles in order to delegate governing responsibilities, giving them a lot of control (D).

4. B   Both the trans-Atlantic and eastern African trade routes took slaves, usually acquired from central Africa before being taken to coastal regions, to European-run plantations. The eastern African slave trade catered to the African, Indian, and Islamic world.

5. **D** The sugar plantations in the Caribbean and Brazil were the primary destination of the Middle Passage, as the trans-Atlantic leg of the triangular trade system was known. Only around 5 percent of slaves were sent to North America. Mortality rates are estimated to be anywhere from 15 to 33 percent, and more men than women were transported.

6. **C** African slaves brought through the Middle Passage will bring along all parts of African they could take with them. Early Africans brought with them highly developed skills in metal working, leather work, pottery, and weaving, as well as cultivation of crops from Africa. With the cultivation of these crops, African-style cooking also arose. This is a common sense question, though. Since Africans were taken against their will to the Americas, it makes sense that they weren't in control of social structures, and regardless of who they were in Africa, they occupied the bottom rung of society on plantations and farms.

7. **A** The British southern colonies are those that relied on slavery for the farming of tobacco, rice, and cotton, all crops which required a lot of labor. The soil in the south was actually better than that of northern colonies, so agriculture flourished there. As a result, so did slavery. High numbers of slaves had to be regularly imported because of the high mortality rate of those who travelled the Middle Passage and were then forced to work in the sugar fields and mines of Latin America; the only way to keep up with demand was to continue importing slaves. Manumission, the freeing of slaves, was not widely practiced in the British colonies. Slavery continued in Latin America until 1888; Brazil was the last hold-out of the practice.

8. **B** The Seljuk Turks are not contemporaries of these other empires. Eliminate (D). This is a bit of a which-one-of-these-is-not-like-the-other game; the only answer choice with empires which were similar to one another is (B), all Islamic empires. "Gunpowder Empires" is a collective phrase which refers to those empires which used gunpowder technology to conquer lands. It includes Safavid Persia, Ottoman Turkey, and Mughal India. Though China invents gunpowder, and Japan and Korea learn to exploit it militaristically, the term refers to the fourteenth-century exploitation of the technology by these Islamic empires.

9. **C** The Spanish came to the new world looking for goods, converts, and fortune. The Spanish were committed to converting the Native Americans to Catholicism, and so set up more permanent settlements than did their French counterparts, who were mostly interested in commercial gain. The French explored and settled parts of the South American coast and kept an outpost in India.

10. **D** Most regions found themselves outside the "global" trade networks, including Russia, Japan, Mughal India, parts of Africa, and the Ottoman Empire. The Polynesians were busy settling New Zealand and Hawaii and won't be bothered by the rest of the world for a little time longer. Though China agreed to trade with the west, it didn't allow much penetration of these societies into China itself; trade was done in specific places.

Drill 3

1. **D**   The Dutch bypassed western Africa by establishing Cape Colony in southern Africa, which served as a way station to Asia. Portugal is the European power you should associate with western Africa. The Dutch also had a North American colony for a few years in what is now New York, and even had trade relations with the Tokugawa Shogunate.

2. **C**   Movable type, or Gutenberg's printing press, influenced by Chinese printing, was developed in Europe in the mid-1400s. The mass production of books made it easier for ideas to spread. Thomas Hobbes and John Locke will most famously discuss the concept that society is defined as when one willingly enters into a social contract with society to protect him/herself, and what a person agrees to give up for that right. Diderot's Encyclopedia is the high point of the Enlightenment; the two are inseparable realities of the other. Though heliocentrism isn't a new idea in the seventeenth century, Copernicus will be the first to prove it mathematically.

3. **B**   The map depicts the breakdown of the initial Lutheran adherents, which began in Wittenberg when Martin Luther nailed his 95 Theses to the door of the Castle Church in 1517. Remember that the Schism between Roman Catholics and Eastern Orthodox Christians happened in the fourteenth century, so it's out of context. So are (C) and (D), since the French Revolution and Napoleonic France are in the late eighteenth and early nineteenth century (the French Revolution begins in 1789 and Napoleon seizes power in 1804). The Thirty Years' War happened later as well, between 1618 and 1648.

4. **A**   Feudalism was already entrenched in Europe by 800 c.e. and ended in the sixteenth century; it wasn't introduced to Japan until the 1100s and lasted until 1868. Peasants were tied to the land and worked for protection, and paid with a portion of their harvest (B). In Europe, lords paid for the harvest they took. Feudal Japan and Europe were built on a system of hereditary classes (C), with nobles occupying the top tier, followed by warriors, with farmers or serfs below. In Japan, merchants made up the lowest level. Finally, (D) constant warfare made warriors the most important class. Knights in Europe and samurai in Japan served local lords and were bound to a code of ethics to protect the peasants they'd sworn to protect.

5. **B**   Islamic elements were pushed out of southern Spain by the powerful Isabella. Spain began the Inquisition in 1478, so you know (A) is no good. POE that out. Use common sense on (C). If the Renaissance spread to Britain and France, some translation work had to happen. The renewal of Catholicism was imposed, not a peasant movement, so (D) also wouldn't make much sense.

    So if Ferdinand and Isabella were fervently pushing the faith (which they were), then they would censor new ideas that may undermine the Church. (B) is your answer.

6. **C**   This one you kinda just have to know. All these answer choices refer to society and economy in Spanish America. The *peninsulares* were colonists who were born in Europe. *Criollos* were colonists born in America, but to European parents. *Mestizos* were people of mixed Spanish and Native

American blood. The hierarchy in Spanish America tended to flow in this way—*peninsulares* on top, followed by *criollos,* then *mestizos,* then *mulatos* (mixed European and African blood).

The *encomienda* system was the feudal system transported to the new world, in which Spanish grant (land) holders could extract labor from the Native American population, which didn't really have a say in all this.

7. **D**   The Glorious Revolution in 1688 was a bloodless coup, unique to the times. James II dissolved Parliament, so Parliamentary leaders brought in Mary (Catholic James' Protestant sister) and her husband William.

Using POE, (A) can't work, because Parliament began the uprising. (B) is not a right gained by any European society in this era. (C) seems a bit weird, so get rid of it.

8. **A**   Once Russia pushed tribesmen of the steppe off its eastern frontier, its monarchs, especially Peter the Great and Catherine the Great, concentrated (among other things) on territorial expansion. Peter will succeed in getting a warm-water port, which was essential for year-round trade. Rulers concentrated on Central Asia and Siberia for natural resources and luxury goods. By the end of Catherine's reign—thanks to her acquisitions of Alaska, Crimea, and northern California—Russia became the largest empire of its time.

9. **A**   Native Americans did not have writing, though the Aztec and the Inca Spanish conquistadors encounter are civilized tribes living in cities, so (B) is out. Though (C) and (D) are both true about the new exchanges with the New World, these sorts of changes happened when Europe opened itself to China, Japan, Africa—just about every other group. Remember that during this time, China and Japan were rather isolationist. They agreed to trade with Europe, but in limited ways.

What's unique about the Americas is the way Europe decimated native life, killing millions of the natives through disease and warfare. With no real resistance, whole economic systems and communities which were clearly European were set up in the New World—think the encomienda system, the structure of the British American colonies, the social structures of these places. They were all exports of the European countries colonists came from.

10. **B**   Though silk, throughout world history, had been a major manufactured product of China, the beginning of the porcelain trade began with the Ming dynasty (1368–1644). Paper, also invented in China, was also being exported. Tea won't actually make it to England until the sixteenth century.

Drill 4

1. **C** The Ming weren't responsible for forcing the Mongols from China (D). They did, however, face threats along their northern border by the horde. This, combined with the Ming's return to Confucian traditions, pushed the Ming into a period of isolation by the 1430s. Russia responded to its previous Mongol occupation by establishing absolute rule. Though Russia eventually entered a period of westernization and allowed women more participation in public events, the subordinate position of women in China was continued by the strict Confucian and Neo-Confucian policies under the Ming (A). Neither the Ming nor the Russians imposed new faiths (B).

2. **D** The difficulty for both the Africans and Native Americans was that both lacked centralized power and so could not rally to fight off the might of the Europeans (A). Neither civilization had the military sophistication (guns, military technology) to keep the Europeans out (B). Europeans caused the death of possibly millions of Native Americans by exposing the Native Americans to diseases they didn't have any natural immunity to. The Middle Passage had a mortality rate of 30%, killing hundreds of Africans on their way to the colonies in the Americas (C). Europe did not take over the African continent in this period (that'll be the Scramble for Africa in the nineteenth century).

3. **B** The reference to "our holy Catholic faith" should make you POE out (A) and (D) since neither was Catholic. The pope doesn't really have control over any cities, at least not the ability to pass public administrative policy, so you can POE out (C) as well.

    The document is the 1492 Edict of Expulsion of the Jews, when Ferdinand and Isabella threw out the remaining Jewish population of Spain. The Jewish and Muslim population had been experiencing persecution for decades, but this Edict was a new level of oppression introduced to the Spanish Inquisition.

4. **D** This question can also be answered as "where did the oppressed of Europe turn in order to escape persecution?" Like Puritans, Jews went to the Americas seeking a place to worship freely. The Ottoman Empire welcomed both Muslims and Jews from Spain, where the Sultan Bayezid II was said to have sent his gratitude to Ferdinand for sending him some of his best subjects, thus 'impoverishing his own lands while enriching his (Bayezid's).' The Netherlands, eager to expand its trade empire, invited educated Jewish bankers to help build its world empire.

5. **C** By the close of the Middle Ages, western Europe began to organize itself along cultural and linguistic lines. By 1500, clear national lines could be drawn by what language one spoke. "Roving nomadic bands" (A) were a thing of the past. Ming China (B) was insular, and therefore didn't compete in the global economy. The Black Plague was a devastating outbreak, but it didn't leave Europe sparsely populated (D).

6. **A** The Zhou Dynasty (c. 1046 B.C.E.–256 B.C.E.) believed in the Mandate of Heaven, meaning that heaven would grant the Zhou power only as long as its rulers governed justly and wisely. In other words, only as long as it had the blessing of heaven, the Zhou Dynasty would remain in power. Both systems claimed that the ruler was divinely chosen [(B) and (C)]. Divine Right claimed that kings were infallible and could do whatever they wanted (D).

7. **B** John Locke wrote *Two Treatises on Government*, in which Locke argued all men are born equal to one another and had natural and unalienable rights to life, liberty, and property. Jean-Jacques Rousseau (A) wrote *The Social Contract*, in which he argued that men enter into a contract with their communities, exchanging some freedoms for protection. *The Book of the Courtier* was written by Baldassare Castiglione, about the ideal behavior of the Renaissance man. Diderot's (C) great work was his authoring of articles and organizing the *Encyclopedie*, the first encyclopedia which gathered myriad information on science, literature, and everything in between. Thomas Hobbes wrote *Leviathan*, which argued that people are naturally greedy and violent. Voltaire (D) was famous for *Candide*, about a young man's education.

8. **C** Mysticism is the belief that one can have a direct relationship, more importantly a direct *experience* with God. Sufis believe they are practicing *ihsan* (perfection of worship): "Worship and serve Allah as you are seeing Him and while you see Him not yet truly He sees you." Ignatius Loyola, founder of the Jesuits, encouraged religious exercises, including direct communion with God. Those who follow Kabbalah believe that there is a part of God that is knowable, and you should work to know this part of God that is understandable, as there is a part of Him that is not.

    The Jesuits were founded by a Spaniard, so (A) has to go. Those who follow Kabbalah are more interested in God, and are rooted in Judaism, so (B) is out. Though you should definitely know that the Jesuits are important evangelists (they reconvert most of Poland back to Catholicism during the Catholic Reformation and converted the New World), those who follow Kabbalah are not (D).

9. **D** The rise of global trade created new realities throughout the world. Demographics (A) shifted significantly—the Aztecs and Incas were wiped out in the sixteenth and seventeenth century. A huge portion of the Native American population was either destroyed or forced to migrate. Millions of Africans were forced against their will to also migrate across the Atlantic as part of the slave trade. Europeans moved to the New World in the hundreds of thousands. Cities in Europe also changed. With the introduction of new crops (B), cuisines and nutrition were changed throughout Europe and Asia. The introduction of the potato in the British Isles, for example, provided a stable crop in a place which had suffered numerous famines, minimizing the number and severity of these famines. Europeans began to see themselves as the benefactors of civilization; some philosophers and missionaries in the Americas claimed that it was better for the African to be sold into slavery, or the Native American person forced to accept European domination, because these communities needed to be civilized.

10. **B** Remember that Japan under the Tokugawa becomes incredibly isolationist, so with that information, you should choose (B), or at least eliminate (D). Japan does take the opportunity of isolation to develop its own art and it's under the Tokugawa that Kabuki theater and the haiku poem are created. Art from this period in wood-blocking prints, detailed scrolls, and paintings thrives. You shouldn't forget the Renaissance was an incredible period of artistic, literary, scientific, and philosophic revival, obviously, so (C) wasn't unique to the Tokugawa. The Renaissance was the one looking for world audiences, though (D). And neither was a mainly literary movement (A).

Drill 5

1. **A** Though Protestants removed some things they didn't agree with concerning the Catholic church, such as indulgences, celibacy of priests, and the nature of Communion, the Catholic church took the opportunity to strengthen much of its teachings (B). Neither Church really contacted the Eastern Orthodox Church (C). Though Catholics did have a strict hierarchy in their Church, it was in part because of this that Protestants rebelled. Protestant churches tend not to have as clearly defined lines as Catholic congregations do (D).

2. **B** Predestination is John Calvin's theory that God already knows who's going to heaven and who's going to hell—it's all predestined. But the way you live your life will tell you where you're headed afterwards. Deism is the religious philosophy that many Enlightenment thinkers ascribed to, which saw God as a watchmaker, who had set the watch at the beginning of time and was now allowing everything to run its course according to natural laws (A). Both Locke and Rousseau stated that the social contracts people tie themselves to have natural rights inherent within them (C). The scientific method became popularized and perfected in the sixteenth century and stated that a fact was only a fact if others could independently verify it by repeating the experiment and obtaining the same results you did (D), which required the use of natural laws.

3. **C** Most cultures don't mind if their cultures spread to other places, so be wary of answer choices like (A). If it looks like it goes against common sense, it probably does. The government wasn't reforming as much as consolidating its power (D). "Reform" usually refers to modernizing and liberalizing. The Tokugawa shogunate was more about strengthening the central government than helping to modernize peasants (B).

   The Tokugawa were concerned about the rising influence of the Europeans in Asia, and didn't appreciate evangelists converting the Japanese to Christianity. Markets were flooded with foreign goods, and the shogunate became concerned that both merchants and missionaries might mess with the social order. So slowly, it closed the borders—in 1616, foreign traders could trade in only a handful of port cities. In the 1630s, Japanese ships were forbidden to trade, or even sail overseas. Eventually, only a handful of ships visited, and Christianity had been violently suppressed.

4. **D** The Ottoman Empire's weakness allowed Russia to expand into Siberia by the sixteenth century (A). Peter the Great seized a portion of the Baltic Sea and built St. Petersburg on its banks (B). Catherine the Great expanded the empire all the way to the banks of northern California (C). Choice (D) is correct because the Mongol hordes were keeping expansion slowed to the west (not the south, as the answer choice specified).

5. **C** Remember that Japan's definitely the most isolationist. (POE out A and B). China comes in a close second due to its willingness to sell Europe its goods (silk, paper, and other similar goods). Africa had traders since classical times, but Europe very much drove the world economy, so you have to go with (C).

6. **B**   Paper (C) and cement (D) are out of era. POE them out. The Chinese began making paper much earlier, and cement was actually invented by the Romans. The spinning jenny (A) was something you should associate with the Industrial Revolution, so it's also out of era. POE.

    Johannes Gutenberg's printing press was probably the most important invention, creating the ability for literature, and therefore ideas and philosophies to spread more rapidly. This will help launch not just the Protestant Reformation, but also the Italian Renaissance and the Scientific Revolution.

7. **C**   The Scientific Revolution was a period in which empirical, testable research was emphasized (A) and was based on the concept that science could improve the condition of humanity, which was basically good (D), which is how the Scientific Revolution and the Enlightenment are tied together. The purpose of scientific inquiry was to try to explain the nature of the world (B). Since the Scientific Revolution proposed a heliocentric model of the world, something that went against Catholic church dogma, the church didn't like it, but it was not a violent revolution, the way the French Revolution was.

8. **D**   Oceania and Polynesia largely sat out the revolution in transoceanic navigation. Portuguese traders generally didn't establish much of a presence in those particular areas, so cross off (A). China was not the dominant power in the region at any point during this period, so cross off (B). And Oceania and Polynesia were not known for their mariners, though they were doubtless skilled, so cross off (C).

9. **C**   Until the mid-eighteenth century, European traders in Asia were largely middlemen. They were rare enough, though their presence increased, but they played a significant role in building foundations and networks for future European presence on the continent, so cross off (A). Transporting laborers was not the primary purpose of these relationships, so cross off (B). There were no significant outposts of European colonists in Asia prior to the mid-eighteenth century, so cross off (D).

10. **A**   Sugar was a rare commodity in Europe until its introduction to the Americas, where an enslaved African workforce undertook its cultivation and processing on a large scale. Fruit trees and grains made the Americas a place to cultivate foodstuffs to sell in Europe and beyond. Cross off (B), as these products went the other direction, (C), because these were not Middle Eastern products spreading into Europe, and (D), because these were not African staple crops.

Drill 6

1. **C** The Dutch were a maritime empire—the others were land-based empires.

2. **C** Rousseau's ideas of freedom were not religious in nature. But he did see men as equals who agreed, rationally, to subject themselves to the rule of law, as they came together to create those laws—so cross off (A), (B), and (D).

3. **C** Disease was the big killer, not guns—so cross off (A)—or human sacrifice—so cross off (B). It was also not the numerical superiority of the Spanish in battle, but rather the comparative might of their germs, so cross off (D).

4. **A** When you think "Martin Luther" you should think "Protestant Reformation"—protesting and re-forming the practices of the Catholic Church. It wasn't about German taxation or German paint-ing—so cross off (B) and (C). Nor was it about Galileo's heliocentric model, though the Church got pretty mad about that, too, so you need to eliminate that, too.

5. **A** China never went so far as to entirely ban trade with Europe, though it was strictly limited under the Manchus. All other policies listed here were employed at some point in time by each nation.

6. **B** Remember: you're looking for the one that *isn't* true. India's economic involvement with South American began in the nineteenth century. (A) and (D) should be easy to eliminate, thanks to colonization and the slave trade. Cross off (C) because Filipino sailors established ties to South and Central America as early as the sixteenth century.

7. **C** They worked within the system they were given to accumulate as much power as possible—this was true in Britain, France, Spain, and the Holy Roman Empire, to name a few. (A) is not correct because this was a period of numerous uprisings by the peasant classes, and many nations took steps during this time to end serfdom, which finally died out completely in the early nineteenth century. While some aristocrats may have believed (B), politics in most countries made it painfully obvious that aris-tocrats held their power at the monarch's whim, not God's, so cross that off. And only in England did aristocrats routinely fund colonization attempts during this period—monarchs elsewhere, such as in Spain, had plenty in their treasuries to bankroll such attempts—so cross off (D).

8. **D** Introduction of new crops had basically the same effect in Europe. It did not cause the Chinese to abandon traditional foods or adopt the European three-field system on any widespread basis, so cross off (A) and (C). While there may have been some immigration from regions where food sources were less available, this would have occurred whatever the Chinese were cooking, as long as they were better off than the other nations, so it isn't really related to the new crops. There were also no "large-scale" migrations, so cross off (B).

9. **B** The Peace of Westphalia ended the Thirty Years' War and the Eighty Years' War, guaranteeing a measure of religious tolerance in the German states of the Holy Roman Empire and laying the foundation for the self-determination of nations by recognizing the princes' sovereignty and right to establish their states with either Catholic ("Ecclesiastick") or Protestant ("Laick") faith. It wasn't about promoting nobles within the Church (which church?), so cross off (A). The Catholic Church also wasn't supporting France's right to German territories with any sort of feudal justification, so cross off (C). Finally, this peace was intended to be as long-lasting as possible, settle two extended wars, and establish a new order in Europe, so cross off (D).

10. **B** These Islamic empires were known as the Gunpowder Empires for their adaptation of this Chinese technology. "The Balkan States" generally refers to the collection of modern states in the area of the Balkan Mountains, formerly united as Yugoslavia—in other words, a long way from India, so cross off (A), even though these states are adjacent to Turkey and were once part of the Ottoman Empire. Cross off (C) because "the Golden Horde" refers to part of the *Mongol* Empire, not the Mughal Empire, and was established to the north of Safavid Persia approximately three centuries before that empire's inception. These also do not represent the other three khanates into which the Mongol Empire was divided, so cross off (D), too.

Drill 7

1. **C** Quebec City (or Cap-Rouge) had a rocky start, established first by Jacques Cartier but abandoned and re-established several times. The iteration that lasted was Samuel de Champlain's, established in 1608. There was no lasting settlement at Charlesfort on Parris Island (which is in South Carolina), and the brief military encampment there had nothing to do with Jacques Cartier, so cross off (A). Henri de Feynes went to China for the French, not to Haiti (a.k.a. Saint-Domingue), so cross off (B). Giovanni da Veranzano explored the coast of much of North America for the French long before any of these others, naming regions he found, but established no permanent settlements, so cross off (D).

2. **D** The English Interregnum was the period "between kings," after the execution of Charles I—so cross off (B), since that's how the Interregnum *began*—and before the restoration of Charles II. Cross off (C) because that refers to the Glorious Revolution, which would end Charles II's brother James II's rule in 1688, and cross of (A) because that was a century and a half prior.

3. **B** All that death got people thinking about humanity and its place in the world, as well as the nature of the human body. That wasn't why feudalism developed, though, so cross off (A). Nor did it result in the oversupply of people or material goods in China or anywhere else, so cross off (C) and (D).

4. **A** All of these are various church councils, but only (A) correctly describes the Council of Trent, which ran intermittently from 1545–1563. (B) is the Second Council of Nicaea, so cross that off. (C) is the Council of Pisa, so cross that off. (D) is the Council of Vienne, so cross that off.

5. **C** Shah Jahan, grandson of Akbar, who unified much of India, built the Taj Mahal as a tomb for his wife and was later interred there himself. Shah Jahan was a Muslim ruler in a Hindu land, and the site was looted by the British in 1857, but the British government sponsored a repair project that concluded in 1908. So cross off (A), (B), and (D). Buddhism, however, is not a part of this story.

6. **C** Staple crops mean foods. These starches, maize/corn and manioc/cassava, brought new sources of carbohydrates and nutrition. Tobacco isn't edible—nor is mint a source of nutrition—so cross off (A) and (B). Okra and rice traveled out of Africa in the Columbian Exchange, not into Africa, so cross off (D).

7. **A** Russia did not have a maritime empire. Portugal (Brazil), the Netherlands (Caribbean, North America), and Spain (lots of places), however, were all transatlantic colonial powers.

8. **C** Gold also came out of South America, but American silver added to the quantity of precious metals available to finance trade, particularly with China.

9. **D** Steamships, the telegraph, and canals were all developments that revolutionized transportation and communication in the nineteenth and twentieth centuries.

10. **A** Anti-imperial resistance in the territories controlled by the Ottoman Empire caused increasing instability in the late nineteenth century. Some of these territories were picked off by other powers capitalizing on the instability. Others, including Serbia, Montenegro, and Romania achieved full independence. Migrations and intermarriage patterns didn't play into it; nor did American and European demand for exports, so cross off (B), (C), and (D).

Drill 8

1. **A** While Australia would ultimately become a British possession, it was Dutch explorers who made landfall in 1606, discovering a continent previously unknown to Europeans and populated by indigenous peoples. So cross off (B) in favor of (A). Though Chinese and Indian explorers may indeed have found their way to Australia before the Dutch in 1606, such visits were not widely recorded, and the question asks which country discovered it in that specific year, so cross off (C) and (D).

2. **D** Constantine XI's reign ended with the overrun of Constantinople by Ottoman forces in 1453—Constantine XI died that day. He was the last of the Byzantine emperors. This began, not ended, Ottoman control of Constantinople, so cross off (A). Roman emperors had been Christian since Theodosius I in the fourth century, so cross off (C). Constantine was not a Mongol so cross off (B).

3.   **A**   Jesuit Missionaries from Portugal arrived in Japan in the late 1500s, initiating cultural and commercial contact between Japan and the West. Marco Polo went to China but did not reach Japan, so cross off (B). The Japanese were well established on the international stage by the time Americans were sailing west from California, so cross off (C). And Ferdinand and Isabella were interested in reaching the Pacific Islands, and Columbus briefly suspected he had landed in Japan after determining he was not in the East Indies, but no Spanish explorer under Ferdinand and Isabella's flag reached Japan in the fifteenth century, so cross off (D).

4.   **B**   The Mughal emperors used the power of their position and the imposition of a common, Persian-based culture to maintain hegemony in Hindu India. While there may have been some instances of violence against minorities, this cannot be described as a primary or even systematic approach so cross off (A). Taxation was not minimal, and the burden fell more heavily on non-Muslim residents, so cross off (C). Finally, "nationalism" is not a word you should associate with anything earlier than the late nineteenth century, so cross off (D).

5.   **B**   Conquering a declining capital of the Byzantine Empire in 1453 officially transformed the Ottoman state into an Ottoman Empire. The Ottoman capture of Baghdad in 1534 occurred nearly a century later, when the Ottomans were well established as an empire, so cross off (C). Similarly, the Ottoman Turks captured Alexandria in 1517, well after they had established themselves as an empire, so cross off (D). Finally, Ankara was part of the Ottoman homeland, so cross off (A).

6.   **B**   Remember that you're looking for the one that *isn't* true. Before the arrival of Spanish conquistadores, horses were unknown to the Americas. Montezuma II's predecessor did conquer the Zapotecs and Mixtecs, as well as work to rebuild Tenochtitlan and particularly the Great Pyramid, or Templo Mayor, so cross off (A) and (C). The Triple Alliance of the Aztecs, rather than engaging in outright war with territories already conquered, demanded human sacrifices through "flower wars" in order to keep the cosmos moving as it should, so cross off (D).

7.   **D**   The English monarchy, more recently established via warfare than the comparatively settled Spanish and Portuguese royal houses, lacked comparable power and resources. As a result, England initially offered state sanction to private exploration rather than financing the expedition with royal funds. It was abundantly obvious that England's territorial ambitions were in potential conflict with France's, so cross off (B). The Church of England was led by the monarch and was thus not in a position to forbid the monarch from doing much of anything, so cross off (A). Finally, while explorers may have sought to make claims for themselves, they were well aware that the English Crown could offer important protections for their holdings, so cross off (C).

8. B   This is a tricky question—you're looking for the primary reason these monarchs established the Inquisition, not just something that resulted from its establishment. Some of the Inquisition's most notorious work may have involved burning witches, and the Inquisition arguably did enforce a measure of fear-driven control over the population, neither was the primary stated purpose of the Inquisition, so cross off (A) and (C). What the Inquisition investigated was not avenues of exploration, so cross off (D). Rather, the intention of the Spanish Inquisition was to maintain the orthodoxy of those who converted from Judaism or Islam, so choice (B) is the correct answer.

9. C   In 1494, the pope settled a Spanish-Portuguese dispute over claims to the New World by dividing the Atlantic in two, granting Spain all territory to the west of the line and Portugal all territory to the east. Brazil was the one piece of South America that jutted east over the line. It was not armed conflict with Spanish settlers, so cross off (B). As a consequence of being shut out of most of the Americas, the Portuguese expanded their efforts to head east around Africa—but to India and the South Pacific. They had first reached South America by the traditional European route, heading west across the Atlantic, so cross off (D). Finally, while the Portuguese and the Dutch were two big names in the slave trade, the Portuguese did not trade the Dutch their (nonexistent) American colonies for rights to Africa—the Portuguese were in Africa long before the Dutch were—so cross off (A).

10. A   The Renaissance began in the fourteenth century in Italy and predated all of the other European cultural movements. The Protestant Reformation is often quoted as having started in 1517 with the posting of his 95 Theses. The Scientific Revolution is often associated with Copernicus' *On the Revolutions of the Heavenly Spheres* in 1543. The Age of Enlightenment wouldn't begin until the mid-seventeenth century.

Drill 9

1. D   Renaissance art still maintained a heavy influence from the Church despite more secular art being generated. Humanism during the Renaissance had a major impact on the development of art. Medieval art was practically all religious in subject having been commissioned almost solely by the Church and appeared flat and stiff in appearance. The Renaissance saw realism and humanism enter art. Both secular and religious leaders commissioned Renaissance art and the subjects were quite broad compared to medieval art.

2. A   The moveable type printing press was actually invented by the Song dynasty in China in the eleventh century in China. However, Europe did not develop and use a printing press until Johannes Gutenberg's invention in the mid-fifteenth century. The development of the press led to increased book production (B), printing of texts in local vernaculars (C), and increased literacy and education (D) in Europe.

3. **B** Martin Luther contested the power of the Catholic Church obtained through the selling of indulgences to lessen the time of purgatory. He viewed this as an abuse of the power of the Church to maintain power and raise money. He maintained that the way to salvation was through grace rather than indulgences. Another critique of the Church was that the word of God and the lessons of God were only available in Latin. Consequently, he was instrumental in translating the first German Bible.

4. **A** The primary reason for Henry VIII's move to separate the Anglican Church from the Roman Catholic Church was so that he may grant himself the right to annul his marriage to Catherine the Great and marry Anne Boleyn. The annulment stemmed from Catherine's inability to produce a male heir (she did have a daughter, Mary, who would become queen approximately 20 years later) and his infatuation with Anne (who would also fail to produce a male heir).

5. **C** Scotland during the Protestant reformation embraced the ideology of John Knox and Calvinism. Spain (A), Italy (B), France (D) as well as Portugal and southern Germany remained largely Catholic during this time.

6. **C** Galileo's ability to observe the motion of planetary objects using his telescope (a new invention of the time) allowed for him to accurately describe the motion of celestial objects and refute Ptolemy's geocentric model. Despite sound proof and evidence, the Roman Catholic Church still placed his work on *The Index* as heretical.

7. **D** Isaac Newton is credited with establishing the mathematical application of calculus. Through calculus he was able to justify the theories of Copernicus, Galileo, Bacon and many others as well as justify scientific phenomenon such as forces and gravity.

8. **B** The scientific method used the principles of observation, reason and experimentation to test and prove scientific hypotheses. This was a major leap from early science which largely used philosophical arguments and reason to find scientific meaning.

9. **B** The first voyages by the Spanish (in 1492) and Portuguese (in 1488) were organized to find new efficient trading routes to Asia. It was later discovered that vast stretches of land and wealth were available and capable of being attained (A and C). The goal of converting natives did not become a focus of nearly all sailing expeditions (D), although it certainly became a part of European conquests.

10. **B** The Treaty of Tordesillas, signed in 1494, established a line of demarcation which ran through South America and gave all lands to the west of the line to Spain (nearly all of the Americas) and all lands east of the line to the Portuguese (which explains why Brazil was settled by Portugal). The Treaty of Guadeloupe Hidalgo in 1848 (A) ended the Mexican American war and had nothing to do with the Spanish and Portuguese. The Treaty of Utrecht signed in 1713 (C) was a series of peace treaties between Spain, Great Britain, Portugal, France, Savoy (a region of France), and the Dutch. The Treaty of Madrid (D) signed in 1750 would ultimately end the discussion about territorial rights in South America between Spain and Portugal.

Chapter 11
Period 5
Industrial and
Global Integration
c. 1750 to c. 1900
Drills

DRILL 1

1. Which of the following is true about the development of world trade between 1750 and 1914?

   (A) World trade brought greater prosperity to China and Japan
   (B) World trade greatly benefitted the West, often to the detriment of other areas
   (C) Desire for New World raw materials made Latin American governments the wealthiest in the world
   (D) The United States, after the Monroe Doctrine, ruled the seas in a way similar to sixteenth-century Spain

2. In what way were the French Revolution of 1789 and the Chinese revolt against the Qing dynasty in 1911 similar?

   (A) Both revolutions ended in dictatorships
   (B) Both revolutions failed to meet their goals
   (C) Neither revolution was a nationalist movement
   (D) Neither revolution was based on Enlightenment theories

3. The American and French Revolutions of the late eighteenth century were similar in all the following ways EXCEPT

   (A) they were based on Enlightenment thought
   (B) they produced important documents defining similar natural rights
   (C) they were initiated by issues of taxation
   (D) they advocated universal male suffrage

4. What was unique about the Haitian revolution at the end of the eighteenth century?

   (A) It was based on Enlightenment philosophies
   (B) It closed with a full democracy in power
   (C) It was led by slaves
   (D) It used foreign mercenaries to balance the sizes of the armies

5. Which of the following is true about the political, social, and economic atmosphere between 1750 and 1914?

   (A) Both China and Mexico reacted against foreign influence.
   (B) Republican governments universally rose throughout the Americas.
   (C) Members of the lower class led most reform movements.
   (D) Latin America became an economic world leader.

6. In which of the following ways was the Brazilian revolution in 1822 unique from other South American revolutions?

   (A) The revolution in Brazil was bloodless.
   (B) The revolution in Brazil concluded with a monarchy.
   (C) The revolutions in the rest of South America were begun by the middle class.
   (D) The revolutions in the rest of South America were fought in the late 1700s.

7. Which of the following did NOT contribute to European imperialism in the late nineteenth and early twentieth century?

   (A) The invention of the steam engine
   (B) Improved European weaponry
   (C) The abolitionist movement
   (D) The desire for commercial plantations

8. All of the following are accurate descriptions of European imperialism in Asia and Africa EXCEPT

   (A) railways, roads, and other public works projects were executed
   (B) natives were not trained to use the new technologies introduced by the Europeans
   (C) hospitals were constructed
   (D) telegraph lines were laid to improve communications with Europe

9. Which of the following is an accurate statement regarding the Nationalism of the nineteenth century?

(A) Nationalism delayed the unification of both Italy and Germany.
(B) Nationalism created tolerance for diversity in the Russian Empire.
(C) Nationalism served as a rallying cry for African independence movements.
(D) Nationalism served as both a unifying and divisive force.

10. In what way were Siam (currently Vietnam) and Liberia similar during the nineteenth century?

(A) Neither nation was colonized during Europe's imperialist period.
(B) Neither nation was in Africa.
(C) Both nations were in Asia.
(D) Both nations traded in slaves.

Check your answers on page 243.

DRILL 2

1. Which of the following was a cause of the American Revolution?

    (A) England's forced abolition of slavery in the American South
    (B) Misrepresentation in Parliament and unfair taxation
    (C) The British loss of territory during the French and Indian War
    (D) Restrictions on universal male suffrage

2. Which of the following was a contributing factor to the French Revolution?

    (A) The Protestant clergy hoped to depose a Catholic monarch.
    (B) Enlightenment thinkers supported the concept of absolute monarchy.
    (C) The middle class wanted better political representation.
    (D) Napoleon Bonaparte's autocratic rule caused peasants to revolt.

3. All of the following were liberal reforms instituted by Napoleon Bonaparte EXCEPT

    (A) a centralized system of secondary schools and universities
    (B) religious freedom
    (C) legal equality for men
    (D) universal male suffrage

4. All of the following are true about the Congress of Vienna in 1815 EXCEPT

    (A) it was attended by Europe's powerful nations after the end of the Napoleonic Wars
    (B) its goal was to make revolution impossible in the future
    (C) it succeeded in stabilizing Europe
    (D) it punished France severely for Napoleon's territorial aggression

"Abstractedly speaking, government, as well as liberty, is good; yet could I, in common sense, ten years ago, have felicitated France on her enjoyment of a government … without inquiry what the nature of that government was, or how it was administered? Can I now congratulate the same nation upon its freedom?"

5. The quote above, from a letter written in 1790, reflects ideas held by which of the following philosophies?

    (A) Conservatism
    (B) Liberalism
    (C) Rationalism
    (D) Nationalism

6. All of the following are true about education in the Western world leading up to 1900 EXCEPT

    (A) by 1900, many American states required a high school education
    (B) most western European countries required the study of a second language by 1900
    (C) by 1900, 90 percent of all adults in the United States and western Europe were literate
    (D) girls were taught the importance of the home and morality

7. Which of the following statements relating to the lives of Europeans by 1900 is true?

    (A) The Industrial Revolution reduced class distinctions.
    (B) Agriculture remained largely unchanged, continuing the tradition of feudalism.
    (C) By 1900, many in the European population lived above a subsistence level.
    (D) Women enjoyed new rights, though none could run for public office.

8. All of the following are ways in which European peasants improved their conditions EXCEPT

    (A) specialized in cash crops
    (B) sought education and new skills
    (C) organized cooperatives
    (D) joined workers' strikes

9. The image above depicts the main players in which eighteenth-century revolution?

    (A) The French Revolution
    (B) The Glorious Revolution
    (C) The American Revolution
    (D) The Russian Revolution

"The history of all hitherto existing society is the history of class struggles."

10. The above quote is from which philosophical tract?

    (A) *The Declaration of the Rights of Man and the Citizen*
    (B) *The Communist Manifesto*
    (C) *The Declaration of Independence*
    (D) *The Magna Carta*

Check your answers on page 244.

DRILL 3

1. Which of the following is true about Europe's partition of Africa in the nineteenth century?

   (A) Germany eventually controlled large portions of Africa.
   (B) The United States joined European nations in a scramble for colonies.
   (C) Only two African nations remained free at the beginning of the twentieth century.
   (D) The slave trade was halted.

2. The Tanzimat Reforms, instituted in the nineteenth century Ottoman Empire, included all of the following modernizing reforms EXCEPT

   (A) railroads were built
   (B) newspapers were established in major cities
   (C) university education was reorganized to mimic Western institutions
   (D) tariffs were introduced to help grow local businesses

3. Which of the following factors played the most significant role in European interest in South Africa in the late nineteenth century?

   (A) The discovery of precious metals
   (B) The desire for additional sources of slaves
   (C) The need for a way station between Europe and India
   (D) The desire for new markets for European goods

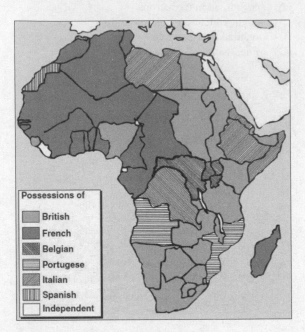

Possessions of
- British
- French
- Belgian
- Portugese
- Italian
- Spanish
- Independent

4. The map depicts Africa during which era?

   (A) Twenty-first century
   (B) Nineteenth century
   (C) Thirteenth century
   (D) Pre-agricultural Neolithic era

5. Which of the following was an element of Russia's industrialization process?

   (A) Access to rich natural resources
   (B) Western philosophies concerning the status of workers
   (C) A large middle class
   (D) A lack of government support

6. Industrialization in Japan had all of the following effects EXCEPT

(A) universal education
(B) a rejection of traditional values
(C) Western influence in fashion and personal care
(D) a drop in the birthrate

7. The nineteenth century woodcut of Commodore Matthew Perry shows his diplomatic connections with which country?

(A) Japan
(B) China
(C) India
(D) Indonesia

The Devilfish in Egyptian Waters

8. The 1882 political cartoon above criticizes the nineteenth-century British policy regarding

(A) the slave trade
(B) imperialism
(C) deep-sea whaling
(D) socialism

9. The British Factory Act of 1883 had a major impact on reforming the labor force because

(A) it limited the length of the workday
(B) it restricted the use of child labor
(C) it mandated safer and cleaner working conditions
(D) of all of the above

10. All of the following responded to industrialization EXCEPT

(A) Karl Marx
(B) the Luddites
(C) labor unions
(D) the Roundheads

Check your answers on page 246.

DRILL 4

1. Which of the following is true about both Social Darwinism and the "White Man's Burden"?

   (A) Both philosophies were racist philosophies which warped the original theories on which they were based.
   (B) Both philosophies emphasized equality of gender and race.
   (C) Both philosophies were adopted by European powers to justify imperialism.
   (D) Both philosophies were based on scientific findings.

2. Which of the following is true about the Indian Sepoy Rebellion in 1857?

   (A) It was caused by violations of Hindu and Muslim soldiers' dietary laws.
   (B) It resulted in a withdrawal of Britain from the Indian subcontinent.
   (C) It was caused by a lack of representation for Indians in the British Parliament.
   (D) It unified the British and French against the native population.

3. The second half of the nineteenth century saw huge global migrations for which of the following reasons?

   (A) Wars in Asia and Europe
   (B) The need for factory laborers and the end of slavery
   (C) The outbreak of disease in Italy and Germany
   (D) The enclosure movement and the rise of socialism

4. Which of the following is true about the 1823 American Monroe Doctrine?

   (A) It invited the British to colonize Latin America.
   (B) It outlined why the United States decided to blockade the Panama Canal.
   (C) It was enforced by the British Navy.
   (D) It helped establish the coffee trade in Brazil.

5. All of the following are examples of American intervention in South America in the 1800s and early 1900s EXCEPT

   (A) the Monroe Doctrine
   (B) the Roosevelt Corollary
   (C) the Spanish-American War
   (D) the creation of a republic in Brazil

6. Late nineteenth- and early twentieth-century imperialism was a result of all of the following EXCEPT

   (A) nationalism
   (B) industrialization
   (C) social Darwinism
   (D) socialism

"All Powers exercising rights of sovereignty or an influence in the Said territories engage themselves to watch over the conservation of the indigenous populations and the amelioration of their moral and material conditions of existence and to strive for the suppression of slavery and especially of the… slave trade."

7. The above quote laid the ground rules for

   (A) the European colonization of Africa
   (B) the opening of Spheres of Influence in China
   (C) colonization in Japan
   (D) exploration of the New World

"The yellow and white races are relatively strong and intelligent. Because the other races are feeble and stupid, they are being exterminated by the white race. Only the yellow race competes with the white race."

8. The 1911 quote above shows the spread of which European philosophy?

   (A) Socialism
   (B) Social Darwinism
   (C) Nationalism
   (D) Darwinism

9. Which of the following is true about the Ottoman, Russian, and Qing Empires of the late nineteenth and early twentieth centuries?

   (A) Each empire attempted to join the Scramble for Africa, but failed to create spheres of influence.
   (B) The Ottoman and Russian Empires attempted to exploit Christianity to control their peasant populations, while the Qing Empire faced no such peasant revolts.
   (C) Prior to their collapse, each of the empires attempted a series of Western-style reforms, but the ruling elites eventually failed to support necessary changes.
   (D) The Qing Empire succeeded in industrializing early; it took the Russian and Ottoman Empires until late in the twentieth century.

10. All of the following are true about the Meiji Reformation in the second half of nineteenth-century Japan EXCEPT

   (A) a bicameral parliament, constructed to mimic Western governments' systems, was created
   (B) Samurai were sent to Western Europe and the United States to study technology, government, and economics
   (C) feudalism ended and the government was centralized
   (D) beards and traditional clothing were discarded for more Western styles

Check your answers on page 247.

DRILL 5

1. All of the following correctly match the political tract to the nationality of its author EXCEPT

   (A) Germany—*The Evils of Revolution*
   (B) France—*Declaration of the Rights of Man and of the Citizen*
   (C) the United States—*Declaration of Independence*
   (D) Great Britain—*A Vindication of Natural Society*

2. Which of the following is one of the main arguments of *The Communist Manifesto*?

   (A) The working class would revolt and seize the means of production.
   (B) Capitalism would peacefully evolve into communism.
   (C) The working class, through education and employment opportunities, would gain wealth and eventually be absorbed into the upper classes.
   (D) Slow, deliberate reform from within the government was a superior reforming tactic, compared to radical revolutions.

3. Which of the following pairs of countries abolished slavery in the 1880s?

   (A) China and Russia
   (B) Japan and Korea
   (C) Brazil and Cuba
   (D) Mexico and Peru

4. The rise of nationalism between the mid-eighteenth and early-twentieth centuries was driven primarily by

   (A) European imperialism
   (B) strengthening of nascent democracies
   (C) technological advances
   (D) explosive population growth

5. Japanese and Ottoman government officials in the nineteenth century modeled their militaries after which of the following country's example?

   (A) The British Empire
   (B) The Austro-Hungarian Empire
   (C) The Roman Empire
   (D) The German Empire

6. One of the initial goals of the Haitian Revolution (1791–1804) was

   (A) to overthrow the planter class
   (B) to expel the French government and military
   (C) to expel the Spanish government and military
   (D) to install Toussaint L'Ouverture as king

7. The Seven Years' War (1756–1763) had which of the following results?

   (A) Spain lost Louisiana to France
   (B) Germany lost the Rhineland and Suedetenland
   (C) Britain lost significant territory in North America
   (D) France lost most of its holdings in India

8. In the late-eighteenth and early-nineteenth centuries, explorers from which of the following governments visited North America, Alaska, and the Hawaiian Islands?

   (A) Tokugawa Japan
   (B) Tsarist Russia
   (C) Qing China
   (D) Ming China

9. Which pair of revolutions created constitutions that granted legal equality to all citizens?

    (A) The French and Serbian Revolutions
    (B) The Haitian and American Revolutions
    (C) The July (France) and Mexican Revolutions
    (D) The Donghak (Korea) Peasant and Egyptian Revolutions

10. Industrialization in nineteenth-century Europe affected women's lives in which of the following ways?

    (A) Married women were less able to balance wage work with family responsibilities.
    (B) The number of women marrying decreased as the century progressed.
    (C) All but the poorest women gained access to higher education.
    (D) As men moved to take urban factory jobs, women dominated the agricultural workforce.

Check your answers on page 249.

DRILL 6

1. Policy changes with Japan's Meiji Restoration had all of the following results EXCEPT

   (A) requiring military service from all males as the samurai warrior class was abolished
   (B) constructing railroads and steamships to revolutionize travel and trade
   (C) slowing Japan's Industrial Revolution out of deference to imperial customs
   (D) westernizing Japan while strengthening imperial traditions

2. Opium most notably linked which of the following three nations in the nineteenth century?

   (A) Afghanistan, China, and the Netherlands
   (B) Great Britain, India, and China
   (C) India, China, and Turkey
   (D) Great Britain, Afghanistan, and China

3. A major difference between nineteenth- and twentieth-century consumerism was

   (A) the decline in time and resources available for leisure
   (B) the professionalization of advertising
   (C) the integration and conglomeration of industries
   (D) the widespread dampening effects of Marxist criticism

4. Unlike the process of industrialization in late eighteenth century Britain, late nineteenth century Japan

   (A) industrialized quickly and deliberately due to government sponsorship
   (B) industrialized reluctantly during a period of cultural isolationism
   (C) experienced a second, distinct wave of industrialization that built on the first
   (D) developed technology unreplicated anywhere else in the world

5. European colonial rivalries in Africa and Asia

   (A) gave Russia an opening to establish a colonial presence in Africa in the twentieth century
   (B) closed down the transatlantic slave trade at the peak of its prosperity
   (C) led to the rise of socialist and communist movements within colonial territory
   (D) contributed to destabilizing the balance of power in the decades before World War I

6. By the end of the nineteenth century, European colonial conquest meant that sub-Saharan Africa's only two free states were Abyssinia (Ethiopia) and

   (A) Morocco
   (B) Liberia
   (C) Angola
   (D) Chad

7. Improved farming techniques led to industrialization because

   (A) better techniques led to less foodborne illness, causing population growth and the expansion of cities
   (B) farmers had to spend more time in the fields to supervise the use of new technologies
   (C) enhanced yield from farmers' fields allowed more fields to be converted into factories
   (D) increased food production allowed for labor specialization and for new technologies to promulgate

8. The Protestant Reformation began in part because of Martin Luther's

   (A) outrage over priests selling absolution to raise money for the Church
   (B) fellow monks at Wittenburg indulging too heavily in wine and luxuries
   (C) belief that important relics of the Church were being forgotten or destroyed
   (D) frustrated desire to be elected pope and lead the Church on his terms

9. Which of the following was NOT the product of a Russian artist in the late nineteenth century?

   (A) *War and Peace*
   (B) *Doctor Zhivago*
   (C) *Swan Lake*
   (D) *Anna Karenina*

10. One of the major components of the Tanzimat Reforms was

   (A) a return to coined currency after a financial crisis caused by paper banknotes
   (B) trade guilds replaced an abusive factory system of production
   (C) common Ottoman citizenship regardless of gender or ethnicity
   (D) limiting military service to Turkish Muslims only

Check your answers on page 250.

DRILL 7

1. One similarity between the process of unification in Germany and Italy is that both countries were

   (A) unified through territorial wars in the late nineteenth century
   (B) predominantly Catholic at the time of unification
   (C) quickly able to build colonial holdings in both Africa and Asia
   (D) forced to expel Spanish forces from their territories

2. Which of the following contributed to the decline of economically productive agriculturally based economies in the eighteenth and nineteenth centuries?

   (A) The proliferation of small family farms in Western Europe
   (B) Significant weakening of international alliances
   (C) The rapid development of industrial production
   (D) An expansion of existing trade routes in the Indian Ocean

3. Liberalism, communism and socialism are all examples of political ideologies that had their development encouraged by

   (A) increased African immigration to Western Europe
   (B) discontent with monarchist and imperial rule
   (C) growing demands for women's suffrage
   (D) new transnational religious movements

4. Which of the following is NOT an example of an empire that collapsed due to a combination of internal and external factors?

   (A) Korean
   (B) Russian
   (C) Ottoman
   (D) Qing

5. Which of the following was used by the British as a penal colony beginning in 1788?

   (A) New South Wales
   (B) Liberia
   (C) Madagascar
   (D) Hong Kong

6. All of the following are true about the Peace of Basel in 1795 EXCEPT

   (A) Prussia withdrew from the conference of powers working out the partition of Poland
   (B) France divided and placated its enemies to regain power after several war-torn decades
   (C) Austria agreed to end its occupation of disputed territories in the northern Italian Alps
   (D) Spain ended the War of the Pyrenees and granted control of half of Hispaniola to France

7. The Anglo-Dutch Treaty of Sumatra included all of the following EXCEPT

   (A) Britain granted the Dutch control throughout Sumatra
   (B) Dutch restrictions on the public practice of Islam, including the call to prayer
   (C) Britain allowed the Dutch equal trading rights in the Sultanate of Aceh
   (D) Dutch concessions to the British in the Gold Coast of Africa

8. Alexander II's Great Reforms in nineteenth-century Russia spurred industrialization, modernized the Russian army, and

   (A) granted freedom and full citizenship to all serfs on private estates
   (B) established the Eastern Orthodox Church as the official state religion
   (C) gave several ethnic groups semi-autonomous self-governance within the empire
   (D) implemented socialist principles in government as a result of industrialization

9. A historian studying women's struggle for political rights in the twentieth century would most benefit from examining which of the following sources?

   (A) Reports from human rights organizations such as NATO
   (B) Economic analysis of matriarchal household budgets
   (C) Diaries of American and British suffragists
   (D) Trends in women's fashion such as trousers

10. After being settled as a British penal colony, settlements in Australia grew in the mid-nineteenth century in large part as a result of

   (A) farming and ranching, as well as a series of gold rushes
   (B) farming and ranching, as well as a growing oil industry
   (C) a series of gold rushes, as well as a growing oil industry
   (D) political opportunities available to British settlers in the colonies

Check your answers on page 252.

DRILL 8

1. The French and Indian War and the War of 1812 had which of the following in common?

   (A) Both were conflicts between Americans and Europeans that resulted in no changes in territorial boundaries.
   (B) In both conflicts, each side allied with various native tribes to advance its respective war aims.
   (C) Each conflict involved one side sacking and burning the other side's capital city.
   (D) Neither conflict was a win for the British.

2. Which of the following pairs of events had the greatest effect on Iranian governance at the beginning of the twentieth century?

   (A) World War I and the fall of the Qajar government
   (B) The Anglo-Russian Convention and the Islamic Revolution
   (C) The Constitutional Revolution and the discovery of oil
   (D) The Crimean War and the invention of the telegraph

3. The case of *United States v. The Amistad* came about because

   (A) after water shortages aboard the slave ship *The Amistad*, the crew threw slaves overboard, and the owners subsequently filed a controversial insurance claim for the losses
   (B) a Spanish ship captain whose crew mutinied and sailed to the United States unsuccessfully sued for repatriation, creating an international incident
   (C) Mende slaves in transit from Africa overthrew the slaver's crew and ended up in the United States, where the African slave trade was illegal
   (D) the United States sued the captain of *The Amistad* for bringing his slave cargo through American waters, where the African slave trade was illegal

4. In late nineteenth-century Europe, all of the following were true of unions EXCEPT that they

   (A) were banned in most countries, as governments considered their activities subversive
   (B) had some success improving working conditions, reducing but not eliminating abuses
   (C) operated with popular support in most communities, even without official sanction
   (D) promoted development of new farming techniques, increasing agricultural output

5. What happened to economically productive, agriculturally based economies in the eighteenth and nineteenth centuries?

   (A) They flourished, providing supplies for the expanding global marketplace.
   (B) They declined as a result of the rapid development of industrial production.
   (C) They maintained a stable level of production, replacing old consumers with new markets.
   (D) They inevitably experienced violent revolts from farmers and the working classes.

6. What was a major similarity between developments in Qing China and those in the Ottoman Empire as global capitalism spread?

   (A) Radicals opposed exploitative business practices and promoted alternative social visions.
   (B) State-sponsored religious leaders pacified rural desires for economic mobility as businesses grew.
   (C) Workers organized themselves to improve wages and working conditions.
   (D) Some government officials tried to preserve preindustrial forms of economic production.

7. What was one negative impact of the rapid urbanization that accompanied global capitalism?

   (A) Unsanitary living and production conditions
   (B) Political corruption and "machine" politics
   (C) The rise of ethnic gangs
   (D) Greater income inequality in rural areas

8. Which of the following was a key difference between the American and French Revolutions?

   (A) One was motivated by economic concerns, though the other was not.
   (B) One was sparked by rights abuses, while the other was not.
   (C) One was a colonial revolt, whereas the other was a domestic revolt.
   (D) One required intervention by multiple foreign powers, but the other did not.

9. Which of the following countries was independent of European rule in 1914?

   (A) Egypt
   (B) Morocco
   (C) Liberia
   (D) Angola

10. Liberated by Simon Bolivar in the early nineteenth century, Gran Colombia included all of the following EXCEPT

   (A) Colombia
   (B) Ecuador
   (C) Venezuela
   (D) Peru

Check your answers on page 254.

DRILL 9

1. The Berlin Conference laid the groundwork for African interethnic and tribal conflicts of the twentieth century by

   (A) legally establishing a system of racial designations that gave some ethnic groups more rights than others
   (B) granting slave trading monopolies to some European nations and their African partners, but not others
   (C) drawing African colonial boundaries based on European political and economic concerns
   (D) assigning mineral rights in perpetuity to European colonizers rather than the Africans indigenous to the land

"If any generation of men ever possessed the right of dictating the mode by which the world should be governed for ever, it was the first generation that existed; and if that generation did it not, no succeeding generation can show any authority for doing it, nor can set any up. The illuminating and divine principle of the equal rights of man (for it has its origin from the Maker of man) relates, not only to the living individuals, but to generations of men succeeding each other. Every generation is equal in rights to generations which preceded it, by the same rule that every individual is born equal in rights with his contemporary."

2. The passage above was written in 1791 by

   (A) Igbo abolitionist Olaudah Equiano, about the transatlantic slave trade
   (B) German philosopher G. W. F. Hegel, about the Haitian Revolution
   (C) British Queen Victoria, about the Sepoy Mutiny
   (D) American political theorist Thomas Paine, about the French Revolution

3. Which of the following had the LEAST impact on the increases in population size and life expectancy during the Industrial Revolution?

   (A) An increase in the birth rates across Europe
   (B) A decrease in the death rates across Europe
   (C) Improved hygiene and sanitation
   (D) Increased agricultural production yielding more available food

4. The Industrial Revolution was characterized by improved technology due to all of the following EXCEPT

   (A) application of new sources of energy
   (B) generation of new materials
   (C) new technological applications
   (D) more raw materials being available

5. When and where did the Industrial Revolution begin?

   (A) Britain in the eighteenth century
   (B) Britain in the nineteenth century
   (C) France in the nineteenth century
   (D) Russia in the nineteenth century

6. Among the following, which was first to begin industrialization during the Industrial Revolution?

   (A) Brazil
   (B) United States
   (C) Russia
   (D) Japan

7. All of the following represent clear differences between industrialization in Great Britain and Japan EXCEPT

(A) use of internal railway systems for transportation and shipping of goods
(B) availability of coal and iron for manufacturing and energy production
(C) development of new technology and machinery
(D) reform of women's rights and ultimately suffrage

8. Which of the following represents a significant invention originating in the United States during the Industrial Revolution?

(A) John Kay's Flying Shuttle in 1733
(B) John Hargreaves's Spinning Jenny in 1764
(C) Eli Whitney's Cotton Gin in 1793
(D) James Watt's Improved Steam Engine in 1769

9. Adam Smith in his *The Wealth of Nations* advocated most closely for which of the following economic systems for prosperity and fairness?

(A) Capitalism
(B) Socialism
(C) Communism
(D) Marxism

10. The Emancipation Act of 1861 had a major impact on Russian societal structure because

(A) serfs were free and no longer bound to land ruled by landowners.
(B) it mandated equal rights for men and women in society.
(C) it provided freedom to Russian republics in Eastern Europe to self govern which ultimately led to the formation of a middle class.
(D) it released wealthy landowners from their obligation to pay taxes on their lands to the Russian monarchy.

Check your answers on page 255.

Chapter 12
Period 5
Industrial and Global Integraton
c. 1750 to c. 1900
Answers
and Explanations

ANSWER KEY

Drill 1
1. B
2. C
3. D
4. C
5. A
6. B
7. C
8. D
9. D
10. A

Drill 2
1. B
2. C
3. D
4. D
5. A
6. B
7. C
8. D
9. A
10. B

Drill 3
1. C
2. D
3. A
4. B
5. A
6. B
7. A
8. D
9. D
10. D

Drill 4
1. C
2. A
3. B
4. C
5. D
6. D
7. A
8. B
9. C
10. D

Drill 5
1. A
2. A
3. C
4. A
5. D
6. A
7. D
8. B
9. B
10. A

Drill 6
1. C
2. B
3. B
4. A
5. D
6. B
7. D
8. A
9. B
10. C

Drill 7
1. A
2. C
3. B
4. A
5. A
6. C
7. B
8. A
9. C
10. A

Drill 8
1. B
2. C
3. C
4. D
5. B
6. D
7. A
8. C
9. C
10. D

Drill 9
1. C
2. D
3. A
4. D
5. A
6. B
7. A
8. C
9. A
10. A

EXPLANATIONS

Drill 1

1. **B**   Once Europe takes over the seas in the fifteenth and sixteenth centuries, and Asia decides to attempt isolation, the West became an overbearing driver of world events. The Opium Wars, spheres of influence in China, the plantations in the Caribbean—all these world events were driven by European powers, mostly England.

    China and Japan were exploited by the West (A), and though the raw materials in Latin America were sought after, England created an exploitative system to extract materials to the detriment of the Latin American economy (C). The United States wasn't really a world power before World War I, but the British kept the rest of the West out of Latin America for the States (D).

2. **C**   Neither revolution meant to break away from a colonial power to become a new nation. Initially, the Chinese revolution attempted to model China's government after Western republics, though the French Revolution did end with the dictatorship of Napoleon (A). Both met their goals of bringing down the respective governments (B). The French Revolution relied heavily on the ideas introduced by Enlightenment thinkers (D).

3. **D**   The United States didn't initially extend the vote to all men, nor did the French. Both revolutions relied heavily on Enlightenment thought, especially on the ideas of Locke and Rousseau (A). The Declaration of Independence and the Declaration of the Rights of Man and Citizen both spoke about natural rights, including life and liberty (B). France's Third Estate reacted to taxation policies, as did the American revolutionaries (C).

4. **C**   The Haitian revolution was led by slaves. It took its cue from other revolutions of the time, of which most were based on Enlightenment ideals (A). It was initially a republic (B). Foreign mercenaries didn't get involved (D).

5. **A**   Both the Chinese and the Mexican revolts were at least in part reactions to foreign involvement. The Americas saw republics arise, but Brazil established a monarchy after its independence movement (B). The middle class led revolts (C). This era sees the rise of Europe as an economic power. Latin America was exploited (D).

6. **B**   The revolution in Brazil took some 6,000 lives (A). Most revolutions during the nineteenth century were begun by the middle class (C). The exception you want to keep in mind is Haiti, where a slave began the revolution there. You want to think of the 1820s as the decade when all of the Latin (South) American revolutions are happening (D).

7. **C**   The abolitionist movement created tension between the Boers (Dutch) and the British in South Africa, but was not a driving force in the imperialist era. The steam engine allowed Europeans to navigate rivers and helped them colonize inland (A). Improved weaponry such as the repeating rifle gave Europeans an upper hand (B). A desire for commercial plantations was driven by the need for raw materials (D).

8. **D**   Telegraph lines were laid in India. Initially, Europeans tried to improve areas that affected the lives of European colonists. That meant improving and laying railways and roads (A), constructing hospitals (C), and improving sanitation. Natives were largely untrained in these new technologies (D), and so could not benefit from them for the most part.

9. **D**   Nationalism did serve as the rallying cry that brought Germany and Italy together (A). It was a divisive force in Russia, though (B). You want to correlate the Scramble (or Colonization) of Africa with this period, so there're no independence movements happening (C).

10. **A**   Liberia, Ethiopia, and Siam (Vietnam) all dodged the bullet of European imperialism. Liberia is in Africa (B) and (C), and Vietnam is in Southeast Asia. Neither country sold slaves (D).

Drill 2

1. **B**   England did not abolish slavery in the South (A). That'll be decided in the American Civil War in the 1860s. The British won the Seven Years' War (also called the French and Indian War), and so did not lose territory (C). The United States did not advocate universal male suffrage at the inception of the nation (D). That's a slightly later development (around the 1820s). American colonists were upset about a lack of representation in Parliament and unfair taxation, and those were the primary causes of the American Revolution, so (B) is the correct answer.

2. **C**   Whenever you're stuck on the reason for a revolt or revolution, blame the middle class. Remember that those in the Third Estate wanted stronger voting rights. France was largely Catholic (A). The monarchy definitely was. Enlightenment thinkers didn't believe in autocratic systems of government (B). Napoleon Bonaparte is a post-revolutionary France figure, so he couldn't have caused the revolution (D).

3. **D**   Education was essential to Napoleon's vision of a new France, and he knew it. He centralized the system for secondary schools and universities to train bureaucrats (A). He allowed Protestants and Jews to practice unmolested while officially recognizing that Catholicism was the religion of the majority (B). The Napoleonic Code created men equal before the law (C), though he didn't give the vote to all men.

4. **D** European powers didn't want to cause strife, so they tried to keep the Congress of Vienna's changes relatively conservative—their goal was stability and a balance of power, not punishment. So, all of Europe's powerful nations were there (A). Again, the balance of power and a lack of revolution was the goal (B). It stabilized Europe for about 50 years, before internal strife began to change countries (C).

5. **A** This quote, from Edmund Burke's *Reflections on the Revolution in France* written in 1790, shows someone critical of the French Revolution. Ask yourself who'd be most critical. Burke, though he initially supported the American colonists in their rebellion, is the father of modern Conservatism, which states that reform and change are essential for governments, but Burke believed change could happen from within the government itself; it didn't need to be radical the way the French Revolution was. All the other answer choices had either no opinion or a positive opinion of the French Revolution.

6. **B** Remember this is the age of Nationalism. This even affects the school system, where children were taught the superiority of the nation's language and history, and often immigrant and minority cultures were attacked. By 1900, many American states required high school, and most Western nations expanded their public secondary school systems (A). 90 to 95 percent of adults in Western nations and the United States could read (C). Female education centered on the role of the woman in the household (D).

7. **C** Due to agricultural improvements and the enclosure system (B), the food supplies of Europe stabilized and populations increased. So many Europeans enjoyed a life that allowed for leisure time. The Industrial Revolution actually increased the gap between the middle and lower classes (A). Women in many European countries actually saw their rights deteriorate (D).

8. **D** In the second half of the nineteenth century, peasants learned to exploit the economy a bit—they organized themselves into cooperatives (C), specialized in cash crops (A), and sent their children to school to learn new farming techniques (B). Worker's unions and strikes were another era.

9. **A** Notice the men standing are dressed as clergy and nobility (or just fancy). Remember that the actors in the French Revolution belonged to the First, Second, and Third Estate. The First was the clergy, the Second the nobility, and the Third everyone else. The Glorious Revolution was in England in the seventeenth century (B), the American Revolution was fought between England and American colonists (C), and the Russian Revolution happened in the twentieth century (D).

10. **B** Remember that Karl Marx, author of the Communist Manifesto, centers his philosophy on class struggles. The Magna Carta (D) is way out of era. You should associate the Declaration of the Rights of Man and the Citizen with France and rights, not class struggles (A). The American Declaration of Independence (C) is also much more about rights than about class.

Drill 3

1. **C** Only two African nations, Liberia and Ethiopia, remained free of European control by the end of the European Scramble for Africa. Germany largely stayed out of land acquisition (A). Otto von Bismarck was more interested in controlling Europe. The United States stayed out of what it viewed as a European affair (B), though the United States was very involved in all things Latin America. The slave trade did not end because of European colonization of Africa (D).

2. **D** Under the Tanzimat Reforms, university education was reorganized on Western lines (C), and training in the European sciences and mathematics was introduced. State-run postal and telegraph systems were introduced in the 1830s, and railways were begun in the 1860s (A). Newspapers were established in the major towns of the empire (B). Merchants and businessmen initially suffered financially, since the Ottoman government did little to protect against European competition.

3. **A** South Africa was initially colonized by the Dutch, called the Boers. The British showed up in greater and greater numbers after diamonds and gold were found. The British ended their slave trade early, and the slave trade was well-established in the more northern coastal areas of Africa (B). Answers related to the Age of Discovery or mercantilism are out of era by the end of the 1800s, so neither (C) nor (D) can work.

4. **B** Notice how the nations are broken up almost arbitrarily, though some straight lines exist. This should tip you off that whatever these entities are, they're not strictly dictated by geological realities; the borders are imposed. That eliminates (D). The first invasive experience Africa had was the European Scramble for Africa in the nineteenth century. By the twenty-first century (A), Africa was broken up into smaller national entities.

5. **A** Russia had access to significant natural resources, which contributed to its impressive development of a steel industry. Russia (and Japan) very much industrialized on its own terms, incorporating as little of Western philosophies as possible (B). Russia lacked a sizable middle class (C), so it had to rely on the government for most industrializing reforms and funding (D).

6. **B** Remember that Russia and Japan are the two industrializing countries that follow their own paths. Japan instituted universal education which emphasized science, technology, and nationalism (A). Western habits and styles found their way into Japanese fashion and grooming (C). Just as in most parts of the world, the rise of the city and industrialization in general caused the birthrate to drop in Japan as well (D).

7. **A** The United States, and specifically Commodore Perry, opened Japan to the rest of the world. In 1853, Perry forced Japan to open its market to the West, ending its isolation.

8. **B** The cartoon shows England getting its hands into all parts of the world. Imperialism relates to a country involving itself in foreign countries, usually creating empires or colonies. England abolished the slave trade in the early nineteenth century (think the Slave Trade Act of 1807) (A). England was whaling as early as the 1600s, so even if this was related to environmentalism, it'd be out of era (C). Socialism is usually a domestic issue, so there'd be no reason to bring in outside countries (D).

9. **D** The British Factory Act was important for changing the labor environment during the late Industrial Revolution in Great Britain. It limited the workday (A), limited use of child labor (B), and mandated safer working conditions (C). Many of these changes would soon be adopted by other industrialized nations such as the United States.

10. **D** The Roundheads was an army led by Oliver Cromwell in 1641 which fought the English Civil War. Karl Marx wrote the Communist Manifesto to explain that all of history is class struggle after observing factory workers (A). The Luddites were groups of workers who destroyed factory equipment to protest poor wages and working conditions (B). Labor unions arose in the late 1800s to protect factory workers (C).

Drill 4

1. **C** Social Darwinism applied Charles Darwin's biological theory of natural selection to sociology. In other words, they claimed that dominant races or classes of people rose to the top through a process of "survival of the fittest." This meant that because Britain was the most powerful, it was the most fit, and therefore the British were superior to other races. The "White Man's Burden" was a poem by Rudyard Kipling which stated that it was Europe's "burden" to "civilize" the rest of the world. Social Darwinism was based on Darwinism, but the White Man's Burden was a theory all its own (A). The philosophies were definitely not about equality (B), and neither was based on scientific findings (D).

2. **A** The Sepoy Rebellion was sparked when Indian soldiers found out their bullet packs for their rifles, which they had to open with their teeth, were greased with pig and beef fat, a violation of both Muslim and Hindu dietary laws respectively. The rebellion largely failed, so the British went nowhere (B). The American Revolution was about a lack of representation (C). Britain and France are deep enemies at this point in history. In fact, the Sepoys were shooting at the French (D).

3. **B** The end of slavery, combined with the need for laborers drove people to cities, and to places of opportunity. Europeans and east Asians immigrated to the Americas, and south Indians moved into other British-controlled territories. Italy and Germany were busy unifying, not fighting diseases (C). Socialism didn't cause migration (D). Wars happened everywhere, but were not driving forces to leave any place (A).

4. **C** The Monroe Doctrine was the United States' attempt to keep the Europeans from recolonizing Latin America. The United States wasn't very strong at the time, but keeping Europe, including itself, out of South America was in Britain's interest, so the United Kingdom actually used its navy to enforce the Monroe Doctrine. The United States helped fund the Panamanian rebels who then sold the land for the Panama Canal to the Americans for a good price (B). The coffee trade was already well-established by the 1800s (D).

5. **D** The United States used the Monroe Doctrine as a shield against a recolonization of Latin America by Europeans (A). The Roosevelt Corollary was added in 1904 when European powers sent warships to Venezuela to collect on loan debt (B). US victory in the Spanish-American war made the United States a world power (C). The creation of a republic in Brazil came about through an internal revolution (D).

6. **D** Socialism was a political movement, unrelated to imperialism. Nationalism promoted the superiority and general awesomeness of a country, and so drove nations to spread their culture (A). Industrialization created a need for raw materials and markets, found in colonies (B). Social Darwinism pushed the idea that you should introduce your awesomeness to the rest of the "uncivilized" world (C).

7. **A** The document quoted is the General Act of the Conference of Berlin, written in 1885 before the Scramble for Africa. You should catch that it reflects some of the ideas of the White Man's Burden. The excerpt didn't talk about commerce (B), Japan was never colonized (C), and exploration of the New World resulted in expanding the slave trade (D).

8. **B** The philosophy that fitness (survival skills) is related to skin color is Social Darwinism. Socialism says the state should help take care of you (A). Nationalism is love of country (C). Darwinism is a biological theory (D).

9. **C** Each empire failed to achieve reform because the basic economic, political, and social structures needed for successful change were not in place (no significant middle class, lack of legal protections for property, government accountability to a large segment of the population). Remember that Russia and Japan will successfully industrialize in the late nineteenth century (D). The empires did not engage in imperialism in Africa (A), and Russians and Ottomans didn't tie themselves to a church or mosque in order to suppress their populations (B).

10. **D** The Meiji Reformation, started in 1868, ended feudalism, centralized the government, and sent samurai to Western Europe and the United States in order to exploit these nations' knowledge to better Japan (B) and (C). The government was restructured to mimic Western governments (A). Cutting off beards and adopting Western styles were forced cultural reforms Peter the Great of Russia instituted in the early 1700s.

Drill 5

1. **A** *The Evils of Revolution* is a book by the Conservative Edmund Burke [who is also the author of *A Vindication of Natural Society* (D)], an Englishman. The Declaration of Independence was written by the American Thomas Jefferson (C). Declaration of the Rights of Man and of the Citizen may have been written by the Frenchman Lafayette. It was an important political tract related to the French Revolution (B).

2. **A** *The Communist Manifesto* (1848) argued that capitalism was ultimately doomed, as the working class would revolt against their powerful employers and seize the means of production. The working class would then establish equal means of production, where no one group of citizens would be more politically or economically powerful than the other. It believed this would happen through violent revolution, so (B) doesn't work. It created clear class lines (C). The last one's a reference to Conservatism (D).

3. **C** Brazil phased out slavery in stages, beginning in 1871 and culminating with 1888's Golden Law, which abolished all remaining slavery in the nation without compensation to the owners. Cuba, which abolished the slave trade in the 1860s, abolished slavery in one fell swoop in 1886. Russia ended serfdom (forced labor) in 1861, and China did not formally end until 1910, so cross off (A). Korea abolished slavery in 1894, though the practice did not fully die out until 1930, and slavery in Japan ended with the country's defeat in World War II, so cross off (B), too. Mexico abolished slavery in the 1810s, but Peru didn't follow suit until 1854, so it's not (D), either.

4. **A** European nations jockeying for territorial conquest, with resources and power at stake, required a consolidation of power and fostered an increasing sense of national identity. Most of these countries were monarchies in some form, even those—such as Britain's—that shared power with parliaments or other representatives of the people, so cross off (B). While this was a time of technological advances, that did not fuel the rise of nationalism—nor did population growth, which was not particularly "explosive"—so cross off (C) and (D).

5. **D** The German Empire's military was widely considered the paragon of a modern, scientific military, in technology and tactics. This was its chief advantage as a model over the Roman Empire's—Rome fell; in the nineteenth century, Germany was ascendant—so cross off (C). After Austria's defeat in the Austro-Prussian War in 1866, the resultant Austro-Hungarian Empire was hardly a power, so (B) isn't the answer. The British Empire was in comparatively good shape, but their stature was no match for the Germans, so (A) isn't the right idea either.

6. **A** At its inception, the Haitian Revolution was a slave rebellion, one long-feared by the French planter class on the island, where death rates outpaced birth rates and slave imports kept the colony populated. While the revolution was ultimately about Haitian independence, a cause for which the Spanish were all too happy to help the rebelling slaves, it was first about slavery, so cross off (B), since (A) is a *better* answer, and (C). Toussaint L'Ouverture did not advocate monarchy for Haiti, so cross off (D).

7. **D** British forces drove the French from their possessions in India, which remained in British hands until India's independence nearly two centuries later. Spain did not lose Louisiana to France—vice versa. The French (who had named the place for their king, Louis) ceded the region *to the Spanish* under the 1762 Treaty of Fontainebleau to settle their wartime alliance agreement, so cross off (A). Remember that Germany, as such, did not exist at this time, so (B) is no good—while Germany would lose the Rhineland and Suedetenland at the end of World War I, *Prussia* suffered no such losses in 1763. And Britain *gained* significant North American territory, seizing Canada from the French under the Treaty of Versailles, so cross off (C).

8. **B** You may recall that Alaska was actually Russian territory before it was purchased by the United States in 1867, but the Russians also visited other parts of North America, as well as the Hawaiian Islands. The Qing dynasty ruled Before the Common Era, so cross off (C). Similarly, while some scholars argue that a Ming fleet did reach North America, it would have done so in the early fifteenth century, so cross off (D). Though the Tokugawa Shogunate did rule Japan during the eighteenth and early nineteenth centuries, they did not explore all of these regions, so cross off (A).

9. **B** Only the pairing of the Haitian and American Revolutions both granted legal equality to all citizens. The Serbian Revolution produced a constitution that maintained some differences among citizens, so cross off (A). The July Revolution in France saw a monarchical change without creating a new constitution, so cross off (C). And the Donghak Peasant Revolution in Korea was crushed and produced no constitutional reform, so cross off (D).

10. **A** The more efficient factories became, the longer factory owners tended to run them, and the more regimented work schedules needed to be. As a consequence, it became harder to reconcile work and home life. This did not, however, dissuade many women from marrying, so cross off (B). Nor, however, did it give them broad access to higher education, so cross off (C). Women also never came to dominate the agricultural workforce, so cross off (D).

Drill 6

1. **C** Remember that you're looking for the one that *isn't* true. The Meiji Restoration of 1868 began an era of Japanese modernization—and Westernization—that had not been possible during the empire's isolationism of the seventeenth and eighteenth centuries. It did not slow Japan's Industrial Revolution; rather, it accelerated it considerably. It did westernize Japan while simultaneously strengthening national identity associated with imperial traditions, so cross off (D). This was also a time of infrastructure building, as (B) suggests, so cross that off, too. Finally, the samurai warrior class was considered an outdated institution of a less progressive era, and it was abolished in favor of military service requirements from all men, so cross off (A).

2. **B** Great Britain and China clashed in the Opium Wars over China's resistance to importing British opium grown in India.

3. **B** Advertising became an end unto itself, as well as the means to an end. Professionalizing this as a field led to a shift in the nature of consumerism, and that shift coincided with the turn of the twentieth century. Time and resources available for leisure generally increased, so cross off (A). The integration and conglomeration of industries had little direct effect on consumerism—the urge of people to buy things—except of course as it affected advertising, so cross off (C) because (B) is better. Finally Marxist criticism had only limited effects on people's interest in buying things, so cross off (D).

4. **A** This was a key part of the Meiji Restoration that began in 1868. Cross off (B), which better describes the Tokugawa Shogunate that preceded the Meiji Restoration in the early part of the century. Cross off (C) because that correctly describes Britain's experience, not Japan's. Cross off (D) because Japan's Industrial Revolution, coming comparatively late, deliberately sought out and replicated Western technologies.

5. **D** Russia never had a colonial presence in Africa, so cross off (A). Closing the transatlantic slave trade also had nothing to do with events in Asia, so cross off (B). (C) is also not an accurate description of African and Asian colonies at this time, so cross it off, too.

6. **B** Liberia was the nation founded in Africa for freed slaves from the United States. Angola is sub-Saharan but was under Portuguese control after the 1884 Berlin Conference, so cross off (C). Neither Chad nor Morocco is sub-Saharan, so cross off (A) and (D).

7. **D** Choice (D) is the only correct cause-and-effect relationship. More food means more nutrition for more people, and better techniques mean fewer farmers are required to produce the more food. So more people have time on their hands to specialize in other things, including developing new technologies. It wasn't about foodborne illness, so cross off (A), or about fields being converted into factories, so cross off (C). Farmers having to spend more time in the fields, even if it were true, wouldn't create progress toward industrialization, so cross off (B).

8. **A** If you were thinking "the sale of indulgences," that's exactly what (A) describes, not what (B) is talking about, so cross (B) off. Relics did figure into the problem, but not in the way (C) describes—Luther was more concerned that people were *too* interested in so-called relics—so cross that off. Luther had no interest in being pope, either, so cross off (D).

9. **B** All four titles are Russian, but *Dr. Zhivago* was written in the twentieth century. The other three are products of Russia's Golden Age of Literature.

10. **C** The Tanzimat Reforms of the Ottoman Empire granted many progressive reforms, including granting common Ottoman citizenship to women and ethnic minorities. (A), (B), and (D) are actually the opposite of what the Tanzimat Reforms included.

1. **A** In both countries, this process spanned the 1860s and involved territorial wars—as well as alliances with each other. Remember that the Protestant Reformation was centered in the German states, and while it was the Catholic states that held out the longest against Bismarck's unification efforts, those, too, were brought under control by 1871, so cross off (B). Germany and Italy were both involved in the Scramble for Africa, but not Asia, so cross off (C). And while the Spanish had to be driven from the Kingdom of the Two Sicilies, the same was not true in Germany, so cross off (D).

2. **C** As industrial production rose, it replaced agriculture as the basis of many economies. At the same time, though, industrialization was only possible due to improved agricultural techniques boosting production while reducing the labor required, so it's not as if agriculture ceased—simply played second-fiddle to industrialization. (A) describes the opposite of what was happening n Western Europe; (B) and (D) were simply not factors in these developments.

3. **B** Industrialization compounded matters, but discontent with monarchist and imperial rule was the key element in the development of liberalism, communism, and socialism. African immigration didn't enter into it at all, so cross off (A). Nor were transnational religious movements really a factor so cross off (D). This era did see a rise in calls for women's suffrage, but that was also not a significant factor in the rise of these belief systems, so cross off (C).

4. **A** The Korean Empire was incredibly short-lived, lasting just over a decade at the turn of the twentieth century. But its fall was purely an external matter. As the empire showed signs of rapid modernization, it was quickly annexed by Japan in 1910. The others faced class, ethnic, and religious conflict, as well as pressure from outside invaders and competing empires.

5. **A** Great Britain claimed Australia (OK, the eastern half of it) in 1770 and established a penal colony at New South Wales in January 1788. Cross off (B), Liberia, as that was a colony established primarily by the United States for freed slaves. While Madagascar and Hong Kong were both under degrees of British control at various points, neither was used as a penal colony, so cross off (C) and (D).

6. **C** Remember that you're looking for the one that *isn't* true. Austria was not a major party to the Peace of Basel, and it wasn't ceding any disputed territories in northern Italy. Prussia did agree that, in exchange for territorial concessions from France, it would withdraw from the coalition partitioning Poland, so cross off (A). France did divide and placate its enemies through a series of concessions and quid-pro-quos, a necessary step after the instability of the French Revolution and the Napoleonic Wars, so cross off (B). Finally, Spain did agree with France to end the War of the Pyrenees and ceded control of half of Santo Domingo, or Hispaniola, which became Saint-Domingue and, eventually, Haiti—so cross off (D).

7. **B** Remember that you're looking for the one that *isn't* true. When the Dutch took control of Sumatra, including the Sultanate of Aceh and other Islamic areas, they placed no such restrictions on the public practice of Islam. They did, however, take control with the permission of the British, who also granted them equal trading rights in Aceh, so cross off (A) and (C). In return, the Dutch ceded territories in the Gold Coast to the British, so cross off (D).

8. **A** This was the Great Emancipation Reform of 1861, which freed serfs from their feudal obligations and gave them the full rights of citizenship. The Eastern Orthodox Church had long been the official state religion, so cross off (B). Russia was not generally in the habit of granting self-governance to the different ethnic groups within its empire, so cross off (C). Finally, while socialist movements arose toward the end of Alexander II's reign and particularly after his assassination, socialist principles were not implemented in government until after the Russian Revolution of 1917, so cross off (D).

9. **C** Primary sources such as diaries are some of a historian's most valuable resources, and the diaries of suffragists (regardless of where they were from) would offer direct testimony on the nature of women's struggle for political rights. NATO is not a human rights organization, so cross off (A). Despite being from matriarchal households, household budgets would say little of use about political rights, so cross off (B). While fashion trends did have links to political trends, (D) is not as good a set of sources on political struggles as (C) would be, so cross off (D) in favor of (C).

10. **A** The ample land in Australia provided many opportunities for agriculture and ranching, which, along with some gold rushes in the mid- to late-1800s, brought thousands of settlers to the continent. By 1901, separate colonies banded together after a referendum approving a federation. Oil was not a significant industry in Australia at this time, so cross off (B) and (C). While there were political opportunities available to some settlers in the autonomous parliamentary democracies the British established in the Australian colonies, these were not the primary draw—the opportunities of the land were—so cross off (D).

Drill 8

1. **B** In the French and Indian War (1754–1763), the American component of the Seven Years' War (1756–1763), both the French and the British allied with various Native American tribes to fight the war. The same was true, though in different alignment, for Britain and the United States, in the War of 1812. While the War of 1812 did not result in any territorial changes in the United States, and the Seven Years' War did not result in any territorial changes in Europe, the French and Indian War reshaped the balance of power in North America, with Britain taking all French holdings on that continent, so cross off (A). In the War of 1812, both the American and Canadian capitals were sacked and burned; this was not the case in the French and Indian War, so cross off (C). And while the British didn't exactly win the War of 1812 (it was more like a draw, *status quo antebellum*), they definitely won the French and Indian War, so cross off (D).

2. **C** While the Anglo-Russian Convention was important because it divided Iran into spheres of British and Russian influence, irrespective of Iranian sovereignty, that meant a *lot* more after the discovery of oil by the British the next year, in 1908. The British had to contend, though, with the constitutional monarchy established in 1906 when a long-running revolution finally forced the shah to accept constitutional limitations on his power. The tension between this constitutional monarchy and the pressures of British commercial influence shaped right up to the British occupation of Iran during World War I. (C) is thus a better answer than (A) or (B)—plus, the Islamic Revolution wasn't until the late twentieth century. Finally, neither the Crimean War nor the telegraph was a factor in any of this, so cross off (D).

3. **C** In 1839, Mende slaves aboard the Spanish ship *The Amistad* successfully overthrew the crew of the slaver—a very rare occurrence in the transatlantic slave trade—and attempted to sail back to Africa. They ended up off the coast of Long Island, where they were captured by an American ship and taken back to the United States. The African slave trade had been illegal in the United States (while the domestic trade carried on), so the ship and its "cargo" were impounded until the Supreme Court of the United States ruled in 1841 that the Mende were to be freed and repatriated to Africa. The United States was not suing the captain, so cross off (D). It was not the crew that overtook the ship (mutiny), but rather the slaves in the cargo, nor was it the captain that sued, so cross off (B). Finally, (A) describes a horrific incident a century earlier on the slave ship *Zong*, so cross that off, too.

4. **D** Remember that you're looking for the one that *isn't* true. Despite being banned as subversive in most countries—cross off (A)—unions in Europe in the late nineteenth century established themselves and thrived on popular support—cross off (C)—and achieved some success in improving working conditions for factory laborers—cross off (B). What they didn't do was work to improve farming techniques, as farmers weren't unionized.

5. **B** Industrialization was the new order of things, crushing independent producers of agricultural as well as other goods, so cross off (A) and (C) in favor of (B). Violent revolts from farmers and working classes, while they did in some cases occur, were neither universal nor inevitable, so cross off (D).

6. **D**   Both Ottoman and Qing government officials made some efforts to prop up pre-industrial methods of production, but neither prevented global capitalism from spreading. (B) is not an accurate characterization of the state's relationship with the rural population or with religion, so cross it off. The sorts of worker organization and protest described in (A) and (C) are not similarities between these regimes, so cross them off, too.

7. **A**   Rapid urbanization always involved a lot of people generating a lot of waste in a comparatively small space/high concentration. Political corruption was not a universal or inevitable development—nor was the rise of ethnic gangs or a differential within rural incomes—so cross off (B), (C), and (D).

8. **C**   The French Revolution was a domestic revolt, whereas the American Revolution was a revolt led by Britain's colonists in North America against the empire. Both involved concerns over economics and taxation, so cross off (A). Both were sparked by violations of the people's rights, and both involved intervention by multiple foreign powers, so cross off (B) and (D).

9. **C**   Egypt was under British rule, so cross off (A), Morocco was under French rule, so cross off (B), and Angola was under Portuguese role, so cross off (D). Liberia had been founded as an independent nation and remained so.

10. **D**   While Peru is right there near the others, it was not technically part of Gran Colombia, as Simon Bolivar and his forces liberated it in the early 1800s. Colombia, Ecuador, and Venezuela all were.

Drill 9

1. **C**   The Berlin Conference saw Africa divided by Europe for Europe. Otto von Bismarck and the other representatives of European nations partitioned the continent according to their own needs, irrespective of tribal boundaries or indigenous arrangements. The conference did not codify racial or ethnic hierarchies, so cross off (A). The transatlantic African slave trade was essentially over by this point, so cross off (B). And while mineral rights were an important concern for the Europeans at the Berlin Conference, they did not assign themselves those rights in perpetuity at this conference, so cross off (D).

2. **D**   This is a quotation from Thomas Paine's *Rights of Man* (1791). This was Paine's commentary on the French Revolution, from which the philosophical language of liberty expressed here should sound familiar. Queen Victoria would never have said such a thing about a mutiny of her own subjects, so cross off (C). While the Haitian Revolution did begin in 1791, this does not accurately express Hegel's thoughts on that conflict, so cross off (B). Equiano's writings about freedom are less formally philosophical in tone than this, so cross off (A), too.

3. **A**   The birth rates in Europe did not increase substantially during the Industrial Revolution. Increases in population and life expectancy were mostly due to people living longer (B) rather than the birth of more people. The primary reason for people living longer was improved hygiene and sanitation in the work place and in medical practice (C) and increased food production due to the agricultural revolution (D).

4. **D** Raw materials and resources used during the Industrial Revolution were available prior to this time. The application of new sources of energy such as the steam power (A), generation of new materials such as steel (B), and technological applications such as the steam engine (C), revolutionized industry and technology.

5. **A** The Industrial Revolution began in Britain in the eighteenth century and eventually spread to Belgium, France, and the United States before ultimately sweeping through the rest of Europe, the Americas, and East Asia.

6. **B** The United States, as former colonies of the British Empire, quickly benefited from the technological growth and application of Great Britain and experienced its Industrial Revolution late in the eighteenth century. Brazil (A), Russia (C), and Japan (D) would not industrialize until the late nineteenth century.

7. **A** Both Great Britain and Japan used extensive railway networks for transportation during their respective Industrial Revolutions. Great Britain had large deposits of coal and iron, whereas Japan had to import most of their coal and iron (B). Most of the technology and machinery developed during the Industrial Revolution originated in Great Britain and was later introduced and incorporated into Japan (C). Suffrage and women's rights emerged as a social change following industrialization of Great Britain, whereas woman remained with little change in social status in industrialized Japan (D).

8. **C** Eli Whitney's Cotton gin was invented in the United Status. The Flying Shuttle (A), Spinning Jenny (B), and Watt's Steam Engine (D) were inventions originating in Great Britain.

9. **A** Adam Smith suggested that economic prosperity and fairness was linked to economic systems that permit private means of production and open free markets or capitalism. Socialism and communism originated from the economic systems described by Karl Marx and others that viewed that privatization failed to protect the workers and resulted in inequality in the workplace.

10. **A** The Emancipation Act gave freedom to the serfs releasing them from their obligation to the land and permitted them to seek work elsewhere.

Chapter 13
Period 6
Accelerating Global Change and Realignments
c. 1900 to Present
Drills

DRILL 1

1. Which of the following best explains why World War I was considered a global war?

    (A) Warring powers held colonies that also participated in the war.
    (B) Battles were fought on every continent.
    (C) The war began in Europe, whose culture dominated the world in the early twentieth century.
    (D) Both Europe and the United States fought in the war.

2. All of the following are true about Russia's role in twentieth-century global conflicts EXCEPT

    (A) it created an ethnic-based alliance with Serbia
    (B) it helped create the League of Nations
    (C) it joined the war against Japan in 1945
    (D) it became highly influential in Eastern Europe

3. Which of the following best explains why Spain did not participate in World War II?

    (A) Its monarchy feared a fascist coup if the country entered the war.
    (B) Its army was devastated during World War I and the country could not commit its military.
    (C) It had just fought a civil war.
    (D) It had signed a treaty of non-intervention with Germany and Italy.

4. Which of the following invasions initiated World War II?

    (A) German invasion of Austria
    (B) German invasion of Czechoslovakia
    (C) German invasion of France
    (D) German invasion of Poland

5. Which of the following is a difference between the periods immediately after World War I and World War II?

    (A) Unlike World War I, World War II was not concluded by one defining peace treaty
    (B) Unlike World War I, World War II concluded with the creation of an international organization
    (C) Unlike World War I, World War II created new colonial possessions
    (D) Unlike World War I, World War II resulted in the immediate independence of all African colonies

6. The twentieth century leader who would have most agreed with the policies of Benito Mussolini would likely be

    (A) Juan Perón
    (B) V. I. Lenin
    (C) Nikita Khrushchev
    (D) Fidel Castro

7. The only communist-controlled country in the twentieth century allowed to have private land ownership and freedom of worship was

    (A) Czechoslovakia
    (B) Poland
    (C) East Germany
    (D) Hungary

8. Mikhail Gorbachev allowed for all of the following in Soviet Russia EXCEPT

    (A) the production of consumer goods
    (B) open discussion of government policy
    (C) democratic local governments
    (D) private land ownership

9. Which of the following correctly lists the countries associated with the Triple Entente, which fought in World War I?

   (A) Germany, Austria-Hungary, Italy
   (B) Germany, Austria-Hungary, Spain
   (C) Great Britain, Russia, Austria-Hungary
   (D) Great Britain, France, Russia

10. Which of the following statements best describes domestic politics at the end of the twentieth century?

    (A) Increased economic prosperity in Japan and Africa
    (B) Ethnic conflicts in Russia and Africa
    (C) A decline in democratic governance throughout Latin America
    (D) A rise in democratization in the Middle East

Check your answers on page 277.

DRILL 2

1. Which of the following events best illustrates the tactic of brinkmanship?

   (A) The Cuban Missile Crisis
   (B) The Korean War
   (C) The Vietnam War
   (D) The Bay of Pigs Invasion

2. Which Communist ruler's policies were most similar to those of Lenin?

   (A) Mao Zedong
   (B) Joseph Stalin
   (C) Fidel Castro
   (D) Deng Xiaoping

3. The economy of which country grew most rapidly during the Second World War?

   (A) France
   (B) The United States
   (C) Great Britain
   (D) Germany

4. The Allied Powers' policy towards Hitler in the 1930s was one of

   (A) support
   (B) containment
   (C) brinkmanship
   (D) appeasement

5. All of the following are examples of how communism affected the post-World War II world EXCEPT

   (A) it divided Korea
   (B) it was most popular in largely agricultural regions
   (C) it caused a pause in the Chinese civil war
   (D) it drove economic policies in Eastern European countries

6. Which of the following nations became a regional power after World War I, only to lose power after World War II?

   (A) Japan
   (B) China
   (C) The United States
   (D) Great Britain

7. Which of the following best characterizes post–World War II Africa?

   (A) Slavery was reintroduced to developing nations in Southeast Asia
   (B) Most African colonies gained national independence
   (C) Most new countries joined either NATO or the Warsaw Pact
   (D) New governments created stability and began trade with European countries

8. All of the following nationalist movements emerged at the turn of the twentieth century EXCEPT

   (A) India
   (B) the Arab world
   (C) Kurds
   (D) the Jewish people

9. Which of the following best characterizes the main difference between the Egyptian and Indian nationalist movements prior to World War I?

   (A) In Egypt, a lack of an educated elite capable of assuming leadership of the nationalist movement stalled progress.
   (B) The two countries were controlled by very different regimes.
   (C) Whereas the Indian nationalist movement benefitted from wealthy patronage, Egyptian nationalists were mostly unsupported peasants.
   (D) In Egypt, several rival parties flourished to populate the nationalist movement, while in India one party directed the movement.

10. All of the following statements are accurate concerning Mohandas Gandhi EXCEPT

   (A) he was a Western-educated lawyer
   (B) he preached the use of nonviolent, but aggressive protest
   (C) he had successfully led a movement against restrictive laws targeting Indians in South Africa
   (D) he was the first leader in India to appeal to the lower classes

Check your answers on page 278.

DRILL 3

1. All of the following are true about the domestic situations in European countries between 1914 and 1919 EXCEPT

    (A) government regulations prevented material shortages and famine
    (B) executive branches of governments became significantly more powerful
    (C) governments manipulated mass media in order to control public opinion
    (D) labor union members were often jailed for voicing dissent

2. Which of the following is an accurate statement about Japan during World War I?

    (A) It remained neutral.
    (B) It profited from the war by seizing German colonies in Asia.
    (C) It formed an alliance with China to defend against Western European aggression.
    (D) None of the answers are correct.

3. All of the following are accurate regarding Western Europe in the 1920s EXCEPT

    (A) fascism gained popularity in Italy and Germany
    (B) the governments of Austria-Hungary and Germany collapsed
    (C) high taxes imposed in England and France caused famine in those countries
    (D) western Europe saw its economic dominance of world markets shift to the United States and Japan

4. All of the following were terms included in the treaties that ended World War I EXCEPT

    (A) a League of Nations was created
    (B) Germany was forced to accept blame for the war
    (C) Russia received vast amounts of territory in Poland and the Baltic regions
    (D) all of the above are correct

"His Majesty's Government view with favour the establishment in Palestine of a national home for the Jewish people, and will use their best endeavours to facilitate the achievement of this object, it being clearly understood that nothing shall be done which may prejudice the civil and religious rights of existing non-Jewish communities in Palestine, or the rights and political status enjoyed by Jews in any other country."

5. The quotation above comes from a 1917 letter which represented which of the following trends of the period?

    (A) Capitalism
    (B) Communism
    (C) Nationalism
    (D) Socialism

6. All of the following are true about the "Roaring Twenties" EXCEPT

    (A) women in several countries gained the right to vote
    (B) consumer items such as the radio and affordable automobiles became icons of the domestic home
    (C) the Decembrist Revolt was violently suppressed in Russia
    (D) the signing of the Kellogg-Briand Pact encouraged Europeans to believe that war was a thing of the past

"Deeply sensible of their solemn duty to promote the welfare of mankind;

Persuaded that the time has, come when a frank renunciation of war as an instrument of national policy should be made to the end that the peaceful and friendly relations now existing between their peoples may be perpetuated;

Convinced that all changes in their relations with one another should be sought only by pacific means and be the result of a peaceful and orderly process, and that any signatory Power which shall hereafter seek to promote its ts national interests by resort to war a should be denied the benefits furnished by this Treaty…

Have decided to conclude a Treaty"

7. The quotation above is an excerpt of which document written in the first half of the twentieth century?

(A) The Treaty of Versailles
(B) The Kellog-Briand Pact
(C) The Balfour Declaration
(D) The Zimmerman Telegram

8. Which of the following was a characteristic shared by countries which saw revolutions in the twentieth century?

(A) Most revolutions were led by the upper class, frustrated with the social mobility now offered to most citizens.
(B) Most revolutions centered on demands for better access to Western influcnce and ideas.
(C) Most revolutions involved an intellectual buildup, and revolutions were led by Western-educated individuals.
(D) Most revolutions followed strikingly similar paths.

9. Which of the following statements about post–World War I Japan are true?

(A) The use of electric power grew faster in Japan than anywhere else in the world in the 1920s.
(B) Primary school attendance became universal in the 1920s.
(C) Rapid expansions occurred in several industrial fields, including shipbuilding and metallurgy.
(D) All of the above are correct.

10. The Great Depression led to the fall of each Western European government EXCEPT

(A) Germany
(B) France
(C) Spain
(D) Italy

Check your answers on page 279.

DRILL 4

1. Which of the following is true about parliamentary governments in the aftermath of World War I?

   (A) Parliamentary governments were weakened by the rise of radical groups from the left and the right.
   (B) Parliamentary governments fell throughout Europe due to economic instability.
   (C) Parliamentary governments were strengthened by their successes during the war.
   (D) Parliamentary governments were rapidly replaced by increasingly liberal governments.

2. Which of the following is true regarding the Chinese and Mexican revolutions during the twentieth century?

   (A) Both promoted communism.
   (B) Both produced new policies regarding land distribution.
   (C) Both successful sides were supported by the United States.
   (D) Both began after the surrender of foreign occupiers.

3. In contrast to Japan's shift towards military dominance after World War I, Germany's shift was more

   (A) complete
   (B) violent
   (C) abrupt
   (D) expansionist

4. In contrast to the end of colonization in Europe's nonsettler colonies in Africa after World War II, the end of colonization in Algeria was

   (A) better organized
   (B) less permanent
   (C) better funded
   (D) more violent

5. Nations successfully born after World War II faced all of the following challenges created by the withdrawal of European powers EXCEPT

   (A) underdeveloped economies
   (B) divisions among different ethnic groups
   (C) a lack of educated leadership
   (D) nations faced all of the challenges listed above

6. All of the following statements regarding World War II are accurate EXCEPT

   (A) the war was initiated by German invasion of Czechoslovakia
   (B) the United States entered the war after the Japanese attack on Pearl Harbor
   (C) nations engaged in a state of "total war," placing their entire economic, industrial, and scientific capabilities in the service of the war effort
   (D) civilian deaths outnumbered deaths of soldiers and combatants

7. Which of the following regions still experienced significant non-native rule after World War II?

   (A) India
   (B) South Africa
   (C) Ghana
   (D) Japan

8. Which of the following best characterizes most
independence movements in Africa and Asia after
World War II?

(A) Native populations used armed revolt to force out
occupying powers.
(B) The United States intervened on behalf of native
populations against European powers.
(C) Activists used peaceful mass demonstrations and
economic boycotts to end colonial rule.
(D) The Soviet Union intervened to help European powers
strengthen their hold on colonial lands.

9. Which of the following is a common problem faced by
both Japan and Russia in the latter part of the twentieth
century?

(A) Economic downturns
(B) Drug cartels
(C) Ethnic conflicts
(D) Political instability

10. By the end of the twentieth century, East Asian nations
began exporting all of the following goods EXCEPT

(A) automobiles
(B) textiles
(C) electronics
(D) films

Check your answers on page 281.

DRILL 5

1. Twentieth-century migration patterns usually followed which of the following patterns?

   (A) From developing to developed countries
   (B) From developed to developing countries
   (C) From urban to rural areas
   (D) From rural to urban areas

2. Which of the following is true about globalization?

   (A) Women's suffrage stalled in Eastern European countries.
   (B) Guest workers became frequent victims of violence.
   (C) The AIDS epidemic became especially prevalent in Latin America.
   (D) Child labor is especially prevalent in the United States.

3. Which of the following best characterizes globalization's effect on religious groups?

   (A) Religious groups embraced the new world order and sought adherents in developing countries.
   (B) Following the example of the Zionist movement, the other monotheistic countries sought their own homelands.
   (C) Reacting against globalism, many religious groups found receptive adherents in impoverished areas.
   (D) Newly empowered women sought and found more significant roles in their churches.

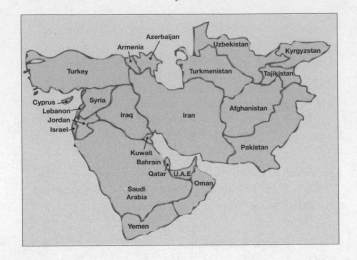

4. The map above depicts the Middle East in the

   (A) 1750s
   (B) 1800s
   (C) 1850s
   (D) 1950s

5. Which of the following is the most important factor in bringing about the end of the Cold War?

   (A) The breakdown of diplomatic relations between the Soviet Union and China
   (B) The economic costs to both the United States and the Soviet Union required to sustain the conflict
   (C) The end of civil conflicts in Southeast Asian nations such as Cambodia, the Koreas, and Vietnam
   (D) The spread to other nations of nuclear technology and the ability to create weapons of mass destruction

6. Which of the following caused the largest displacement of people in the twentieth century?

   (A) The post–World War II partition of Pakistan and India
   (B) The Korean War
   (C) Illegal immigration to France
   (D) World War II

7. Which of the following is an accurate interpretation of the political cartoon above?

    (A) The United States. and Russia hoped to learn from China how to make an atomic bomb in the twentieth century
    (B) The United States and Russia were concerned about China's development of the atom bomb in the twentieth century
    (C) China under Mao Zedong used its atom bomb to make itself a world power
    (D) China under Mao Zedong made great leaps in science and technology

8. Which of the following nations did NOT need a new government in the latter years of the twentieth century?

    (A) The Soviet Union
    (B) Germany
    (C) Japan
    (D) Nicaragua

9. All of the following are new political issues debated on among international actors EXCEPT

    (A) global warming
    (B) universal human rights
    (C) the AIDS epidemic
    (D) tariffs and trade relations

10. Which of the following is a result of "McDonaldization," or the globalization of American culture?

    (A) An increase in quality of life in most countries
    (B) Anti-Western backlash in some developing nations
    (C) More cultural tolerance globally
    (D) The exploitation of child labor in most countries

Check your answers on page 282.

DRILL 6

1. All of the following are true about the Iranian Revolution EXCEPT

   (A) it caused war with Iraq
   (B) its leaders were adherents of Sunni Islam
   (C) it was led by Islamic fundamentalists
   (D) its leaders strongly rejected Western culture as satanic

2. Post-industrial economies tend to employ the highest number of people in

   (A) agricultural industries
   (B) manufacturing industries
   (C) service industries
   (D) nuclear sciences

3. World War I was considered "total war" because it involved

   (A) mobilizing every aspect of nations' resources
   (B) Europe's near-total destruction
   (C) Asian as well as European nations
   (D) chemical warfare, as well as traditional tactics

4. Mao Zedong's Great Leap Forward

   (A) resulted in positive economic growth for China
   (B) collectivized farms and diverted labor to steel production
   (C) was enforced primarily through nonviolent means such as taxation
   (D) was the first of Mao's five-year plans adapted from the Soviet model

5. Which of the following is an accurate description of this political cartoon?

   (A) U.S. President Woodrow Wilson made a mistake when he chose to enter World War I.
   (B) German U-boat attacks on American ships speeded an inevitable war only slightly.
   (C) Indecision about when to seek vengeance for American lives lost cost Woodrow Wilson political capital.
   (D) Congress should not have disputed Woodrow Wilson's decision to enter World War.

6. One impact of improved military technology and new tactics in the twentieth century was

   (A) increased levels of wartime casualties
   (B) shorter duration for military conflicts
   (C) decreased reliance on diplomatic solutions
   (D) longer postwar occupation periods

7. NATO and the Warsaw Pact are examples of

   (A) new military alliances produced by the Cold War
   (B) mutual defense agreements signed by Asian leaders
   (C) organizations that participated in proxy wars in Africa
   (D) vehicles for the spread of nationalist ideologies world-wide

8. Which of the following characterized the economic policy decisions of many governments in the late twentieth century?

   (A) Increased government influence in economic life
   (B) Tightened controls on imports to strengthen demand for local goods
   (C) Efforts to decrease immigration from the Indian sub-continent
   (D) Encouragement of free market policies and promotion of economic liberalization

9. U.S. President Jimmy Carter initiated the process of returning the Panama Canal to Panamanian control in 1977 primarily in response to

   (A) France and the United Kingdom applying pressure on American trading interests
   (B) increased economic pressure from Asia for equitable access to the canal
   (C) security concerns over South American proxy conflicts during the Cold War
   (D) several decades of Panamanian agitation over American control of the canal

10. Woodrow Wilson's proposed Fourteen Points included free trade, open diplomacy, and

   (A) independence for Poland
   (B) Russian protectorship of the Balkan states
   (C) cession of Belgian territory to the French
   (D) maintaining the status quo in Africa

Check your answers on page 283.

DRILL 7

1. The World Health Organization was founded primarily in order to

   (A) coordinate nutrition campaigns in the Third World
   (B) monitor reproduction rates in developing countries
   (C) eradicate communicable diseases worldwide
   (D) support U.N. efforts to pass global health laws

2. The global influenza pandemic of 1918

   (A) had the highest mortality rates among children and the elderly in infected populations
   (B) was stopped due to development of an effective vaccine for the virus in late 1918
   (C) began in Spain during World War I and spread throughout the world as a result of troop movement
   (D) resulted in a comparable death toll to that of the Black Death in medieval Europe and Asia

3. Which of the following is NOT an accurate statement about the Suez Crisis of 1956?

   (A) It occurred in part because the United States and the United Kingdom would not support construction of the Aswan Dam in Egypt.
   (B) The United Nations refused to intervene because key members of the Security Council believed Egypt should control the Suez Canal.
   (C) The Western response to close Soviet-Egyptian relations sparked a backlash against the West and Egypt's nationalizing the Suez Canal.
   (D) It resulted in Israel provoking Egypt by invading the Sinai Peninsula as pretext for drawing the British and French into a war with Egypt.

4. The Declaration of Independence Ho Chi Minh penned for Vietnam in 1945 was based primarily on

   (A) the United States *Declaration of Independence*
   (B) the French *Declaration of Rights of Man and Citizen*
   (C) the United Nations *Universal Declaration of Human Rights*
   (D) Karl Marx's *The Communist Manifesto*

5. In January 1959, official United States policy toward the new government of Cuba called for

   (A) friendly relations with the new non-Communist leadership
   (B) a hard-line embargo against the newly-installed Castro regime
   (C) supporting opposition forces both financially and militarily
   (D) American ability to review any decision of the Cuban government

6. Betty Friedan's *The Feminine Mystique* raised awareness of

   (A) the role of women in environmental activism
   (B) women's unhappiness with their opportunities
   (C) discrimination against women in religious patriarchies
   (D) women's struggle to achieve equal voting rights

7. Which of the following is NOT an accurate statement about Africa in the late twentieth century?

   (A) Independence movements strengthened as European powers weakened after World War II.
   (B) Some leaders aggravated existing ethnic conflicts in order to maintain their positions of power.
   (C) Civil wars decimated the young, leaving a disproportionately elderly population and workforce.
   (D) Supplying aid to Africa was another means of proxy conflict between the United States and U.S.S.R.

8. Chinese leader Sun Yat-sen differed from his successor Chiang Kai-shek in that

   (A) Sun was more socially liberal, embracing western democratic ideas Chiang rejected in favor of conservative nationalism
   (B) Chiang was respected by the increasingly powerful Communist Party, while Sun was often in open conflict with the party
   (C) Sun respected the rights of China's Christians but was not one himself, whereas Chiang converted against his family's wishes
   (D) Chiang sought diplomatically negotiated solutions to China's problems, reluctant to use military force as Sun had preferred

9. Which of the following is an accurate statement about colonies in the twentieth century?

    (A) All colonies that achieved independence did so through negotiation.
    (B) All colonies that achieved independence did so through armed conflict.
    (C) Some colonies negotiated their independence, while others achieved it through armed conflict.
    (D) No colonies achieved independence after the end of World War I.

10. What was one key factor in maintaining cultural and economic ties between newly independent colonies and their former metropoles in the twentieth century?

    (A) The proliferation of ethnic conflicts and the flood of refugees
    (B) The ease of travel and communication between the new nations and imperial metropoles
    (C) The shifting of former colonies' newly established national borders
    (D) The migration of former colonial subjects to imperial metropoles

Check your answers on page 285.

DRILL 8

1. Which of the following was NOT an ideology employed by twentieth-century governments to mobilize state resources for war?

   (A) Transcendentalism
   (B) Fascism
   (C) Communism
   (D) Nationalism

2. What event led a number of western governments to take a significantly more active role in economic life in the mid-twentieth century?

   (A) The Great Awakening
   (B) The October Revolution
   (C) The Second Bantu Migration
   (D) The Great Depression

3. Vladimir Lenin's 1918 April Theses called for all of the following EXCEPT

   (A) an end to Russian involvement in World War I
   (B) the abdication of Czar Nicholas II
   (C) land allocated for the peasantry
   (D) expanded powers for the local soviet councils

"The study of the powers that shape, maintain and alter the state is the basis of all political insight and leads to the understanding that the law of power governs the world of states just as the law of gravity governs the physical world."

4. The above quotation, penned in 1853, describes a political philosophy followed by all of the following leaders EXCEPT

   (A) Mao Zedong
   (B) Otto von Bismarck
   (C) Neville Chamberlain
   (D) George H. W. Bush

5. The 1919 Amritsar Massacre

   (A) was the bloodiest episode of the Armenian genocide
   (B) marked the beginning of the decline of the Ottoman Empire
   (C) horrified abolitionists and prompted a final push to end Caribbean slavery
   (D) galvanized Indian resistance to colonial rule across religious lines

6. The 1960 Sharpeville Massacre led to all of the following EXCEPT

   (A) the establishment of apartheid government in the Union of South Africa
   (B) the African National Congress began advocating guerilla warfare
   (C) a break with the tradition of nonviolent resistance inspired by Gandhi
   (D) a United Nations resolution condemning the actions of the South African government

7. The above images are most appropriately associated with

   (A) the separation of Slovakia and the Czech Republic
   (B) the reunification of Ireland and Northern Ireland
   (C) post–World War II Japanese and Chinese reconciliation
   (D) French and British cooperation during World War II

8. All of the following contributed to the participation of much of the modern world in World War I EXCEPT

(A) most of the world had either been colonized or formerly colonized by Europe
(B) alliances had been established to maintain the balance of power in Europe
(C) the Industrial Revolution resulted in new advances in technology, which allowed for more weapons and means of transporting them
(D) most of the monarchs of Europe were now genetically related to one another

9. Germany's Triple Alliance in the 1880s was formed between Germany, Italy, and which other nation?

(A) Japan
(B) Austria-Hungary
(C) Russia
(D) Switzerland

10. All of the following contributed to the United States shift from a policy of isolationism during the early years of World War I to its entry in 1917 EXCEPT

(A) American sympathy for Central Europe
(B) sinking of passenger liners en route to Europe
(C) the Zimmerman Telegram
(D) attack of U.S. merchant ships en route to Britain

Check your answers on page 287.

DRILL 9

1. The Treaty of Versailles signed in 1919 had a devastating effect on postwar Germany including all of the following EXCEPT

   (A) payment of war reparations to the allies
   (B) dissolution of the German state
   (C) territorial losses
   (D) high inflation and economic meltdown

2. Why was the League of Nations a failure?

   (A) Nations were reluctant to join and support the league.
   (B) The United States was given too much power in the decision-making of the organization.
   (C) It lacked the monetary means to effect real change in the world.
   (D) It established biased and unacceptable standards of fairness and international conduct.

3. Ataturk was responsible for forming which of the following modern nations?

   (A) Turkey
   (B) Greece
   (C) Ottoman Sultanate
   (D) Macedonia

4. Which of the following was the result of the Munich Conference in 1938?

   (A) Germany would cease all attempts to acquire more territory in exchange for the Rhineland.
   (B) Germany would cease all attempts to acquire more territory in exchange for Czechoslovakia.
   (C) Germany would cease all attempts to acquire more territory in exchange for the Sudetenland.
   (D) Germany would cease all attempts to acquire more territory in exchange for monetary support to rebuild.

5. All of the following contributed to the ability of Britain to resist German invasion EXCEPT

   (A) use of newly developed radar to help protect Great Britain from aerial attack
   (B) alliance with the United States
   (C) alliance with France
   (D) Germany focused its attention on the Eastern Front

6. Which of the following was part of the Allied powers during WWI and Axis powers during WWII?

   (A) Germany
   (B) Japan
   (C) France
   (D) Turkey

7. Which of the following prompted the surrender of Japan to end World War II?

   (A) Surrender of Germany earlier that year
   (B) Threat of mainland invasion by the United States
   (C) Threat of more atomic bombings
   (D) Death of Emperor Hirohito

8. The Marshall Plan was meant to

   (A) settle territorial borders at the end of WWI
   (B) establish war reparations at the end of WWII
   (C) help rebuild Europe at the end of WWI
   (D) help rebuild Europe at the end of WWII

Check your answers on page 288.

Chapter 14
Period 6
Accelerating Global Change and Realignments
c. 1900 to Present
Answers and Explanations

ANSWER KEY

Drill 1
1. A
2. B
3. C
4. D
5. A
6. A
7. B
8. C
9. D
10. B

Drill 2
1. A
2. D
3. B
4. D
5. C
6. A
7. B
8. C
9. D
10. D

Drill 3
1. A
2. B
3. C
4. D
5. C
6. C
7. B
8. C
9. D
10. B

Drill 4
1. A
2. B
3. C
4. D
5. C
6. A
7. B
8. C
9. A
10. D

Drill 5
1. A
2. B
3. C
4. D
5. B
6. A
7. B
8. C
9. D
10. B

Drill 6
1. B
2. C
3. A
4. B
5. B
6. A
7. A
8. D
9. D
10. A

Drill 7
1. C
2. D
3. B
4. A
5. A
6. B
7. C
8. A
9. C
10. D

Drill 8
1. A
2. D
3. B
4. C
5. D
6. A
7. B
8. D
9. B
10. A

Drill 9
1. B
2. A
3. A
4. C
5. C
6. B
7. C
8. D

EXPLANATIONS

Drill 1

1. **A**   European nations held Asian and African colonies that participated in the war. Colonial populations hoped to earn their independence by fighting in the war. No battles were fought in Australia or South America (B). A war started by a global power doesn't make it a global war (C), and Britain and the United States didn't make up the world (D).

2. **B**   Since Russia had left World War I early and it was governed by Communists, it wasn't allowed to help form, or even join, the League of Nations. Russia's Pan-Slavic movement worked to unite all Slavic people, including the Serbs (A). At Yalta, the Soviet Union agreed to go to war with Japan for territory in Manchuria (C). After World War II, Latvia, Lithuania, and Estonia became Soviet provinces and Czechoslovakia, Hungary, Bulgaria, and Romania were occupied by the Soviet Union, making the Soviet Union influential in the region (D).

3. **C**   Spain fought a civil war between 1936 and 1939. Spain was Fascist by World War II (A). It didn't fight in World War I (B). The non-intervention treaty was signed by European powers to not intervene in Spain's civil war (D).

4. **D**   Remember Neville Chamberlain believed in the policy of appeasement, so when Hitler announced the unification of Germany and Austria in 1938 (A), the other Western powers did nothing. Hitler "annexed" the Sudetenland, part of Czechoslovakia, in 1938, taking the rest of the country the next year (B). When he invaded Poland on September 1, 1939, France and Britain *finally* declared war. Germany invaded France and occupied Paris only during the war (C).

5. **A**   World War II was concluded by three separate peace meetings; one meeting—the Tehran Conference—happened even before the end of the war. The Yalta and Potsdam Conferences rounded out the three meetings to plan peace. Keep Treaty of Versailles in mind for World War I. World War II had the United Nations, but World War I had the League of Nations (B). No new colonial territories were carved out (C). African colonies didn't gain their independence until the 1950s.

6. **A**   Mussolini was a fascist and Perón's government followed fascist models; he was said to have fascist sympathies. Lenin (B), Khrushchev (C), and Castro (D) were all communists and, therefore, were opposed to fascism.

7. **B**   Remember that Poland was the only country in the USSR that was allowed private ownership and religious freedom. This will give rise to the Solidarity movement. Though the other countries had uprisings (A), (C), and (D), it was the lack of freedom they chafed against.

8. **C**   You'll want to associate Gorbachev with *glasnost* (openness), when the Soviet Union finally started loosening the reins of communism. He instituted *perestroika* (restructuring) of the Soviet economy, allowed for some measure of free market economy, a more open press and society which could more openly discuss the government's policies, and private land ownership. The state remained the supreme controller, however, and no element of democratic politics was introduced.

9. **D**   Otto von Bismarck had set up the Triple Alliance—originally Germany, Austria-Hungary, and Italy (A)—all the way back in the 1880s. England signed on with France and Russia to form the Triple Entente by the early years of the twentieth century.

10. **B**   Russia attempted to suppress independence movements from its ethnic groups, such as the Chechens, while Africa faced conflicts regarding political and economic dominance fought among different ethnic groups. In the 1990s, Japan's economy crashed and Africa continued to face weak economies (A). Latin America actually experienced a period of democratization (C), whereas hopes for democratic change in the Middle East floundered (D).

Drill 2

1. **A**   "Brinkmanship" is the policy of ratcheting up rhetoric, fighting through diplomacy to the brink of war, though not actually engaging in it, which explains the Cuban Missile Crisis. The Korean War (B) and the Vietnam War (C) were hot wars, where bullets *were* fired. The Bay of Pigs Invasion (D) was a botched attempt at a coup in Cuba, which also led to casualties.

2. **D**   Deng Xiaoping allowed some elements of a market economy and some foreign investment; Mao and Stalin did not (A, B). Castro has allowed such change only VERY recently (C).

3. **B**   By initially staying out of the war, the United States protected itself from the destructive force of the war. Though industries grew throughout the warring world to respond to the demand of the respective militaries, the United States' economy took off as it sold to the Allied Powers.

4. **D**   The Allies didn't really support (A) Hitler's land grabs, but they tried to minimize them, which they thought the Munich conference and other agreements to allow him certain parts of Europe would accomplish. Containment (B) and brinkmanship (C) are phrases, or policies, that you should associate with the Cold War, after World War II, starting much more in the 1950s.

5. **C**   World War II is what forced a pause in the Chinese civil war. Korea became split geographically by the communist North and the Western South (A). Most of the nations that the Soviet Union occupied in Eastern Europe, creating its economic policy through the philosophy (D), were agricultural, rather than industrial, nations (B).

6. **A** Japan's initial strength gained from World War I turned it into a belligerent regional actor. Its empire fell after World War II, however, after joining the losing Axis powers. China was a Japanese protectorate after World War I (B). The United States rose in power after both wars (C), while Great Britain saw its world stance decline both times (D).

7. **B** In 1957, Ghana became the first African colony to gain its independence. It took until 1990, though, for Namibia, the last former colony, to gain independence. African countries, however, still lag behind in the world economy. Slavery was not reintroduced (A). Countries did not join any world networks (C), and Africa still has a way to go to create stability (D).

8. **C** Mohandas Gandhi was most effective at rallying nationalist spirits in India (A). Egypt led the Arab world in nationalist movements as the Ottoman Empire began to crumble (B). Zionism, the Jewish nationalist movement for a homeland, also became a more political reality around this time (D). The Kurdish nationalist movement is a much more recent struggle.

9. **D** Women, students, intellectuals, and politicians all voiced their opposition to British colonialism in Egypt; in India, Mohandas Gandhi had effectively put an end to violent protest. Under his leadership, nationalist protest swelled in the 1920s and 1930s. In most places where nationalist movements sprang up, protests tended to be run by Western-educated elites (A), which is a theme you want to remember for nationalist movements in general. Britain controlled both places (B). In Egypt, the nationalist movement was strongly funded and run by the middle class. Journalists became leaders. In India, lawyers predominated nationalist leadership (C).

10. **D** Gandhi's success came, in part, from his ability to appeal to both the middle and lower classes, but others had tried to appeal to one or the other group, with varying levels of success. Gandhi was a Western-educated lawyer by trade (A), but had worked with South African activists, before his return to India, to end discriminatory laws there (C). This is where he honed and perfected his strategy of peaceful resistance (B).

Drill 3

1. **A** Governments took control of most aspects of everyday life during the First World War. Rationing and media control most affected all Europeans (C). In order to organize the wartime effort, executive branches of governments became much more powerful (B) and, often, average citizens who voiced dissent were jailed (D). Labor union members happened to be some of the most vocal. All this rationing did little, in some countries, to stave off hunger, however.

2. **B** Japan took advantage of the general chaos of the war by moving into German-held areas in China's Shantung region, in China's northeast. Japan came in on the side of Britain and France during the war (A), and used the war to expand its aggressive stance, so did not ally with China (C).

3. **C** England and France were paying back debt, but they didn't tax their countries to famine. All the others are true of post-World War I Europe.

4. **D** American President Woodrow Wilson pushed aggressively for the creation of the League of Nations, though the Unite States failed to join the organization (A). The Treaty of Versailles included a "war guilt clause" in which Germany was required to accept responsibility for the war (B). Russia took large parts of Poland and the Baltic Region (Lithuania, Latvia, Estonia, around the Baltic Sea) (C).

5. **C** The quote comes from the Balfour Declaration, a letter written by the United Kingdom's Foreign Secretary Arthur James Balfour supporting the creation of a Jewish state, the goal of the Zionist movement, which called for a Jewish state for the Jewish people. Remember that post–World War I, many different countries began advocating for their own independence, among them the Jewish people, Egypt, and India.

6. **C** The Decembrist Revolt happened in 1825; that's out of era. In the middle of the 1920s, economic prosperity lifted hopes throughout Europe—industrial production boomed (more in the United States than in Europe), mass consumption standards rose (radios and cars became widespread) (B), and household appliances entered the home in high numbers. Women in Great Britain, Germany, and the United States gained the right to vote (A). The Kellogg-Briand Pact, signed by the United Kingdom, the United States, Germany, and France, which outlawed war, raised European hopes that war would not mar daily life again (D).

7. **B** The excerpt mentions "a frank renunciation of war as an instrument of national policy," which means that nations should not wage war, the main point of the Kellogg-Briand Pact. The Treaty of Versailles ended World War I (A). The Balfour Declaration called for a Jewish nation (C). The Zimmerman Telegram is a document you should associate with World War I, and is one of the causes for the United States entering the war (D).

8. **C** Revolutions throughout the twentieth century occurred for vastly different reasons, and happened in markedly different ways (D). They occurred in Mexico, China, Russia, Cuba—to name a few. These revolutions were often to assert greater national autonomy, and therefore were usually some sort of negative response to Western influence (B). Most of the revolutions had a large number of peasant participants (A), but were usually led by Western-educated people who still had ties to the lower classes.

9. **D** You want to associate the post–World War I period with the rise of the United States and of Japan as industrial and economic powers, so all these answer choices are correct. Silk and rice production also exploded during this time, helping fund new government initiatives. The Japanese began to develop a strong consumer culture, at least in cities, during this time.

10. **B** France, along with Britain, did not change government structures and remained a democracy during the Great Depression. Germany and Italy turned to fascism (A, D). A civil war broke out in Spain in 1936 and authoritarian and military leaders won out against republicans and leftists (C).

Drill 4

1. **A** The rise of radical philosophies, parties, and movements weakened governments throughout Europe. The governments fell in Germany, Italy, and Spain, France and England weathered the changes (B). Though France and England were declared victors, no government was strengthened by the outcome of World War I (C). Many countries moved to more conservative and, some, radical right governments (D).

2. **B** Mexican and Chinese revolutionaries gained early success with peasant classes by taking land out of the hands of the wealthy and returning the land to the peasants. China's revolution in the 1940s was meant to promote Mao Zedong's communism (A). The United States backed Chiang Kai-shek in China's civil war, not the more successful Communists (C). The United States also skirmished with Mexican revolutionaries, but never became directly involved in the revolution. China's revolution began, in part, upon Japan's surrender of Chinese lands (D). Mexico's revolution, however, began when Francisco Madero, a reformist writer and politician, challenged the rule of President Porfirio Diaz.

3. **C** Both Germany's and Japan's new militaristic governments completely controlled the government (A), suppressed dissidents when they felt it was necessary (B), and were interested in expanding the borders of the country (D). By World War II, Japan controlled Manchuria, Korea, Taiwan, and large parts of China. Germany took over Czechoslovakia, Poland, and lots of Europe.

4. **D** The main difference during the end of the colonial period after World War II in Africa between nonsettler and settler colonies (as in, Europeans hadn't moved to the area in nonsettler colonies) was that the places where Europeans did not live, Ghana most notably, withdrew control peacefully. In settler colonies such as Algeria, Kenya, and Southern Rhodesia, to name a few, guerilla warfare and violent clashes between the European power and the native population universally broke out.

5. **C** Most of the successful revolutions in post–World War II developing countries were led by Western-educated individuals (think India and nonsettler African colonies). Many of these countries' borders had been made arbitrarily by Europe—colonial India, though still divided by ethnic and religious divisions, initially split into India and Pakistan in order to try to accommodate these different groups. Africa was a hot mess of random divisions, and still is mostly (B). The economies of many of these places had been structured on European needs, not on a proper, fully developed economic scale (A).

6. **A** Keep in mind the Allies attempted to appease Hitler by allowing him to occupy parts of Czechoslovakia. It's Hitler's invasion of Poland that starts the war. The United States entered the war formally after the bombing of Pearl Harbor (B). "Total war" meant all resources—economic, industrial, and scientific—were dedicated to the war effort. The main powers used this strategy to keep their war machine going (C). Estimates put civilian deaths as high as 45 million. Battle deaths are thought to be around 15 million (D).

7. **B** South Africa experienced a long period of apartheid, a system of racial segregation against the black population enforced through the government which didn't end until the early 1990s. India (A) and Ghana (C) gained their independence after World War II. Japan (D) was already powerful in its own right.

8. **C** Though there were violent nationalist movements, such as those in Rhodesia and Algeria (A), most African and Asian colonies negotiated with European powers for a peaceful transition to independence. What happened after withdrawal was not so calm, unfortunately. The United States and the Soviet Union did not get involved with any of the independence movements in Africa (B, D).

9. **A** Japan's economy tanked in the 1990s and Russia struggled to build a market economy. Neither really dealt with problems regarding political instability or drug cartels (B, D) and only Russia dealt with ethnic conflicts (C).

10. **D** The United States is known for its film production. Japan and South Korea began producing automobiles (A). Taiwan, South Korea, and Singapore were exporting textiles (B). Japan, Singapore, and South Korea began exporting electronics (C).

Drill 5

1. **A** Most twentieth-century migrants were leaving developing countries for developed countries, hoping for a better economic future. (C) and (D) are examples of internal migration. The twentieth century was marked by international migration.

2. **B** Guest workers from Africa and Asia have experienced violence from antiforeign protestors in Europe. Most women have the right to vote but many fewer opportunities to hold office than men (A). Sub-Saharan Africa faced the biggest epidemic of AIDS (C). South Asia and Southeast Asia are still challenged by issues of child labor (D).

3. **C** Religious movements reacted against globalization because of their opposition to sexuality, freedom for women, and consumerism. Orthodox Christianity, Protestant fundamentalism, Hinduism, and Islam found eager adherents in impoverished groups which weren't profiting from globalization. This surge of conservatism kept the church from any of those other answer choices.

4. **D** Pay close attention to the East of the Mediterranean. We see Israel in this map, which means this has to be after 1948.

5. **B** The various treaties signed by the United States and the Soviet Union, such as SALT I and II and the Intermediate Range Nuclear Forces Treaty did signal the success of détente and diplomacy, and they were also a sign that neither nation was in a position to continue unchecked military spending. The most important reason for the resolution of the Cold War was, simply, the economic costs.

   Using POE, remember that, while tension did increase between the Soviet Union and China beginning in the 1950s, this had little impact on the end of the Cold War between the USSR and the United States, so choice (A) is not the correct answer. Choice (C) is out because tensions between North and South Korea remained high, and the resolution of conflict in Vietnam and Cambodia did not play an important role in ending the Cold War. While Choice (D) is a true statement, it is not the correct answer. Numerous nations now have the ability to create nuclear, chemical, and biological weapons, but this issue was not relevant to the Cold War.

6. **A** Hindus and Muslims moved to India and Pakistan, respectively, after the countries were partitioned after World War II. Some estimates say as many as 12.5 million were displaced.

7. **B** Communist China exploded its first atomic bomb in October 1964. Herb Block's menacing, blossoming caricature of leader Mao Zedong suggests that China's emergence as an unbridled nuclear power was, and continues to be, a world-wide concern. The United States was the first to make the bomb (A). China did not become a world power under Mao Zedong (C), and it took until Mao's death for China to begin on its current path of science and technology (D).

8. **C** Japan kept the same government since after the United States ended its occupation after World War II. The Soviet Union was completely dissolved and communism ended (A). Germany was reunified in 1990, and a new government had to be built (B). Nicaragua, no longer under the control of the Sandinistas, forged a new path with President Violeta Chamorro leading the new government (D).

9. **D** Tariffs and trade relations were topics debated since the beginning of civilization, really. Global warming (A), universal human rights (B), and the AIDS epidemic, and health issues in general (D) all became topics for debate among nations after World War II.

10. **B** Though some parts of Americanization—the spread of American culture—definitely changed the experience of those around the world, making the world a *better* place may be a bit of a stretch (A). In many places, Western culture has replaced, or clashes with, religion and local culture. It didn't lead to more cultural tolerance (C) and child labor, which is mostly practiced in Southeast Asia, can't be blamed on the spread of American culture (D).

Drill 6

1. **B** The leaders of the Iranian revolution were Shi'ites, which separates them from the majority of the Arab world, predominantly Sunni. The leaders felt the *shah* wasn't running the country with enough respect shown to Islam (C). Once Ayatollah Khomeini took control, he instituted strict Islamic law, including a requirement for women to veil themselves and rejected Western culture (D). Saddam Hussein of Iraq, hoping to take advantage of the weakness of the nation, attacked in 1980 (A).

2. **C** Post-industrial economies exist where the service sector (where people don't *make* things; they *do* and *think* things) makes more money than the manufacturing sector (B). These economies are characterized by high production of agriculture (A), mining, and industry, but have nothing to do with nuclear sciences (D).

3. **A** "Total" war referred to the total mobilization of a nation's economic, financial, natural, technological, and human resources for the war effort. In Europe, this very much described World War I, even if it didn't rise to this level on American soil during the United States' short involvement in the war. While the other three statements are true, they aren't descriptions of why this was "total" war.

4. **B** When you think Mao, you should think communism, and that's exactly what (B) should sound like. It went terribly—negative economic growth and tens of millions dead, some from starvation and others from the violence associated with enforcing the plan. So cross off (A) and (C). It was also not Mao's first five-year plan but his second, so cross off (D).

5. **B** This is not implying anyone made a mistake, neither Wilson nor Congress, so cross off (A) and (D). While (C) may be a true statement, it's not what this cartoon represents. The best assessment of what's depicted in the cartoon is (B).

6. **A** Advances in warfare in the twentieth century were pretty much all about finding better ways to kill more people while reducing the risk of dying yourself. This didn't necessarily make wars any shorter (Vietnam, for example) so cross off (B). (D) may be true, but it isn't an impact of improved military technology so cross it off. And there was still significant reliance on diplomatic solutions, so (A) is the better bet than (C).

7. **A** Choice (A) is the best description of what NATO and the Warsaw Pact were. Asia didn't enter into the picture, so cross off (B). These organizations didn't engage in proxy wars in Africa, so cross off (C). They were also decidedly military alliances not about spreading nationalist ideologies, so cross off (D).

8. **D** The list of free trade agreements forged in the late twentieth century is quite long, but two prominent examples are NAFTA, the North American Free Trade Agreement signed in 1992 allowing free trade among Mexico, Canada, and the United States, and APTA, the Asia-Pacific Trade Agreement signed in 1975 and reaffirmed in 2005 which allowed free trade among eight South and East Asian nations. While some have opted for increased government influence, that has not characterized the significant bulk of policy decisions in the late 1900s, so cross off (A). (C) is also not a global phenomenon, so cross it off. (B) is more characteristic of the eighteenth and nineteenth centuries, so cross it off, too.

9. **D** Both domestic and international pressure resulted in the United States's willingness to hand over control of the canal to Panama—domestically, protests, particularly by students, called for Panamanian control of the canal at the same time that the international community increasingly believed that the United States was operating by a double standard in blocking French and British reclamation of the Suez Canal in the 1950s but itself insisting on control of the Panama Canal. Asia wasn't a direct factor in the equation, so cross off (B). While concerns over proxy conflicts were significant, that would have been a reason for the United States to maintain control, not give it up, so cross off (C). And despite French and British feelings on the Suez matter, any pressure they exerted on American trading interests was not directly responsible for Carter's decision so cross off (A).

10. **A** Wilson's Fourteen Points—his plan for peace following World War I—was an ambitious plan to foster international cooperation and respect for national sovereignty and territorial integrity. That included protecting Poland, which had been conquered and subdivided many times before. Anything giving one country control over another is against the spirit of Wilson's ideas, so cross off (B) and (C). Wilson also called for European colonial holdings in Africa, where the balance of power had been upset by German conquest during the War, to be readjusted and more fairly distributed, so cross off (D).

Drill 7

1. **C** While the W.H.O. has coordinated nutrition campaigns and monitored reproduction rates, one of its primary goals has always been to wipe out diseases such as smallpox, malaria, and tuberculosis, so cross off (A) and (B) in favor of (C). Also, the U.N. does not pass laws, only resolutions, so cross off (D), even though the W.H.O. is an organization within the United Nations.

2. **D** While an accurate death toll has been hard to calculate for either, scholarly estimates place the death toll from both the Black Death and the 1918 "Spanish" Flu between 50 million and 100 million worldwide. Though it was called the "Spanish" flu, there has been little definitive evidence to pin its origins in Spain—rather the comparatively loose restrictions on the Spanish press during a time marked elsewhere by wartime media censorship meant Spain was the source of most if not all news about the early stages of the pandemic. In the public perception, then, it was the "Spanish" flu—but not in reality, so cross off (C). While there were attempts to develop a vaccine, and researchers even believed they had in 1918, flu is a virus and not something for which a vaccine could be developed at the time, so cross off (B). And unlike most influenza strains, which do primarily affect the very young and very old, the 1918 flu claimed more young adults than victims from any other demographic, so cross off (A).

3. **B** Remember that you're looking for the one that *isn't* true. The United Nations intervened in the Suez Crisis in November 1956 with the very first U.N. peacekeeping force, whose presence in Sinai was mandated by U.N. resolution until both Egypt and Israel agreed to their departure. The United States supported this action. (A), (C), and (D) are all true, occurring in approximately that order.

4. **A** Ho Chi Minh's declaration was based primarily on the U.S. *Declaration of Independence*, which he greatly admired. It's worth realizing the *Declaration of Rights of Man and Citizen* (B) was penned after the *Declaration of Independence* (A), and the former was based on the latter—meaning cross off (B) as you keep (A). The United Nations document was written in 1948, three years after Ho Chi Minh delivered his declaration in Vietnam, so cross off (C). And while the government Ho proposed was a communist government, Marx's *Communist Manifesto* was not the basis of his declaration, so cross off (D).

5. **A** This policy was short-lived, but just after the Batista regime lost power, the United States adopted a wait-and-see policy of friendly relations with a regime they presumed to be "free of Communist taint." Before the year was out, Castro was in power and Eisenhower had approved support for opposition forces, but that was not where things stood in January of that year, so cross off (C). The United States soon thereafter implemented Operation Mongoose, the complete commercial and diplomatic embargo of Cuba, so cross off (B), too. Finally, (D) describes the Platt Amendment, put in place after the Treaty of Paris ended the Spanish-American War in 1898, so cross that off, too.

6. **B** Friedan studied American housewives in the late 1950s and early 1960s (publishing in 1963) and found women unfulfilled in their limited (socially enforced) role as housewives. Her book, which sparked second-wave feminism in the United States was subsequently translated into other languages and resonated with women internationally who faced similar social limitations. It did not, however, focus on discrimination in religious patriarchies, so cross off (C). It was also not about environmental activism or voting, so cross off (A) and (D).

7. **C** Remember that you're looking for the one that *isn't* true. During the late twentieth century, Africa's younger population bloomed, despite bloody civil strife in a number of regions. The weakening of European powers' hold on their African colonies after WWII did indeed facilitate the success of independence movements in a number of countries from the 1950s onward, so cross off (A). Some of those independence leaders, once in power, maintained their stations by military force, stirring ethnic conflict to justify martial control, so cross off (B). Finally, African aid was very much another proxy battle between the United States and U.S.S.R., with each side alternately funding existing leadership or native insurgencies in order to win the balance of power in the continent—so cross off (D).

8. **A** Sun Yat-sen was very interested in western democratic ideas, governing based on his Three Principles of the People: nationalism, democracy, and the people's livelihood. Chiang Kai-shek's nationalism was especially conservative, though he opened himself to some western ideas, carefully cast in Chinese terms, later in his career. He engaged in major purges of suspected Communists, shattering the fragile cooperative equilibrium Sun had established with the Communist Party of China before his death—so cross off (B). Chiang also relied heavily on the military to enforce his will for China, where Sun did not—so cross off (D). Finally, Sun converted to Christianity against his family's wishes as a young man—Chiang, on the other hand, converted to Christianity much later in life to appease his wife's mother, and he subsequently incorporated his Christian values into his New Life Movement, conceived as an antidote to communism. But (C) does not correctly describe either leader, so cross it off.

9. **C** Singapore, for example, negotiated its independence from British rule in 1957, whereas other colonies, such as Vietnam, won it in through armed conflict with the colonial power (in Vietnam's case, France, after World War II).

10. **D** Former colonies maintained ties with their former metropoles enough that migration was both easy and popular. This was true within the former bounds of the British and French Empires especially, but also the Dutch, Spanish, and other empires. While (B) is part of the equation, that alone wasn't enough—the people actually had to move, so cross off (B) in favor of (D). Shifting borders didn't play a major role, so cross off (C), nor did ethnic conflict, so cross off (A), even if these things occasionally factored in.

Drill 8

1. **A** Remember, you're looking for the one that *isn't* true. Transcendentalism was an American philosophy of the early nineteenth century, whereas fascism, communism, and nationalism were used by governments from the Nazis to the Soviets to the Americans in the twentieth century, both during the World Wars and other periods—so cross off (B), (C), and (D).

2. **D** The Great Depression shook the United States and several other western countries out of the laissez-faire approach to business and economics that had allowed business to run unchecked, even into corruption, in the nineteenth and early twentieth centuries. Government took on the responsibility of protecting the people from business. The Second Bantu Migration was an African event, so cross off (C), and the October Revolution was a Russian event that did not involve the United States, so cross off (B). Finally, the Great Awakening was not an economic event, so cross off (A).

3. **B** Lenin's April Theses did not call for the czar's abdication, as he had abdicated the previous year. They did, however, call for an end to Russian involvement in World War I (which came with the Treaty of Brest-Litovsk later that year), land for the peasantry to cultivate, and soviet governance, so cross off (A), (C), and (D).

4. **C** Remember that you're looking for the one that *isn't* true. This is a definition of realpolitik, a political philosophy embraced by Mao Zedong, Otto von Bismarck, and George H. W. Bush that aims to analyze international political power in pragmatic terms, so cross off (A), (B), and (D). Chamberlain, with his philosophy of appeasement, is the odd man out here, and thus our answer.

5. **D** The Amritsar Massacre involved the deaths of Muslims and Hindus alike at the hands of the British, unifying both groups in the push for Indian independence. It was not part of the Armenian genocide, nor anything to do with the Ottoman Empire, so cross off (A) and (B). Cross off (C), as 1919 is too late for anything to do with Caribbean slavery.

6. **A** The Sharpeville Massacre was an episode in which anti-apartheid protesters were cut down by government forces—they were protesting apartheid, so it wasn't what led to apartheid government's establishment. It was, however, what prompted the African National Congress and its supporters to break with its prior Gandhi-styled message of nonviolent resistance and advocate guerilla tactics—so cross off (B) and (C). The U.N. Security Council responded to the massacre with Resolution 134, condemning the South African government's actions, so cross off (D).

7. **B** These images are of reconciliation and reunion. Separation is the wrong idea, so cross off (A), and (D) doesn't really reflect the distance and sadness of the images, so cross that off, too. Cross off (C), as there's no reflection of Asian artistic influences here.

8. **D** Although many of the leaders of Europe were genetically related due to years of formalized marriages, this played very little role in the power struggle during World War I. Much of the world was pulled into World War I due to colonial ties (A), alliances (B), and advancements in technology (C).

9. B   The Triple Alliance negotiated by Otto von Bismarck set the stage for Germany's attachment to Austria-Hungary and the formation of the Central Powers. Germany would not ally with Japan (A) until World War II. Germany did form alliances with Russia (C); however these alliances were not as formal and did not constitute part of the German Triple Alliance.

10. A   The United States was much more sympathetic to Western Europe due to close history and trade with Great Britain and France than Central Europe. It was in part this sentiment that contributed to the United States' entry on the side of the Allies. The sinking of the *Lusitania* (B) in 1915 and other passenger liners and merchant ships (D) angered Americans who had tried to maintain their policy of isolation during the early years. The Zimmerman telegram (C) sent by Germany to convince Mexico to join forces and attack the United States was intercepted and prompted the Americans to enter the war.

Drill 9

1. B   Germany remained after the Treaty of Versailles; however they were forced to make war reparations (A), they lost many of the territories that they had acquired over the last century (C), and they faced years of high inflation and an economic meltdown in the 1920s (D). All of these factors led to the growth of the Nationalist Party (Nazis) in the late 1920s and eventual power of Adolf Hitler.

2. A   The League of Nations was meant to bring all nations together to deal with the world's problems. However, many nations were reluctant to join including the United States (who never joined the organization despite having suggested it). Since the United States never participated, it did not have any decision-making capacity, eliminating (B). It did have monetary support from member nations (C) and did attempt to establish acceptable standards of fairness and conduct (D).

3. A   Mustafa Kemal also known as Ataturk (meaning Father of the Turks) led the overthrow of the Ottoman sultan and formed the modern state of Turkey. In 1923, he became the first president of the nation.

4. C   During the Munich conference, Hitler was given the Sudetenland in exchange for his promise to stop expanding his territory. This appeasement policy failed to prevent further expansion as Hitler ultimately would seize Czechoslovakia (C) and Poland the following year. Hitler had already seized the Rhineland (A) by 1935 at the time of the conference.

5. C   By the time Hitler was planning on conquering Britain, France had already fallen to the axis power. Great Britain was able to fend off the Germans at great cost during the Battle of Britain using radar technology (A) and in later years because of American military and financial support (B). Around the same time, Hitler decided to invade the Soviet Union, which focused a large amount of military resources and money to the Eastern Front (D).

6. **B**   Japan (like Italy) was part of the Allied powers during World War I, but formed an alliance with Germany and Italy during World War II. Germany (A) was part of the axis during both wars. France was part of the allied powers (while free) in both wars (C). Turkey (D) had yet formed by the end of World War I and remained neutral during World War II.

7. **C**   The atomic bombs dropped on Hiroshima and Nagasaki forced the Japanese to accept surrender. By the time of their surrender, Germany had already surrendered (A) and the Japanese knew that they were close to being invaded (B); however these had not deterred them from continuing to fight. Emperor Hirohito (D) did not die in 1945 and would maintain power (albeit as a figurehead) for years later).

8. **D**   Through the Marshall plan, the United States would make billions of dollars available to rebuild Europe following World War II. Although only Western Europe accepted American assistance, it did have a stabilizing role in helping reestablish the Western European economies.

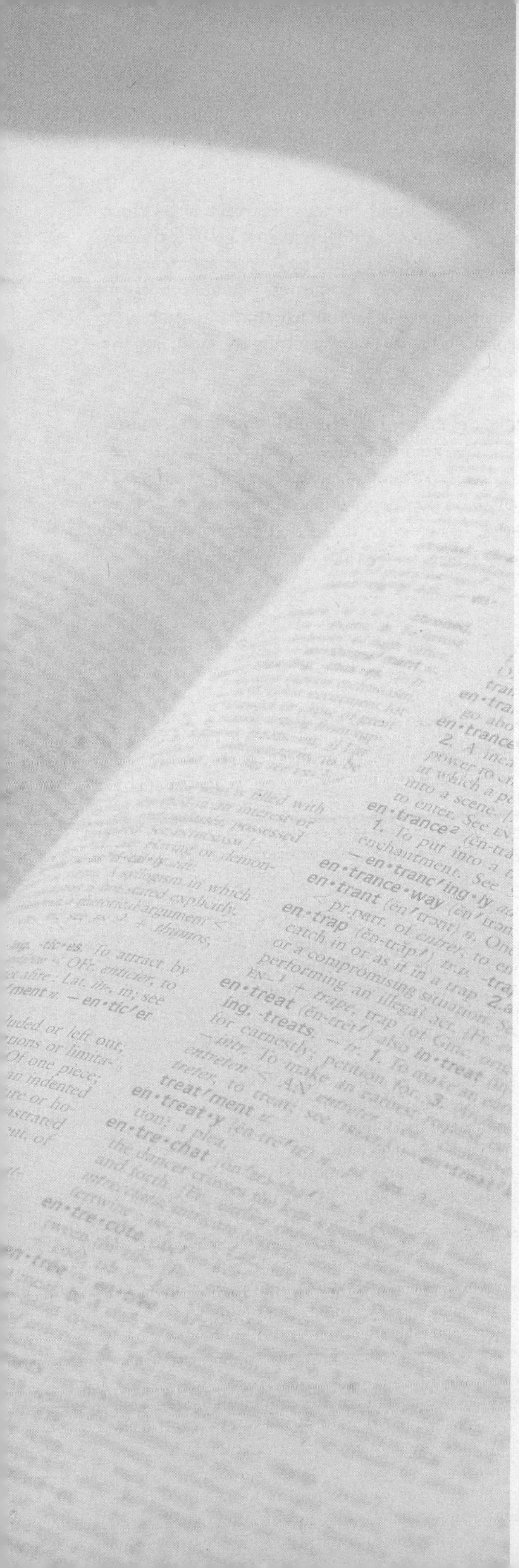

Chapter 15
Essays Drills

ESSAYS

As you know, the essay section of the AP World History Exam includes three types of essays: one document based questions (DBQ), one change-over-time essay, and one comparative essay. In this chapter you will find a wide assortment of practice essay prompts. When you tackle these during your test preparation, try to mimic real testing conditions as best you can—give yourself the same time limit that you'll have on test day, sit in a desk and write out everything by hand, and use the essay tips that we shared in Chapter 2.

In Chapter 16 you'll find an assortment of detailed explanations and scoring rubrics. For the first 14 essay prompts, we have written detailed brainstorms for you. Topics to remember, important historical eras, battles, issues, and people. For the next batch of essay prompts, we have focused on how to get the best score that you can by sharing point-by-point scoring rubrics. Between our detailed content overview and scoring rubrics, you'll be ready to rock when you see these essays on exam day.

Batch 1

1. Compare Islam's effects on Northern Africa and the Indian Subcontinent during the period 600–1450. Be sure to address both similarities and differences.

2. For the period from 1500 to 1860, describe the continuities and changes in trading patterns of North America with Europe OR within the Indian Ocean basin.

3. Analyze the changes and continuities in race relations in South America OR the Caribbean region between the 1750s and the 1950s. Be sure to include evidence from specific countries within that region.

4. Compare ONE of the following sets of conquests, being sure to discuss both similarities and differences: Alexander the Great's conquest of the Eurasian landmass (336–323 B.C.E.) with Genghis Khan's (1206–1227 C.E.) OR Napoleon Bonaparte's conquest of Europe (1803–1815 C.E.) with Adolf Hitler's (1936–1945 C.E.).

5. Discuss how technological innovations since 1750 affected the lives of women in ONE of the following nations. Be sure to include continuities as well as changes.

   Japan
   India
   Brazil
   England

6. Analyze major changes and continuities in the social and political lives of people that came with the adoption of communist government in the twentieth century in ONE of the following countries.

   Vietnam
   Hungary
   Venezuela

7. Within the period from 1580 to 1860, compare the development of the British Empire (e.g., political, social, and economic processes) with that of ONE of the following.

   The Ottoman Empire
   The Mughal Empire

8. Compare the effects of the Columbian Exchange on the North American continent to its effects on ONE of the following from the sixteenth through the nineteenth centuries C.E. Be sure to discuss both similarities and differences.

   Europe
   Africa

9. Compare and contrast the aims and results of the revolutionary process in TWO of the following countries, beginning with the dates specified.

   Haiti   1791
   Italy   1848
   Japan 1866

10. Describe and explain the political, social, and cultural continuities and changes in the Roman Empire in the period 27 B.C.E. to 476 C.E.

11. Discuss the effects of Silk Road trading routes on economic and cultural exchange among the regions connected by these routes from the period 200 B.C.E. to 1450 C.E. Be sure to address both continuities and changes, and cite evidence from specific regions or kingdoms.

12. Compare the development of early Chinese civilization (2500–250 B.C.E.) with the development of civilizations in the area known as the Fertile Crescent (4000–1000 B.C.E.). Be sure to cite evidence from specific societies, addressing both similarities and differences.

13. Compare the status of women in TWO of the following ancient societies (2500 B.C.E. to 600 C.E.), examining similarities and differences in women's status, as well as the cultural forces that affected it.

    China
    India
    Greece
    Rome

14. In the period 500 B.C.E. to 1000 C.E., India's religious landscape experienced many changes. Discuss both the changes and the continuities in Hinduism's relationship with Buddhism and Islam during this time.

Batch 2

1. Analyze similarities and differences in political and economic effects Mongol rule had on TWO of the following regions:

    China
    The Middle East
    Russia
    Europe

2. Analyze the changes and constants in trade on the Indian Ocean between 650 B.C.E. and 1750 C.E.

3. Compare and contrast the philosophies and spread of Islam with the conquest and spread of ONE of the following faiths until 1492 C.E.

    Christianity
    Buddhism

4. Describe and explain continuities and changes in the status of women in ONE of the regions from 600 B.C.E. to 1450 C.E.

    Europe
    Arabia
    India

5. Compare and contrast the philosophical and religious developments in TWO of the following regions from 1450 to 1750.

    Western Europe
    Russia
    China and Japan

6. Compare and contrast the economic and social impacts of trade with the New World from 1450 to 1750 on TWO of the following regions.

    Europe
    Africa
    Asia

7. Analyze the development and impact of the continuities and changes to technology from 1450 to 1914.

8. Describe and explain continuities and changes to governments in TWO of the following regions from 650 C.E. to 1750 C.E.

    Europe
    Asia
    Russia
    Africa

9. Compare and contrast the social and political impacts of the Industrial Revolution on TWO of the following regions.

    Europe
    Asia
    Africa

10. Compare and contrast the philosophies and actions leading from ethnocentrism in Europe from 1750 to 1914.

11. Describe and explain continuities and changes to social class structures before and after the introduction of the industrial work model in the eighteenth century.

12. Analyze the continuities and changes of European Imperialism from 1800 to the present.

13. Compare and contrast the reasons for the rise of extremist governments and their governance policies in the twentieth century in TWO of the following countries.

    Germany
    Italy
    China
    Russia

14. Compare and contrast the reasons and impacts of nuclear weapons development in TWO of the following countries

    The United States
    The USSR
    Israel
    Iran
    North Korea

15. Analyze major continuities and changes to the impact of global institutions and governance from the eighteenth century to the present.

16. Analyze the social and political changes and continuities in ONE of the following countries or regions in the recent past

    The USSR (1917 to present)
    Iran (1979 to present)
    China (1911 to present)
    Africa (1950s to present)

DOCUMENT BASED QUESTION (DBQ)

1. Using the documents below, analyze the roles and perceptions of women in the Chinese and Vietnamese revolutions of the twentieth century. Identify an additional type of document and explain how it would help your analysis of women's roles or images in these nations.

   Historical Background: In the turn of the twentieth century, nationalist movements swept the non-Western world. In Asia in general, and China and Vietnam specifically, a rising tide of Communism gained popularity.

Document 1

Excerpt from: *Nationalism*, by Sir Rabindranath Tagore, 1918.

Source: He Zhen, wife of the anti-Manchu leader Liu Shipei. From *Sources of Chinese Tradition: From 1600 Through the Twentieth Century*, compiled by Wm. Theodore de Bary ahnd Richard Lufrano, 2nd ed., vol. 2 (New York: Columbia University Press, 2000), 389–392. © 2000 Columbia University Press.

…those of us who are women suffer untold bitterness and untold wrongs in order to get hold of this rice bowl. My fellow women: do not hate men! Hate that you do not have food to eat. Why don't you have any food? It is because you don't have any money to buy food. Why don't you have any money? It is because the rich have stolen our property…

There is now a kind of person who says that if women only had a profession, they would not fear starvation. Middle-class families, for example, are sending their daughters to school. … Then if they get married they can become teachers. They won't need to rely on men in order to survive. Likewise, families that are very poor are sending their daughters and daughters-in-law to work in factories. … However, as I see it schools too are owned and operated by certain people, and if you teach in a school, then you are depending on those people in order to eat. Factories too are built by investors, and if you work in a factory, you are depending on its owners in order to eat.

…

I have a good idea that will exempt you from relying on others while still finding food naturally. How? By practicing communism. Think of all the things in the world. They were either produced by nature or by individual labor. Why can rich people buy them but poor people cannot? It is because the world trades with money. … If every single woman understands that nothing is more evil than money, and they all unite together to cooperate with men to utterly overthrown the rich and powerful and then abolish money, then absolutely nothing will be allowed for individuals to own privately.

Document 2

Source: Sharon L. Sievers. "Women in China, Japan, and Korea."

The following quotations are taken from Vietnamese and Chinese revolutionary writings and interviews with women involved in revolutionary movements in each country. They express the women's goals, their struggle to be taken seriously in the uncharacteristic political roles they had assumed, and some of the many ways women found self-respect and redress for their grievances as a result of the changes wrought by the spread of the new social order.

"Women must first of all be masters of themselves. They must strive to become skilled workers ... and, at the same time, they must strictly observe family planning. Another major question is the responsibility of husbands to help their wives look after children and other housework."

"We intellectuals had had little contact with the peasants and when we first walked through the village in our Chinese gowns or skirts the people would just stare at us and talk behind our backs. When the village head beat gongs to call out the women to the meeting we were holding for them, only men and old women came, but no young ones. Later we found out that the landlords and rich peasants had spread slanders among the masses saying 'They are a pack of wild women. Their words are not for young brides to hear'."

"Brave wives and daughters-in-law, untrammelled by the presence of their menfolk, could voice their own bitterness encourage their poor sisters to do likewise, and thus eventually bring to the village-wide gatherings the strength of "half of China" as the more enlightened women, very much in earnest, like to call themselves. By "speaking pains to recall pains," the women found that they had as many if not more grievances than the men, and that given a chance to speak in public, they were as good at it as their fathers and husbands."

"In Chingtsun the work team found a woman whose husband thought her ugly and wanted to divorce her. She was very depressed until she learned that under the Draft Law [of the Communist party] she could have her own share of land. Then she cheered up immediately. "If he divorces me, never mind," she said. "I'll get my share and the children will get theirs. We can live a good life without him.""

Source: Florence Ayscough, *Chinese Women: Yesterday and Today*, 1938.

TRADITIONAL WOMEN

"To be unassuming, to yield; to be respectful, to revere, to think first of other people afterwards of herself, if she performs a kind of action, to make no mention thereof, if she commits a find, to make no denial; to endure reproach, treasure reproof, to behave with veneration and right fear; such demeanor is described as exemplify humility and adaptability....

To lie down to sleep when it is late, to be at work, early, from dawn till dark not to shirk puffing forth strength, to bend the mind to domestic affairs, nor to evade such, be they troublesome or easy, to accomplish that which must be done, to be orderly, to systernatize the way of conduct; such behavior is said to be absorption in diligent too..... .

To be sedate in manner, of upright purpose, to serve her lord her husband; to keep herself pure, composed, not being given to misplaced jest or laughter; free from pollution, reverently to arrange the wine and food to be placed before tablets of progenitors, ancestors, the oblations of dead forefathers....

Nothing equals in importance the imperative duty of obedience! If the mother-in-law say, 'It is not so' and it be so, assuredly, it is right to obey her order. If the mother-in-law say, 'It is so' even if it be not so, nevertheless, act in accordance with the command. Do not think of opposing, or of discussing what is, what is not; do not struggle to divide the crooked from the straight. This is what is called the imperative duty of obedience. The ancient book Nu Hsien-Patterns for Woman-states: "A wife is like the shadow from high sunlight, the echo following sound."

MODERN WOMEN

'... You'd better think it over and choose some other job. Driving tractors is no work for a slip of a girl like you.'

The man in charge of registration for the tractor-drivers' training class had clearly made up his mind that I was unsuitable. I felt angry because it seemed unjust that he should try and turn me down without even a trial.

'Let me take the entrance examination anyway,' I said. 'If I fail, I shall have nothing more to say.'

I passed the examination. In the six years that followed I achieved my ambition of becoming a tractor driver, worked for a while as instructor to a women's tractor-drivers team, and became the vice-director of the Shuangchiao State Farm near Peking. That is still my work today."

Document 4

Source: *Ling long* women's magazine, published in Shanghai from 1931 to 1937.

Caption: "From these few pictures you can see female sentiment. There is absolutely no way men can express this. These so-called good friends are inseparable. The unfortunate thing is that after marriage they suddenly become cold and indifferent."

Document 5

Source: Nguyen Quang Thieu, "The Examples," in *The Women Carry the River Water: Poems*, 1997.

My village widows—the examples—without shoes or sandals, they avoid roads that lead them to moonlight. Their breasts are tired and almost deaf, and could not hear love calling from the village men. And only the house mice eating rice in the casket can wake them. And they lie still, fearing their wooden coffin will be eaten hollow by termites.

And when I have nobody to count, my village widows come back from the grass. They walk moonlit lanes. Their hair spills over moonlight. Their breasts reach for the sexual fire just kindled. After footsteps, after doors opening, I hear the strange song. The song penetrates the skulls of lunatics who cannot sleep, and who stand looking up at the moon.

And the lunatics open the doors and go out. They go with the song—further and further, to the place where there are no examples.

Document 6

Source: Phan Boi Chau, Vietnamese nationalism leader, "The New **Vietnam**," 1907

With regard to education, that of the military and women is the most important…

Women will become good mothers, loving wives, knowledgeable in literature and poetry, well trained in commerce; they are also expert educators of our children and efficient assistants to our soldiers. A good mother will have nice children; she will be a virtuous wife to a perfect husband. Moreover in politics women will possess many rights. Only with education will one know how to neglect one's private interests in order to take care of the public good, so as to make one's country accumulate its riches and increase its strength. A country that has no patriotic women is bound to be subjugated by another country… In all matters related to finance, in industrial schools… in trading outlets, in banks… it is best to employ well-educated women. They will strive to serve the country as much as men. Their pride and dignity will be equal to men's… Every woman in the country should of course endeavor to become a good mother, a virtuous wife, but also a talented woman… Women shall not be inferior to men. That's the aim of women's education.

Document 7

Source: Communist political pamphlet, 1930

Oh, unhappy patriots, let us struggle alongside our men. Let us destroy the French capitalists, the mandarins, in order to establish a social government that will give us freedom, equality, and happiness… Let us work and act energetically in order to achieve the Revolution, to obtain equality, between men and women.

Document 8

Source: Statement by Le Duan, Vietnamese communist party politicial, speech at the Vietnamese Women's Fourth Congress, 1974.

The Viet Nam Fatherland owes its heroic sons and daughters to the contributions of heroic, undaunted, faithful and responsible mothers. For many centuries, the Vietnamese mothers have handed down to us the mettle of the Trung Sisters and Lady Trieu, the tradition of industrious labour and love of country and of home. We can rightly be proud of our Vietnamese mothers.

Chapter 16
Essays
Answers
and Explanations

EXPLANATIONS

Batch 1

1. Compare Islam's effects on Northern Africa and the Indian Subcontinent during the period 600–1450. Be sure to address both similarities and differences.

This question asks you to **compare and contrast** Islam's effects on Northern Africa and India between 600 and 1450. You should immediately recognize the two dates, as they are also the parameters of the second periodization in AP World History—the foundation of Islam in Arabia around 600 C.E. and the conquest of Constantinople in 1453. Luckily, if you did not know those dates, the regions listed in the question specifically involve neither instance, but an excellent essay would include the birth of Islam and how it spread out from Arabia as a starting point.

In fact, a great way to go about tackling Compare and Contrast essays is to come up with several big concept fields in which the two things you're comparing had an overall similar situation (for example, that Islam certainly spread to both North Africa and India), but had different ways of happening, outcomes, or effects (the former by conquest, the latter more by diffusion through trade routes than outright conquest). Here are some suggestions for key points regarding this essay.

- Military Conquest and Political Control: The founding of Islam had an immediate unifying effect on the Arab tribes in the Arabian Peninsula whose energies were now turned outwards against Sassanid Persia, which they completely overran by around 650, and the Byzantine Empire, whose southern provinces (the Levant, Egypt) were overrun by around 640. Successive campaigns conquered the remnants of Byzantine North Africa by around 700. All these campaigns were conducted under the rule of the Umayyad Caliphs, so these wayward western territories were directly under the control of the Umayyad Caliph in Damascus and the Abbasid Caliph in Baghdad, and would be until the Caliphate was delivered a crushing blow by the Mongols in 1258. India, on the other hand, was not directly conquered by the armies of the Caliph. Parties raiding southwards from Afghanistan occupied Indian territories in the north, but set up their own Sultanates, and by 1450, most of India was a patchwork of Muslim sultanates, all independent from the control of the Caliph.

- Social - Conversion: It would be very difficult to mention many specifics about the social fabrics in these individual regions that would be different from Islamic civilization as a whole, so avoid that. Instead, emphasize the differences inherent in conversion patterns on account of how these places came into the House of Islam. North Africa was conquered by Muslim armies, and while the territory was allowed to practice Christianity as a fellow faith of the book, the Christian inhabitants were charged a poll tax to practice that belief. As such the population gradually converted to Islam, and by the period of the Crusades, the vast majority of the population of North Africa was Muslim. On the other hand, India did not convert so completely since the primary vehicle of Islam's spread was trade and merchants. Certainly the conquest of northern India impelled people there to convert, but southern India, conquered later and not completely, had its fair share of converts. Overall the population of India was a patchwork of Hindus and Muslims, with more Hindus than Muslims, and certainly not as complete a conversion as North Africa was. A great essay would also include that on account of this, even in Muslim-controlled areas, the Hindu caste system still was practiced by the Hindu community, whereas local cultural traditions in North Africa were subsumed and integrated into Islamic practices there.

- Economics - Trade: A good essay would illustrate in the case of trade and economics how Islam's penetration into India was conducted mainly by trade, and that by 1450, the Indian Ocean was nothing more than a Muslim lake, dominated by Arab and other Muslim merchants sailing all across the vast expanse. On the other hand, the Muslim conquest of North Africa did not necessarily change the course of trade routes so much as ensure Muslim participation on key trade centers on said routes. North Africa, as a part of the old Roman Mediterranean trade networks, maintained trade connections with Spain and Western Europe until the rise of Manorialism in Europe cut off long-distance trade networks that had been in place for centuries. Despite this, North Africa still connected to Spain, which was also controlled by the Umayyad Caliphs, and Spain was a central stopping point for Viking traders in the seventh to tenth centuries. By the time of the Crusades, however, the Italian mercantile city-states of Genoa and Venice had supplanted Muslim merchants on the Mediterranean and had begun to re-establish trade links long broken.

2. For the period from 1500 to 1860, describe the continuities and changes in trading patterns of North America with Europe OR within the Indian Ocean basin.

This essay asks you to discuss the **changes and continuities over time** in either North America's trading patterns with Europe **or** the trading patterns within the Indian Ocean between 1500 and 1860 C.E. Please be careful to do only one of these! Any extra work you might do on the AP Exam's essays will not be graded!

Let's start with the first option: North America's trading patterns with Europe. Remember that as this is a Change and Continuity over Time essay, it can be quite easy to approach this prompt by stating how the regions were at the beginning of the prompt's periodization, certain major events or developments that caused them to change, and then how the regions ended up at the end of the periodization. So a good essay would emphasize how unconnected the two continents were in 1500. While Europe had strengthening trade links with the rest of the Old World, and the Aztecs had developed an extensive trade system in Mexico, the two land masses simply were not connected, though Columbus's voyages of discovery had resulted in Spanish colonies dotting several islands in the Caribbean.

There are a myriad of possibilities for causes of great changes and events that brought such changes about, so we can't list them all in this book, but a good essay would certainly hit upon the European settlement or conquest of Native American peoples by guns, germs, and steel, in the New World. Cortez's conquest of the Aztecs in 1521 opened the whole of Mexico to Spanish occupation and exploitation, while French settlement in Canada and English settlement along the Eastern Seaboard of the continent guaranteed those regions were linked to international trade routes. In an essay about trade systems, a good essay would also include some mention of the kinds of goods transported at this early stage—raw materials, gold, silver, and New World crops such as maize, potatoes, tomatoes, tobacco, and sugar were shipped from North America to Europe, which instead sent immigrants, Old World crops and pack animals, and diseases back to North America. Good essays would also mention the wars between European powers over the possession of North America, and how, in these wars, the British would outmuscle the French and Spanish to be the hegemon of North America. Finally, a good essay would also mention the impact of Enlightenment thought and how this inspired Mexico and the United States to revolt from Spain and Great Britain, and their mercantilist trade practices, respectively, though Canada remained a loyal British colony.

By 1860, industrialization would go into full force in at least the United States, but the trade relationships between Europe and North America were certainly changing before that. With Mexico and the United States independent of their former colonial possessors, mercantilism gave way to free trade, especially as the United States promulgated the Monroe Doctrine in an attempt to protect the newly independent New World nations from being reconquered by European powers. The growing industrial juggernaut of the United States started to compete with countries like Great Britain, who for centuries prior had enjoyed a monopoly on exporting manufactured goods to North America. The native populations who had for so long resided on their ancestral lands had largely been eradicated or assimilated into the new order, but on the Great Plains and the vast western expanses of North America, native Americans still reigned supreme, not yet subdued by Mexico, Great Britain, or the United States.

Now let's consider the other option, the Indian Ocean trading system. In 1500, the Portuguese had just begun their penetration into the area, which up till this point was completely dominated by Arab and other Muslim merchants. Spices, silks, and other fine goods made their way from Indonesia and India across the Indian Ocean, as merchant ships sailed according to the monsoon seasons. Slaves, ivory, and other goods from the East African coast were brought north, and all these goods were imported into the Middle East. From there, these products eventually departed to make their way towards their eventual buyers further west.

Some major events and developments that good essays would discuss include the following:

- The Age of Discovery, and Portugal's adventures in India: After Bartolomeu Dias rounded the Cape of Good Hope in 1488, Portuguese fleets sailed into the Indian Ocean in earnest. Portugal's victories at the Battle of Calicut and Diu led to establishments of trading posts on the coasts of India, and inspired other European nations to establish their own.
- The development of joint stock companies: When wise merchants realized how it would be less risky to pool their money into companies (sharing the costs, but sharing the presumably greater profits) instead of bearing the full costs of trading alone, East India Companies popped up all around Europe, the famous ones being the British and Dutch East India companies. These companies acted like countries within countries, attacking each other as well as native Indian kingdoms to further expand their holdings. Compare this to the centralized attempts of the Portuguese and even Mughal Empires and their less successful attempts to control the riches of India.
- The Scientific Revolution: While the Scientific Revolution may have started and occurred principally in Europe, there is no doubt that technological innovations made were quickly implemented by the East India Companies. The result was that these companies were often better equipped with more powerful, advanced weapons, rather than Indian kingdoms, making the native Indians easy pickings for more modern European-style armies. Even the mighty Mughal Empire was completely destroyed by the British East India Company.

The end result of all these developments was that by 1860 the Indian Ocean had become a British lake. The British East India Company's domination, and mismanagement, of India meant that the subcontinent was annexed directly into the British Empire as the "Crown Jewel" of British holdings. British and Dutch merchant ships, and certainly not the Muslim merchants from centuries prior, sailed the trade routes of the ocean. Since the British, no single power has since conquered the entire subcontinent. Though, while the British and European powers may have gained control of the Indian Ocean basin, their control was not through colonization or assimilation as it was in the New World. Rather, Europeans were just another group of invading minorities that Indian cultures were all too familiar with throughout their history.

3. Analyze the changes and continuities in race relations in South America OR the Caribbean region between the 1750s and the 1950s. Be sure to include evidence from specific countries within that region.

This essay asks you to analyze the **continuities and changes over time** in race relations in either the Caribbean or in South America between the 1750s and 1950s by using specific examples of countries in the regions. Good essays will address the varieties of people who lived in these Latin American regions: Creoles, descendants of original white European settlers; Mestizos, descendants of whites and Native Americans; and Mulattos, descendants of whites and Africans.

Let's start with the Caribbean. If you choose this prompt, your initial instincts should strongly indicate you should write about Haiti. Another good country to choose in the region would be Cuba. The Caribbean, on account of all of its sugar wealth, was an area especially populated with African slaves. Consequently racial tensions simmered in both Cuba and Haiti where the Creole minorities were quite afraid of the massive slave populations they managed, lest these slaves revolt. When the slaves of Haiti revolted from France, whatever independence movements that might have occurred through the cooperation of Creoles and slaves stopped entirely. The newly freed Haitians sacked plantations and ran out their former oppressors creating a society of former slaves and equals, though this society quickly degenerated into despotic periods in which despots ruled the country with an iron fist. Meanwhile slavery continued on Cuba until the late 1880s, by which point racial tensions were simmering to such an extent that Cuban patriots fought a revolution against Spain. When the United States fought the Spanish American War and freed Cuba from Spain, a limited democracy resulted, and this era was often punctuated by strong men using existing racial and economic inequalities to continue their rule.

Let's turn to South America now. If you choose this prompt, you should mention Brazil, as it too was an important destination for African slaves imported to the New World. In fact, African descendants accounted for over 30% of Brazil's population by 2000. Brazil's important sugar plantations guaranteed that slavery would remain as a critical source of labor for the Brazilian economy. When Brazil became independent from Portugal, the country remained a monarchy supported by European descended plantation owners. Race politics continued to remain an important institution of Brazilian politics, until slavery was finally abolished, along with the monarchy, in 1888. When slavery was abolished, the former slaves became second-class citizens, though hugely important contributors to Brazil's culture. Brazil's inequalities would continue unabated since continued racism on the part of conservative elements of society encouraged European migration to the country at the expense of other races and economic inequalities maintained the status quo. Compare Brazil to Argentina. Argentina revolted successfully from Spain with its creole elite, but Spanish assimilation and intermingling with native populations allowed for a more heterogeneous, but still biased, political situation which favored the creole elites. While slavery and other harsh policies like those in Brazil were not as widespread in Argentina, a pro-European bias still existed with Native populations and African descendants largely discriminated against. A large wave of European immigration in the late 1800s also contributed new populations into the country, further exacerbating a complex social issue. Nevertheless, even though mestizos were integral to the operation of the country, their disadvantaged socio-economic situation guaranteed the supremacy of the creoles in the country.

4. Compare ONE of the following sets of conquests, being sure to discuss both similarities and differences: Alexander the Great's conquest of the Eurasian landmass (336–323 B.C.E.) with Genghis Khan's (1206–1227 C.E.) OR Napoleon Bonaparte's conquest of Europe (1803–1815 C.E.) with Adolf Hitler's (1936–1945 C.E.).

This essay asks you to **compare and contrast** the campaigns of either Alexander the Great and Genghis Khan, or Napoleon Bonaparte and Adolf Hitler. There is certainly a lot of history to be covered in this essay, so please take care to make comparisons between the campaigns rather than write narratives—big ideas and comparisons are exactly what AP World History is all about!

Several bases of comparison you could discuss in your essays would include the following:

- Regions of the world affected and nations involved—Alexander was king of Macedonia, and he managed to conquer Greece, Egypt, Persia, Afghanistan, and the Indus River Valley; Genghis Khan managed to unify the disparate Mongolian tribes and then conquer Northern China, Central Asia, and Siberia; Napoleon became the emperor of Revolutionary France and then managed to subdue the whole of Europe up to Russia by force of arms or by alliances, though he was reversed by defeats against the United Kingdom and Russia; Adolf Hitler too managed to secure a great deal of territory for Germany by treaties with other European powers, and then managed to conquer almost all of continental Europe before being reversed by the Soviet Union, the United Kingdom, and the United States
- Results of campaign—Alexander's campaigns ended with his troops mutinying at the Indus River, and when he passed away in Babylonia on his way back home to Macedon, his empire was divided by his generals, never to be unified again; Genghis Khan's campaigns ended when he passed away, though unlike Alexander's empire, Genghis's empire stayed whole for at least two more generations before it too split apart; Napoleon's empire was brought down first by his disastrous defeat in Russia which allowed the other members of the Coalition against him, like the United Kingdom, to help land the final blows at the Battle of Waterloo in 1815, though France itself would remain an independent country; Adolf Hitler's Reich too was brought down following its failed invasion of Russia, when the Allied powers of the United States, United Kingdom, and the Soviet Union all invaded his empire from all sides and completely destroyed Germany, splitting the remains amongst themselves.

Good essays would also emphasize nuances between the campaigns that focus on knowledge of the civilizations that undertook them. For instance, Genghis Khan's empire was won by hardy Mongolian horse archers, whereas Alexander's was won by pike wielding infantry in the deadly Phalanx formation. Adolf Hitler's armies largely employed Blitzkrieg (lightning war) tactics against their foes, while Napoleon's armies too were renowned for their speed in getting to battlefields before their adversaries. While both Alexander and Genghis personally commanded most if not all the parts in their campaigns, Napoleon did so as much as he could though often had to delegate to generals to command in other theaters of battle, and Adolf Hitler was involved in planning campaigns but always delegated commands to generals as he himself was not a career soldier, only serving as a volunteer in World War I. Finally, essays could focus on the motivations for the campaigns, with Alexander's being motivated by his desire to conquer the Persian Empire, Genghis's to seek plunder in order to keep his Mongols united, Napoleon's to spread and secure the ideals of the French Revolution, and Adolf Hitler's to seek more resources and living space from undesirables and "less worthy peoples" than Germans.

5. Discuss how technological innovations since 1750 affected the lives of women in ONE of the following nations. Be sure to include continuities as well as changes.

Japan
India
Brazil
England

This essay asks you to discuss the **continuities and changes over time** of the status of women from 1750 to the present in only one of four nations. A good essay will recognize that the date 1750 corresponds roughly to the beginning of the Industrial Revolution in the United Kingdom, so this essay's prompt could more directly be stated as, "Explain the impact of industrialization on the role of women." Therefore the essays should follow the usual paradigm of women's roles with industrialization and insert country-specifics when the situation calls for them. The paradigm is essentially that while a nation is an agrarian society, women were hardly needed in the wage-paying workforce, so women were tenders of the home and children and related chores. However, when the society undergoes industrialization, women have an opportunity to work in these factories (and were often especially chosen) and thus joined the workforce alongside men. The more important women become in these roles (such as in the case of World War I, when Women worked in the factories principally while men were drafted to fight in the war and earned the right to vote after the war ended), the more politically and potentially socially equal they become.

Japan: Japan was a patriarchal society under the Tokugawa Shogunate, with many legal protections, such as the right to an inheritance, not existing for them. All this changed when the Meiji Restoration overthrew the Tokugawa Shogun and put in his place the Emperor Meiji and his court of modernizers. Industrialization and urbanization quickly opened up opportunities for poor women to move out from the countryside and seek employment in the new factories. Nonetheless, the Meiji Civil Code of 1898 did not permit women any legal rights and put them at the mercy of their household head. The demands of World War II forced Japanese women to work in the factories only very late in the war, but Japan's defeat and occupation by the United States allowed the United States to modify Japan's social fabric itself. The new Japanese constitution allowed for women to have legal rights as men did, such as the right to vote and the right to inherit. Women were able to be educated, and often were. As economic growth returned to Japan, so too did the demand for labor, and Japanese women leapt at the chance. But the Japanese culture interestingly remained patriarchal, as Japanese women, when married, usually stayed home to raise their children than remain in the workforce. There is a growing trend for women to focus on their careers, a development that is compounded with a decline in the Japanese population growth rate.

India: India's strong Hindu and Muslim traditions and agrarian culture meant that women had few rights in 1750s India. The British domination of the continent, however, changed that. Importing Western concepts of social equality as well as Western standards of decency, the British outlawed "barbaric" practices like Sati, in which women would immolate themselves on the pyre of their dead husbands. British missionaries also worked to spread Christianity in India and established schools and other social programs for women. These educated women worked along with their fellow men to pine for Indian independence. When the Indians achieved independence from the United Kingdom in 1947, women participated in all rungs of society, with Indira Gandhi (not related to the famous Mohandas Gandhi commonly known as Mahatma Gandhi) becoming Prime Minister of the country and serving as Prime Minister for fifteen years. The Indian constitution grants legal and social equality to women in the country, but despite all this, women are still threatened by a rape culture and violence. Even though the Indian Parliament is obligated to be staffed with 1/3 of its members as women, and despite the economic growth India has undergone in past decades, there is much more that can be done for women.

Brazil: Brazil started out in 1750 as a colony of Portugal, but while the country achieved independence in 1822, industrialization did not truly take place in the country until recent decades. As such, Brazil largely remained an agricultural society until after World War II. But with the advent of industrialization and with true democracy restored to the country from military juntas by 1988, women have gained a variety of rights, such as equality under the law. Education for all women expanded dramatically as prosperity came to Brazil, and along with education came political participation. Even the current president of Brazil, Dilma Rousseff, is a woman. Nevertheless, despite accounting for more than half of the electorate, women account for a minority in government.

England: English women largely follow the paradigm above as England was the birthplace of the Industrial Revolution. Women were very attractive as factory workers in the outset of the Industrial Revolution because they would often work for less pay than male equivalents. As prosperity came to Britain, women were largely siphoned off from the workforce. Campaigns for women's suffrage and other policies of social equality started around the turn of the century, but were often disregarded. The First World War and its demands necessitated that women be involved in the Home Front. Their reward for their hard work was the right to vote, started in 1918, but expanded to all adult women by 1928. World War II imposed the same demands on women as did World War I, but following World War II, Women maintained their jobs in the factories and gained greater and greater acceptance. Today, women in the UK are more or less considered social equals to their male counterparts.

6. Analyze major changes and continuities in the social and political lives of people that came with the adoption of communist government in the twentieth century in ONE of the following countries.

    Hungary
    Vietnam
    Venezuela

This essay asks you to discuss the **continuities and changes over time** regarding the effects on the social and political lives of people by communist governments in Hungary, Vietnam, or Venezuela in the twentieth century. Good essays would thusly give an account of the rise of the communist government in the country the student has chosen, explain what the communist government has done to the social and political fabric of the country, and then explain what the outcome of the communist government was or is.

- Hungary: The Soviet Union imposed a communist government onto Hungary like the other Eastern European nations it overran following Germany's defeat in World War II. This government replaced an Axis-friendly Fascist government, so one totalitarian system replaced another. Despite being at peace with Russia by 1947, the Soviets had soldiers still within Hungarian territory, and dictated what Hungary should do from this position of strength. The country joined the Warsaw Pact as soon as the alliance structure was established, guaranteeing that it would be a satellite of Soviet interests in Eastern Europe. However, public support for the communist system quickly faded, and the Hungarian people rose up against the communist government in 1956, and the revolt was just as quickly crushed by Soviet troops. While Communist social policies brought central planning and economic benefits to the dispossessed, the single-party system communism brought effectively disenfranchised the citizenry. As a result, so long as the government was propped up by Soviet troops, Hungary would remain communist, but with the withdrawal of Soviet forces by Gorbachev in 1989 the communist government quickly collapsed and a multi-party democracy took hold.

- Vietnam: When partisans led by Ho Chi Minh finally secured Vietnamese independence from the French, the new country was divided between a Communist north and a pro-Western South. These Communists immediately implemented a social program of purging the intelligentsia, Catholics, large-scale landowners, and anyone else who was considered to be an enemy of the revolution. Politically the communists implemented a single-party system guaranteeing their control of the country for the foreseeable future. However, the government of Vietnam, which used to enjoy somewhat warm relations with China, grew distant as China moved into the orbit of the United States and especially became envious as China enacted capitalist reforms. In recent days, though the communists still retain control of Vietnam, they too have enacted very similar capitalist reforms, rewinding the social and economic policies of their revolutionary forebears, but not their political ones.
- Venezuela: Unlike the other two countries in the list, Venezuela actually did not fall under the sway of a communist government by means of force of arms. Instead, the Venezuelan people elected Hugo Chavez and his socialist party to lead the country. Ironically, the very same Hugo Chavez had attempted earlier to overthrow the standing government through a coup but the coup was unsuccessful. Nevertheless, once he was elected, Chavez utilized the immense oil wealth that Venezuela possessed, enacting nationalizing policies to gain greater control of that wealth and distribute it to the people in the form of subsidies and other relief. By promising and providing the people with all sorts of government gifts, Chavez rallied his formerly disaffected people behind him, though irking some of the more conservative elements of the population. However, to perpetuate his brand of the revolution, Chavez sought, successfully, amendments to the Venezuelan constitution granting him longer terms in power and an eventual end to term limits. His passing in 2013 forced power to fall to a fellow member of the party, confirming at least a sense of single-party rule over the country to this day, perhaps rendering the people as disaffected as they were prior to Chavez's presidency.

7. Within the period from 1580 to 1860, compare the development of the British Empire (e.g., political, social, and economic processes) with that of ONE of the following.

    The Ottoman Empire
    The Mughal Empire

This essay asks you to **compare and contrast** the development of the British Empire to either the Mughal Empire or the Ottoman Empire between the years 1580 and 1860. An astute student would recognize the significance of these dates—the Spanish Armada was defeated by the English in the 1580s and the whole of India, including the Mughal Empire, was absorbed directly by the British by the 1860s. Remember that AP World History craves big picture ideas and concepts, so organize your essay around those. A good essay would mention the following points:

- Territorial Expansion: While the British Empire was a colonial and mercantile empire expanding in the New World and in India, both the Mughal and Ottoman Empires were land-based Islamic Gunpowder Empires that conquered contiguous and often non-Muslim enemies. As such, the British Empire was certainly more in a position to take advantage of shifting trade routes as discoveries of direct sea routes to Asia and the New World reduced the importance of the Silk Road and terrestrial trade links between East and West.
- Economic Policies: The British certainly practiced mercantilist policies with their colonies and granted monopolies to the large state-subsidized companies like the East India Company, but neither the Ottomans nor the Mughals, themselves extremely mercantilist, established similar companies or even sent merchants abroad like the British did. Indeed, both the Ottomans and Mughals contented themselves with allowing foreigners to come to them (and sign treaties) in order to conduct business.

- Technological Developments: While the Ottomans and the Mughals are two of the so-called Muslim Gunpowder Empires, named after the fact that these states used cannon and musket frequently in their armies, these powers' innovation never seemed to catch up to the kinds of developments going on in Europe, developments that the British often seemed to be at the leading edge in. It is telling that both the Mughals and Ottomans imported European experts in order to domestically produce the very muskets and cannons their armies relied upon. As the Enlightenment Age caught on in Europe, both the Mughals and Ottomans were hopelessly behind in terms of technology, and the disparity would only become worse as time went on.
- Governments/Religious Policies: While the British Empire by 1580 was just starting its transition to a Constitutional Monarchy, with Parliament taking the leading role in the government of the state, both the Ottoman and Mughal Empires were absolute monarchies. The Religious policies of the governments therefore differed dramatically, with the British embarking on a Protestant path in the outset of Elizabeth's reign in the 1560s and mandating that Protestantism be the state religion so long as Parliament was in charge. The Ottomans and Mughals, ruling as diverse empires as the peoples they conquered, were officially Sunni Muslims and allowed Islam to dictate their policies. However, as time passed and these empires became more entrenched, conservative elements of society seemed to be more prominent with the effect that the successful policies of tolerance promulgated by men such as Akbar the Great or Mehmed II were undone and ignored by their successors with disastrous results.

Ultimately, by 1860, the British Empire, through a variety of reasons, had more or less been entrenched as the world's superpower with a powerful fleet and a vast colonial empire which at that point included even the mighty Mughal Empire. While the Mughals had been entirely absorbed into the British colony of India, the Ottoman Empire still limped on, badly bloodied by successive defeats from European powers and internal rebellions. It was no longer the powerful state it had been centuries prior.

8. Compare the effects of the Columbian Exchange on the North American continent to its effects on ONE of the following from the sixteenth through the nineteenth centuries C.E. Be sure to discuss both similarities and differences.

   Europe
   Africa

This essay asks you to **compare and contrast** the effects of the Columbian Exchange between the 1500s and 1800s on North America and one of either Europe or Africa. Remember that the Columbian Exchange is a particularly beloved subject to AP World History Exam writers because it focuses exactly on the kind of big picture developments the subject is primarily about. Consequently, expect to see at least one question about the Columbian Exchange (whether it is in essay or multiple-choice form) on your exam. Since the AP Exam graders like big ideas, it would be easier for you to organize your essay along the same lines.

A good essay would discuss topics like the following:

- New contacts and new trade routes: While North America was completely separate from Old World trading systems in 1500, that changed drastically once exploration and colonization went in full swing. New World crops like maize, sugar, and tobacco were exported to Europe and Africa, and received livestock like cows and horses, and diseases like smallpox from the Old World in turn. Europe and Africa also exported population to the New World, willingly or otherwise. Immense amounts of gold and silver were plundered from Mexico following the conquest of the Aztecs and mined from the ground wherever they could be found, and then shipped back to Europe, or used to purchase goods from Africa.

- Population effects: The obvious impact of the importation of Old World diseases on North America was that native populations were almost wiped out through their lack of resistance. The population of North America plummeted, despite all the replacements that Europe and Africa were sending to the continent. By 1800 the continent's population had just managed to recover to its zenith in the 1500s. On the other hand, Europe's population only continued to grow as starvation and other nutrition-based maladies were overcome with new crops brought in from North America. Africa's population growth, on the other hand, was certainly aided by the introduction of North American crops, but the carrying off of so many Africans surely stymied growth rates so much so that the continent may have stagnated between 1500 and 1800.
- Political developments: The colonization of North America largely by Spain, France, and England more or less had carved up the whole continent by 1776. While there certainly still were some independent Native American polities in the deep interior of the continent, the rest of the continent had been divided among the major colonial powers. Following the American and French Revolutions, the remainder of these colonies, save Canada, successfully declared their independence and became independent Western-style states. Africa's tribal kingdoms that had engaged in trade with European merchants grew stronger and consolidated their power, though were certainly not as powerful as the European nation-states that had congealed largely by the 1800s.
- Technological disparity: Though an indirect result of the Columbian Exchange, the great engine of the Industrial Revolution was certainly made possible only by the massive population growth rates achieved by the Columbian Exchange. While North America, as an extension of Europe on a different continent, largely had access to European technologies, only the United States industrialized at a fever pace in the middle part of the 1800s. Africa did not industrialize at all.

Remember to summarize the main points of your essay in a conclusion paragraph, restating the end results of the effects of the Columbian Exchange on North America and whatever region you chose to write about.

9. Compare and contrast the aims and results of the revolutionary process in TWO of the following countries, beginning with the dates specified.

    Haiti   1791
    Italy   1848
    Japan 1866

This essay asks you to **compare and contrast** two of the following three revolutions:

    Haiti—1791: The Haitian Revolution
    Italy—1848: Italy's first nationalist movement (the beginning of the Risorgimento)
    Japan—1866: The Meiji Restoration

It is incredibly important that you know exactly what revolution is being asked about in each of these cases. An essay that discusses a revolution which did indeed occur but is not the correct revolution cannot receive full credit, no matter how good it might be! Since all these revolutions are very different, let's treat them in separate paragraphs below.

- Haiti: The Haitian Revolution was a large-scale slave revolt on the island of Santo Domingo. Inspired by the American and French Revolutions and the Enlightenment ideals that followed those revolutions, the slaves of Haiti revolted against their plantation owners, laying waste to the most profitable colony in the New World. Attempts by the British and Spanish and even Napoleon's armies to put down these slaves, who were led by the charismatic and ingenious Toussaint

L'Overture, were solidly defeated. While Toussaint died, his revolutionary spirit continued to inspire his followers who successfully declared Haiti's independence from France in 1803 to make Haiti the first and only successful New World Slave Rebellion in history. Unfortunately for Haiti, however, fear of the spread of anti-slavery sentiment led the United States and other New World states and colonial powers to suspend trade with the newly independent nation, rendering it completely helpless and impoverished within a few years of achieving independence.

- Italy: The Risorgimento, or Resurgence, was the process by which the disparate Italian states eventually unified under the guidance of the Kingdom of Sardinia-Piedmont. Inspired by the nationalistic fervor Napoleon and his armies carried with them across Europe, suffering under the squalid conditions of urbanization and industrialization, and chafing under the boots of their Austrian occupiers, Italy was a powder keg waiting for the right minute to explode. The right minute came in 1848 when a wave of nationalist and republican revolts exploded across continental Europe. Austria itself was struck particularly badly as the Austrian Empire was vast and composed of many different nationalities. Seeing their chance, many Italian states revolted from Austria and attempted to establish a new Italian republic. However, as this republic was a grave threat to the established conservative order that had guaranteed decades of peace in Europe, the monarchies of Europe all joined forces to squash each of these nationalist movements. Austria herself managed to summon the strength to put down these revolts and the nationalist revolution of 1848 would have to wait another ten years before Italy would be free.

- Japan: The Meiji Restoration was a revolution on the part of the daimyos of Japan to restore authority to the Emperor, whose position was more or less that of a figurehead for centuries, from the Shogun. These Daimyos were inspired to take such a drastic step on account of the grave threat that Western countries posed to Japan, as well as outrage over the "unequal" treaties that the Tokugawa Shogunate had signed with these Western powers giving them great trading and legal concessions in exchange for technological aid and foreign experts. With the slogan "Revere the emperor, expel the barbarian!" as their watchword, these daimyos sought to raise Japan to parity with the West much faster than the Tokugawa were doing so as to preserve Japan's independence. The Tokugawa were quickly defeated and deposed, and Japan modernized at a break-neck pace, abolishing all the old trappings of feudal Japanese society. When disaffected samurai and other conservative elements of society revolted against the Imperial Government these rebels were quickly put down and crushed. The Meiji Restoration had indeed caught hold in Japan and guided the country well enough that by 1914 it was one of the world's Great Powers.

10. Describe and explain the political, social, and cultural continuities and changes in the Roman Empire in the period 27 B.C.E. to 476 C.E.

This essay asks you to analyze the social, political, and cultural **changes and continuities over time** in the Roman Empire between 27 B.C.E. and 476 C.E. Note that these dates correspond directly to the beginning of the Imperial period of Roman history with the rise of the first emperor Augustus in 27 B.C.E. and the fall of the Western Roman Empire in 476 C.E. This essay is therefore asking you more directly, "How did the imposition of an autocratic form of government modify Roman civilization?"

A good essay would begin by establishing the stage and explaining the immediate history of ancient Rome at 27 B.C.E., that the Republic had been immensely successful but had collapsed under the weight of competing aristocrats and mounting social issues. Through a series of civil wars only one man emerged with any authority and ability remaining to bring peace to the shattered Roman world—the emperor Augustus. The Roman people accepted his style of monarchy, a veiled despotism which retained the outward show of the old Roman republic while guaranteeing the emperor absolute power, in exchange for the peace and stability they craved.

Of course, certain things modified this new arrangement in the government of Rome. Harsh rulers like Nero, Caligula, Commodus, and other insane or despotic rulers established more naked authoritarian policies. Barbarian invasions on every frontier of the empire taxed the army's strength, forcing Roman emperors to invest in ever-expanding armies. To finance these ever-larger armies, the emperors had to increase taxes, further diminishing public support for the empire. To make matters even worse, Augustus' imperial form of government did not have a rule for succession. With the empire heavily militarized, any general who commanded the loyalty of his soldiers could make himself emperor and fight his rivals for the throne. A perfect storm of all the above things happened in the middle of the 200s, when, starting in 235 C.E., the Roman Empire underwent a period of fifty years of civil war, barbarian invasion, and economic stress. The Roman Empire survived, but the end result was very different from what had been in the past.

This new Roman Empire had abandoned any trappings of the old Republic and had become a pure military despotism. The constant civil wars and barbarian invasions had sapped the public's faith in the traditional gods and ways of the Empire, fostering the rise of Christianity which went from being a banned faith to the official religion of the empire by 400 C.E. The old order of the Republic where leading citizens felt it to be an honor to serve the state had disintegrated and turned into a huge bureaucratic system in which working for the imperial government conferred honors. In terms of the social fabric of the Roman Empire, while citizenship had expanded across the entire empire, two classes of citizens legally arose between aristocrats and peasants, with the aristocrats receiving many legal protections against capital punishments. The large-scale slave society which characterized the Republic and early empire had diminished greatly over time, though the use of slaves was still widespread. Women had many legal rights too, but still were disenfranchised.

By 476 C.E., constant barbarian attacks, rebellious provinces, and disenchantment with the Imperial system caused the Western half of the empire to fall, but the Eastern Roman Empire still survived, strong and intact.

11. Discuss the effects of Silk Road trading routes on economic and cultural exchange among the regions connected by these routes from the period 200 B.C.E. to 1450 C.E. Be sure to address both continuities and changes, and cite evidence from specific regions or kingdoms.

This essay asks you to explain the cultural and economic **changes and continuities over time** of the regions along the Silk Road between 200 B.C.E. and 1450 C.E. Note that 200 B.C.E. roughly matches with the imposition of the Pax Romana and the consolidation of major civilizations such as the Iranian empire of the Parthians as well as the Han Dynasty in China. The year 1450 of course is approximately the date of the conquest of Constantinople by the Ottoman Turks (1453). This is quite a tall order for an essay, but there are some major events and developments that this prompt clearly is asking for.

Firstly, a good essay will note that the Silk Road gained prominence quickly as major empires along the Silk Road consolidated and allowed for peaceful and stable travel along this overland route. The vast distances that the Silk Road traveled forced the trade to really only carry luxuries which were almost unheard of in the West but plentiful in the East, such as silks and spices. Major world faiths such as Christianity, Zoroastrianism, and Buddhism spread along the Silk Road as well. This explosion in world trade was somewhat mitigated, however, by the collapse of these civilizations between 200 and 500 C.E., as barbarian invasions affected China, Persia, and Rome almost simultaneously. Nevertheless, the trade survived but in a muted form.

A good essay would absolutely have to include the development of Islam around 600 C.E. as Islam's area of influence would come to encompass almost the entire Silk Road. Muslim merchants became the middlemen of choice as the Caliphate assumed the role as an arbiter of stability that the old Sassanid Persian Empire once served. These merchants also carried the faith of Islam with them, and the faith spread quickly in their wake. Many territories that had not seen conquest by Muslim warriors, such as southern India, found many people convert to the new faith. Not all societies welcomed Islam, however. Western Europeans embarked upon the titanic Crusades in an attempt to rescue the dying Byzantine Empire and regain control of the Holy Land from the infidels. Centuries of war ensued, guaranteeing the two faiths would be on quite bad terms for centuries to come.

In addition to the rise of Islam, a good essay would have to discuss the impact of the Mongols on the Silk Road. The Mongols quickly overran Song China, and then followed the Silk Road routes west, crushing any resistance that stood in their way. Whole civilizations in Central Asia were wiped out, their cities plundered and exterminated. Baghdad was sacked in 1258, and the stability that the Caliphate provided disintegrated quickly afterwards. Russia was overrun too, and Mongol warriors even invaded Eastern Europe before falling back to the pastures of the Russian steppes. While the Mongols had brought much destruction, they also were interested in fostering commerce and connections throughout their widespread empire. For the first time Westerners could travel unmolested from Europe to China. Despite their destruction of Baghdad, the Mongols who subjugated the former realm of the Caliph converted to Sunni Islam. Of course, Mongol rule was not permanent, and in many locations—Russia and China chief among them—the Mongols had either assimilated into their subject societies or reduced to such a minority part of the population that they could not retain their power.

By 1450, the Silk Road was still prominent but not as important as it was in the past as the sole route for goods to travel from East to West. Unifying forces like Islam and the Mongolian empire allowed for alternate routes to arise and changed the dynamics of the merchants travelling the routes, but they also caused no small amount of destruction to the societies they affected. With the Turkish capture of Constantinople in 1453, the Europeans had received a symbolic awakening that, in order to avoid Muslim middlemen who straddled the Silk Road, they should instead seek out Asia itself.

12. Compare the development of early Chinese civilization (2500–250 B.C.E.) with the development of civilizations in the area known as the Fertile Crescent (4000–1000 B.C.E.). Be sure to cite evidence from specific societies, addressing both similarities and differences.

This essay asks you to **compare and contrast** Ancient China with Mesopotamia. As these were both ancient river valley civilizations, their similarities are actually quite numerous, while their differences, nevertheless, are pronounced.

A good essay would touch on the following points:

- Both regions had civilizations that arose out of labor organization for irrigation. This means that the societies developed stark and rigid class structures, putting kings and mystical religious figures at the top, and the gangs of peasants that were essential for powering agriculture at the bottom.
- Both regions had civilizations that organized into governed states, though the scope of these states varied. Mesopotamia first featured small city states that eventually coalesced into larger empires, while China had different dynasties, the Xia, Shang, and Zhou, which, unlike the later Chinese dynasties, appeared to be distinct states and overlapped with each other in various points in history.
- While Mesopotamia was able to be united under city-state empires, like Akkad, these empires were often short-lived, and were consumed by foreign invasion by civilizations such as the Hittites. By 1000 B.C.E., the Eastern Mediterranean started headlong into a decline that has yet to be explained, but by that point ancient Mesopotamian civilization had been lost. Meanwhile, the Chinese states all retained their culture despite wars with outsiders and with themselves. The Zhou dynasty survived a particularly long time because it had developed huge armies and the logistics to support them, but to do so the dynasty had decentralized rule, allowing local strongmen to split it apart

around the year 400 B.C.E. which brought about the Warring States period in Chinese history. Still, despite all this, Chinese civilization survived and thrived.

13. Compare the status of women in TWO of the following ancient societies (2500 B.C.E. to 600 C.E.), examining similarities and differences in women's status, as well as the cultural forces that affected it.

    China
    India
    Greece
    Rome

This essay asks you to **compare and contrast** the status of women in two of four ancient societies. Since your answers can come in any pattern, we have put each of the societies below with our explanations:

- China: Ancient Chinese civilization was extremely patriarchal. Sons were preferred to daughters, especially since opportunities for social advancement were connected with working in the Confucian government bureaucracy. Confucianism itself insists that women have a subordinate social role than men. As such, women in Ancient China were treated as second-class members of society. Women of wealthy families would have their feet bound, and men would often have concubines while in marriage. There are exceptions to this rule. Zhou sources suggest female rulers at certain points in time. Wu Zetian became empress of China during the T'ang dynasty, around 700, which is slightly outside the parameters but serves as a good reminder to look for counter-examples on these essays!

- India: Ancient Indian civilization too was patriarchal. Hinduism's caste system ensured that society's view of women and their role was just as rigid. Women were expected to manage and maintain the household, and do weaving, and they were expected by their husbands to be available for pleasure at any time. One might consider Buddhism would serve as a powerful counter-force to this, but the faith, with its emphasis on Monks and monasteries, was not as welcoming to women as Hinduism which had shrines in the very houses women were in charge at.

- Greece: Ancient Greek treatment of women varied depending upon what city-state the woman was a citizen of, but the very organization of the polis ensured that women would be held to high moral standards, as citizenship was not earned or given in Ancient Greek societies—it could only be born into. Consequently, classical Athens' aristocratic women were shut inside their homes, lest illegitimate children be born to them, or property be inherited outside the family line. Spartan women were given considerably more freedom than their Athenian counterparts, such as the complete authority to maintain their households (especially since their husbands were in the army until they were forty), but were also responsible for procreating with their husbands to generate more Spartans to carry on the line. Roman conquest did not change Greek society too much, but the spread of Christianity found willing converts in Greece, and early Christianity certainly employed females in rites and services, providing an escape to an otherwise objectifying reality.

- Rome: Roman women were also subject to a patriarchal society, but unlike those from all the other societies above, Roman women were guaranteed certain rights to property and inheritance and business. While Roman women needed custodians to form legal documents and conduct other affairs, Roman women were treated so liberally because Roman citizenship could and often was conferred based on merit and the needs of the Republic and could be transmitted if any parent was a citizen. The Emperor Augustus even promulgated a law granting women more freedoms if they successfully bore three children. The spread of Christianity in the Roman Empire allowed women the right to participate in Christian ceremonies and rites, something that traditional Roman society did not necessarily approve of.

14. In the period 500 B.C.E. to 1000 C.E., India's religious landscape experienced many changes. Discuss both the changes and the continuities in Hinduism's relationship with Buddhism and Islam during this time.

This essay asks you to analyze the **changes and continuities over time** with Hinduism's relationship with Buddhism and Islam between 500 B.C.E. and 1000 C.E. An astute student would recognize these dates as bookends—Buddhism came into being around 500 B.C.E., while the first Muslim invasions of India occurred around 1000 C.E.

A good essay would mention the significant differences Hinduism had with Buddhism. Buddhism arose as a challenge to the socially stifling caste system that Hinduism strictly imposed. As such, it quickly gained a following among those who were lower on the caste system, such as merchants and the poor. It gained so much traction that even the emperor Asoka of the Mauryan Empire converted to it after his pyrrhic victory at the battle of Kalinga. Nevertheless, Hinduism remained the favorite religion of aristocrats. Hinduism's emphasis on the home and cult sites and shrines differed vastly from Buddhism's monks and monasteries, guaranteeing that women would at least have some greater attraction to Hinduism than they did to Buddhism. An excellent essay would mention how the changes in Buddhism, such as the development of Mahayana Buddhism, despite making Buddhism more accessible to mainstream Hindu populations, ended up making Buddhism a bit too similar to Hinduism, since Mahayana Buddhism featured many gods and many Buddhas. In fact, by the time of the decline and fall of the Gupta dynasty, Buddhism's strength in India was waning. For whatever reason, the popularity of Hinduism grew back as the Gupta Dynasty crumbled, probably directly in response to such a disaster. While Buddhism exploded outside of India as it was carried by the very merchants who supported it, Hinduism reigned supreme in India.

All that changed when Islam came on the scene. Good essays would indicate how the relationship between Islam and Hinduism was very peaceful. Muslim merchants, who imported the religion into India, were among its front-rank missionaries. Islam spread unabated, and Muslims noted how Hinduism did not seek to convert or proselytize like Islam did. Many people then in India converted to both. Of course, Islam was spread by the sword as well, and by 1000 C.E., Muslim invasions into Northern India overran several Hindu kingdoms there. These Muslim sultanates ruling over a majority Hindu population would become the norm in India for the next 600 years, with a sort of peaceful coexistence reached between Hinduism and Islam.

Batch 2

1. Analyze similarities and differences in political and economic effects Mongol rule had on TWO of the following regions:

   China
   The Middle East
   Russia
   Europe

BASIC CORE (competence) (0–6 points)

1. Has acceptable thesis (1 point)

The thesis has to be at the beginning or the end of the essay.
The thesis must
- Be more than just a restatement of the question. DO NOT quote the prompt
- Clearly state similarities and differences—"Though political differences appeared, economic similarities characterized these societies" is minimally acceptable. "There were some similarities and differences" is not.

2. Addresses all parts of the question (2 points)

To earn 2 points, cover all FOUR parts (Region 1 + political, Region 1 + economic, Region 2 + political, Region 2 + economic)

To earn 1 point, write on TWO or THREE of the parts listed above.

No points are awarded if only one of the four is discussed.

3. Substantiates thesis with appropriate historical evidence (2 points)

To earn 2 points, present FOUR or more correct and relevant pieces of information (as in, historical facts).

To earn 1 point, TWO or THREE *correct/relevant* facts are necessary.

One piece of information can be used as evidence for both regions, but you need to explain *how* it's relevant to both. For example, "The Mongol rulers reinvigorated the Silk Road, which benefitted the economies of both Region 1 and Region 2, by doing *x* in Region 1 and *y* in Region 2."

4. Makes at least TWO relevant, direct comparisons between or among societies (1 point)

Make at least TWO direct, clear comparisons or contrasts between the two regions. One *has* to be about politics and one *has* to be about economics. If you contribute examples of only one or the other, you don't get this core point.

Comparisons obviously have to be relevant and pertinent to the question.

Subtotal: 6 points

EXPANDED CORE (excellence) 0–2 points

Expands beyond the basic core of 1–6 points. The basic core score of 6 must be achieved *before* you can get any extra points.

Examples:

- Has a "clear, analytical, and comprehensive" thesis, so remember to break down exactly what you'll talk about—which two regions and how each of them were effected in political and economic ways (that's four things—Region 1 + political, Region 1 + economic, Region 2 + political, Region 2 + economic)
- Provides balanced information on both regions
- Shows a balance between similarities and differences
- Proves balanced information on political and economic effects
- Provides ample historical evidence to support thesis
- Includes comparisons related to the global impact(s), for example
  - Significant and relevant connections between Mongol rule and the periods after Mongol rule ended
  - Places Mongol societies in historical context or compares them with other nomad/settler interactions
- Makes direct comparisons between regions regularly

2. Analyze the changes and constants in trade on the Indian Ocean between 650 B.C.E. and 1750 C.E.

BASIC CORE (competence) 0–7 points

1. Has acceptable thesis (1 point)

The thesis has to be at the beginning or the end of the essay, though you can split it.
The thesis must
- Be more than just a restatement of the question. DO NOT quote the prompt
- Clearly discuss both the things that change and the things that remain the same

2. Addresses all parts of the question (2 points)

To earn 2 points, address the changes and the constants, but this is separate from the thesis. The thesis can never count for double points.

To earn 1 point, address the changes or the constants.

3. Substantiates thesis with appropriate historical evidence (2 points)

To earn 2 points, at least FIVE pieces of evidence must be presented which illustrate change *and* constants
- At least one must explain a constant, and at least one must explain a change
- Each example must be clearly appropriate to the task—facts illustrating material exchanged, people/groups involved, or new technologies
To earn 1 point, write about at least FOUR pieces of evidence which illustrate change *and/or* constants
- Think materials traded, nations involved, new technologies

4. Uses relevant historical context effectively to explain change over time and/or continuity (1 point)

Remember to mention somewhere in the essay something relating to the global aspects of the trade during the period that remained constant OR changed. For example, how did the spice trade affect global politics?

5. Analyzes the process of change over time and/or continuity (1 point)

Explain the *why* of something that stayed the same or changed—"this happened because…"

Subtotal: 7 points

EXPANDED CORE (excellence) 0–2 points

Expands beyond the basic core of 1–7 points. The basic core score of 7 must be achieved *before* you can get any extra points.

Examples:

- Has a "clear, analytical, and comprehensive" thesis, so remember to break down exactly what you'll talk about
- Mentions several changes and constants
- Gives lots of evidence

3. Compare and contrast the philosophies and spread of Islam with the conquest and spread of ONE of the following faiths until 1492 C.E.

Christianity
Buddhism

BASIC CORE (competence) 0–6 points

1. Has acceptable thesis (1 point)

The thesis has to be at the beginning or the end of the essay.
The thesis must
- Be more than just a restatement of the question. DO NOT quote the prompt
- Clearly state similarities and differences—"Though the spread of Islam followed violent conquest, the beginning years of Christianity were not as successful" is minimally acceptable. "There were some similarities and differences" is not.

2. Addresses all parts of the question (2 points)

To earn 2 points, cover all FOUR parts (Islam + philosophies, Islam + spread, Religion 2 + philosophies, Religion 2 + spread)

To earn 1 point, write on TWO or THREE of the parts listed above.

No points are awarded if only one of the four is discussed.

3. Substantiates thesis with appropriate historical evidence (2 points)

To earn 2 points, present FOUR or more correct *and* relevant pieces of information (as in, historical facts).

To earn 1 point, TWO or THREE *correct/relevant* facts are necessary.

One piece of information can be used as evidence for both regions, but you need to explain how it's relevant to both. For example, "Both Islam and Christianity are monotheistic, which affected the philosophies of Islam by *x* and Christianity by *y*."

4. Makes at least TWO relevant, direct comparisons between or among societies (1 point)

Make at least TWO direct, clear comparisons or contrasts between the two regions. One has to be about the philosophies and one has to be about the spread of the faiths. If you contribute examples of only one or the other, you don't get this core point.

Comparisons obviously have to be relevant and pertinent to the question.

Subtotal: 6 points

EXPANDED CORE (excellence) 0–2 points

Expands beyond the basic core of 1–6 points. The basic core score of 6 must be achieved before you can get any extra points.

Examples:

- Has a "clear, analytical, and comprehensive" thesis, so remember to break down exactly what you'll talk about
- Makes several comparisons and contrasts between the faiths
- Makes several comparisons and contrasts concerning the spread of these faiths—where they spread, how they spread, where they are practiced today

4. Describe and explain continuities and changes in the status of women in ONE of the regions from 600 B.C.E. to 1450 C.E.

    Europe
    Arabia
    India

BASIC CORE (competence) 0–7 points

1. Has acceptable thesis (1 point)

The thesis has to be at the beginning or the end of the essay, though you can split it.
The thesis must
- Be more than just a restatement of the question. DO NOT quote the prompt
- Clearly discuss both the things that change and the things that remain the same

2. Addresses all parts of the question (2 points)

To earn 2 points, address the changes *and* the continuities but this is separate from the thesis. The thesis can never count for double points.

To earn 1 point, address the changes *or* the continuities.

3. Substantiates thesis with appropriate historical evidence (2 points)

To earn 2 points, at least FIVE pieces of evidence must be presented which illustrate change *and* constants.
- At least one must explain a continuity, and at least one must explain a change
- Each example must be clearly appropriate to the task—facts illustrating rights obtained or taken away, the status of girls in society, employment opportunities, and so on

To earn 1 point, write about at least FOUR pieces of evidence which illustrate change *and/or* continuities.
- Think rights, education, livelihoods

4. Uses relevant historical context effectively to explain change over time and/or continuity (1 point)

Remember to mention somewhere in the essay something relating to the global aspects of the status of women that remained constant OR changed. For example, how were women expected to dress in every society?

5. Analyzes the process of change over time and/or continuity (1 point)

Explain the *why* of something that stayed the same or changed—"this happened because…"

Subtotal: 7 points

EXPANDED CORE (excellence) 0–2 points

Expands beyond the basic core of 1–7 points. The basic core score of 7 must be achieved *before* you can get any extra points.

Examples:

- Has a "clear, analytical, and comprehensive" thesis, so remember to break down exactly what you'll talk about
- Mentions several changes and continuities
- Gives lots of evidence

5. Compare and contrast the philosophical and religious developments in TWO of the following regions from 1450 to 1750.

Western Europe
Russia
China and Japan

BASIC CORE (competence) 0–6 points

1. Has acceptable thesis (1 point)

The thesis has to be at the beginning or the end of the essay.
The thesis must
- Be more than just a restatement of the question. DO NOT quote the prompt.
- Clearly state similarities and differences—"Though religious differences characterized these regions, philosophical developments were similar in some ways" is minimally acceptable. "There were some similarities and differences" is not.

2. Addresses all parts of the question (2 points)

To earn 2 points, cover all FOUR parts (Region 1 + philosophical, Region 1 + religious, Region 2 + philosophical, Region 2 + religious)

To earn 1 point, write on TWO or THREE of the parts listed above.

No points are awarded if only one of the four is discussed.

3. Substantiates thesis with appropriate historical evidence (2 points)

To earn 2 points, present FOUR or more correct *and* relevant pieces of information (as in, historical facts).

To earn 1 point, TWO or THREE *correct/relevant* facts are necessary.

One piece of information can be used as evidence for both regions, but you need to explain *how* it's relevant to both. For example, "The Westernization of Russia led to similar governmental philosophies; however, in Russia, this philosophy resulted in *x*, while in Western Europe, it resulted in *y*."

4. Makes at least TWO relevant, direct comparisons between or among societies (1 point)

Make at least TWO direct, clear comparisons or contrasts between the two regions. One *has* to be about philosophy and one *has* to be about religion. If you contribute examples of only one or the other, you don't get this core point.

Comparisons obviously have to be relevant and pertinent to the question.

Subtotal: 6 points

EXPANDED CORE (excellence) 0–2 points

Expands beyond the basic core of 1–6 points. The basic core score of 6 must be achieved *before* you can get any extra points.

Examples:

- Has a "clear, analytical, and comprehensive" thesis, so remember to break down exactly what you'll talk about
- Shows a balance between similarities and differences
- Provides balanced information on both regions
- Proves balanced information on philosophical and religious effects
- Provides ample historical evidence to support thesis
- Includes comparisons related to the global impact(s), for example
  - "Europe's new dominance led to its controlling of seaports, which Russia hoped to imitate. This led to Peter the Great's desire for a warm water port in the Baltic, and Peter, too, became expansionist."
- Makes direct comparisons between regions regularly

6. Compare and contrast the economic and social impacts of trade with the New World from 1450 to 1750 on TWO of the following regions

Europe
Africa
Asia

BASIC CORE (competence) 0–6 points

1. Has acceptable thesis (1 point)

The thesis has to be at the beginning or the end of the essay.
The thesis must
- Be more than just a restatement of the question. DO NOT quote the prompt.
- Clearly state similarities and differences—"Though trade with the New World had significant economic impacts in this region, its effect on social life was not as consequential" is minimally acceptable. "There were some similarities and differences" is not.

2. Addresses all parts of the question (2 points)

To earn 2 points, cover all FOUR parts (Region 1 + economic, Region 1 + social, Region 2 + economic, Region 2 + social)

To earn 1 point, write on TWO or THREE of the parts listed above.

No points are awarded if only one of the four is discussed.

3. Substantiates thesis with appropriate historical evidence (2 points)

To earn 2 points, present FOUR or more correct *and* relevant pieces of information (as in, historical facts).

To earn 1 point, TWO or THREE *correct/relevant* facts are necessary.

One piece of information can be used as evidence for both regions, but you need to explain *how* it's relevant to both. For example, "Food from the New World helped stabilize populations in Asia and Europe, which did *x* in Europe and *y* in Asia."

4. Makes at least TWO relevant, direct comparisons between or among societies (1 point)

Make at least TWO direct, clear comparisons or contrasts between the two regions. One *has* to be about economics and one *has* to be about social impacts. If you contribute examples of only one or the other, you don't get this core point.

Comparisons obviously have to be relevant and pertinent to the question.

Subtotal: 6 points

EXPANDED CORE (excellence) 0–2 points

Expands beyond the basic core of 1–6 points. The basic core score of 6 must be achieved *before* you can get any extra points.

Examples:

- Has a "clear, analytical, and comprehensive" thesis, so remember to break down exactly what you'll talk about
- Shows a balance between similarities and differences
- Provides balanced information on both regions
- Proves balanced information on philosophical and religious effects
- Provides ample historical evidence to support thesis
- Includes comparisons related to the global impact(s), for example
    - "Stabilized populations around the world made populations which demanded certain things from their governments, ushering in new ideas."
    - "The slave trade, fueled by a demand of labor in the New World, was a global empire."
- Makes direct comparisons between regions regularly

7. Analyze the development and impact of the continuities and changes to technology from 1450 to 1914.

BASIC CORE (competence) 0–7 points

1. Has acceptable thesis (1 point)

The thesis has to be at the beginning or the end of the essay, though you can split it.
The thesis must
- Be more than just a restatement of the question. DO NOT quote the prompt.
- Clearly discuss both the things that change and the things that remain the same.

2. Addresses all parts of the question (2 points)

To earn 2 points, address the changes *and* the continuities, but this is separate from the thesis. The thesis can never count for double points.

To earn 1 point, address the changes *or* the continuities.

3. Substantiates thesis with appropriate historical evidence (2 points)

To earn 2 points, at least FIVE pieces of evidence must be presented which illustrate change *and* continuities.
- At least one must explain a constant, and at least one must explain a change
- Each example must be clearly appropriate to the task—facts illustrating new technology developed, but also old technologies that either remained the same or were improved

To earn 1 point, write about at least FOUR pieces of evidence which illustrate change *and/or* constants.
- Think transportation (boats, roads), mathematics

4. Uses relevant historical context effectively to explain change over time and/or continuity (1 point)

Remember to mention somewhere in the essay something relating to the global aspects of technology during the period that remained constant OR changed. For example, how did new ships affect politics and world dominance?

5. Analyzes the process of change over time and/or continuity (1 point)

Explain the *why* of something that stayed the same or changed—"this happened because…"

SUBTOTAL: 7 points

EXPANDED CORE (excellence) 0–2 points

Expands beyond the basic core of 1–7 points. The basic core score of 7 must be achieved *before* you can get any extra points.

Examples:

- Has a "clear, analytical, and comprehensive" thesis, so remember to break down exactly what you'll talk about
- Mentions several changes and constants
- Gives lots of evidence

8. Describe and explain continuities and changes to governments in TWO of the following regions from 650 C.E. to 1750 C.E.

Europe
Asia
Russia
Africa

BASIC CORE (competence) 0–7 points

1. Has acceptable thesis (1 point)

The thesis has to be at the beginning or the end of the essay, though you can split it.
The thesis must
- Be more than just a restatement of the question. DO NOT quote the prompt
- Clearly discuss both the things that change and the things that remain the same

2. Addresses all parts of the question (2 points)

To earn 2 points, address the changes *and* the continuities, but this is separate from the thesis. The thesis can never count for double points.

To earn 1 point, address the changes *or* the continuities.

3. Substantiates thesis with appropriate historical evidence (2 points)

To earn 2 points, at least FIVE pieces of evidence must be presented which illustrate change *and* continuities.
- At least one must explain a constant, and at least one must explain a change
- Each example must be clearly appropriate to the task—facts illustrating representation of social and political groups, organization of government

To earn 1 point, write about at least FOUR pieces of evidence which illustrate change *and/or* constants.
- Think who gets to vote, what the priorities of the governments were

4. Uses relevant historical context effectively to explain change over time and/or continuity (1 point)

Remember to mention somewhere in the essay something relating to the global aspects of technology during the period that remained constant OR changed. For example, how did the government's policies reflect their role on the world stage?

5. Analyzes the process of change over time and/or continuity (1 point)

Explain the *why* of something that stayed the same or changed—"this happened because..."

Subtotal: 7 points

EXPANDED CORE (excellence) 0–2 points

Expands beyond the basic core of 1–7 points. The basic core score of 7 must be achieved *before* you can get any extra points.

Examples:

- Has a "clear, analytical, and comprehensive" thesis, so remember to break down exactly what you'll talk about
- Mentions several changes and constants
- Gives lots of evidence

9. Compare and contrast the social and political impacts of the Industrial Revolution on TWO of the following regions.

    Europe
    Asia
    Africa

BASIC CORE (competence) 0–6 points

1. Has acceptable thesis (1 point)

The thesis has to be at the beginning or the end of the essay.
The thesis must
- Be more than just a restatement of the question. DO NOT quote the prompt
- Clearly state similarities and differences—"The social impacts of the Industrial Revolution were much more significant than the political fall-out the movement created" is minimally acceptable. "There were some similarities and differences" is not.

2. Addresses all parts of the question (2 points)

To earn 2 points, cover all FOUR parts (Region 1 + social, Region 1 + political, Region 2 + social, Region 2 + political)

To earn 1 point, write on TWO or THREE of the parts listed above.

No points are awarded if only one of the four is discussed.

3. Substantiates thesis with appropriate historical evidence (2 points)

To earn 2 points, present FOUR or more correct *and* relevant pieces of information (as in, historical facts).

To earn 1 point, TWO or THREE *correct/relevant* facts are necessary.

One piece of information can be used as evidence for both regions, but you need to explain *how* it's relevant to both. For example, "The rise of factories resulting from the Industrial Revolution impacted England by *x*, though this rise of factories in another country effected Africa by *y*."

4. Makes at least TWO relevant, direct comparisons between or among societies (1 point)

Make at least TWO direct, clear comparisons or contrasts between the two regions. One *has* to be about social impacts and one *has* to be about politics. If you contribute examples of only one or the other, you don't get this core point.

Comparisons obviously have to be relevant and pertinent to the question.

Subtotal: 6 points

EXPANDED CORE (excellence) 0–2 points

Expands beyond the basic core of 1–6 points. The basic core score of 6 must be achieved *before* you can get any extra points.

Examples:

- Has a "clear, analytical, and comprehensive" thesis, so remember to break down exactly what you'll talk about
- Shows a balance between similarities and differences
- Provides balanced information on both regions
- Proves balanced information on philosophical and religious effects
- Provides ample historical evidence to support thesis
- Includes comparisons related to the global impact(s), for example
    - "England's new dominance in industry allowed it to become a world power within the powerful European-dominated world economy."
    - "Technology continued to leave Africa behind, making its entry into world economics more challenging."
- Makes direct comparisons between regions regularly

10. Compare and contrast the philosophies and actions leading from ethnocentrism in Europe and Asia from 1750 to 1914.

BASIC CORE (competence) 0–6 points

1. Has acceptable thesis (1 point)

The thesis has to be at the beginning or the end of the essay.
The thesis must
- Be more than just a restatement of the question. DO NOT quote the prompt
- Clearly state similarities and differences—"The Europeans and Chinese were both ethnocentric, though these regions reacted differently to their self-obsessions" is minimally acceptable. "There were some similarities and differences" is not.

2. Addresses all parts of the question (2 points)

To earn 2 points, cover all FOUR parts (Region 1 + philosophy, Region 1 + actions, Region 2 + philosophy, Region 2 + actions)

To earn 1 point, write on TWO or THREE of the parts listed above.

No points are awarded if only one of the four is discussed.

3. Substantiates thesis with appropriate historical evidence (2 points)

To earn 2 points, present FOUR or more correct *and* relevant pieces of information (as in, historical facts).

To earn 1 point, TWO or THREE *correct/relevant* facts are necessary.

One piece of information can be used as evidence for both regions, but you need to explain *how* it's relevant to both. For example, "Insularity and a healthy dose of self-confidence was an important piece of each of these regions' pursuit of world dominance, but Europe used its own ideas of self-importance to do *x* while Asian societies did *y*."

4. Makes at least TWO relevant, direct comparisons between or among societies (1 point)

Make at least TWO direct, clear comparisons or contrasts between the two regions. One *has* to be about the philosophies of ethnocentrism and one *has* to be about actions. If you contribute examples of only one or the other, you don't get this core point.

Comparisons obviously have to be relevant and pertinent to the question.

Subtotal: 6 points

EXPANDED CORE (excellence) 0–2 points

Expands beyond the basic core of 1–6 points. The basic core score of 6 must be achieved *before* you can get any extra points.

Examples:

- Has a "clear, analytical, and comprehensive" thesis, so remember to break down exactly what you'll talk about
- Shows a balance between similarities and differences
- Provides balanced information on both regions
- Proves balanced information on philosophical and religious effects
- Provides ample historical evidence to support thesis
- Includes comparisons related to the global impact(s), for example
  o "Ethnocentrism in Europe played out on a global scale, as Europe controlled significant parts of the world economy."
  o "China's ethnocentrism led to isolationism, and the region pulled away from the global stage."
- Makes direct comparisons between regions regularly

11. Describe and explain continuities and changes to social class structures before and after the introduction of the industrial work model in the eighteenth century.

BASIC CORE (competence) 0–7 points

1. Has acceptable thesis (1 point)

The thesis has to be at the beginning or the end of the essay, though you can split it. The thesis must
- Be more than just a restatement of the question. DO NOT quote the prompt
- Clearly discuss both the things that change and the things that remain the same

2. Addresses all parts of the question (2 points)

To earn 2 points, address the changes *and* the continuities, but this is separate from the thesis. The thesis can never count for double points.

To earn 1 point, address the changes *or* the continuities.

3. Substantiates thesis with appropriate historical evidence (2 points)

To earn 2 points, at least FIVE pieces of evidence must be presented which illustrate change *and* continuities.
- At least one must explain a continuity, and at least one must explain a change
- Each example must be clearly appropriate to the task—facts illustrating how people lived under feudalism versus the factory system

To earn 1 point, write about at least FOUR pieces of evidence which illustrate change *and/or* constants.
- Think how they lived, where they lived, who they lived with

4. Uses relevant historical context effectively to explain change over time and/or continuity (1 point)

Remember to mention somewhere in the essay something relating to the global aspects of these social classes during the period that remained constant OR changed. For example, how did the new family structure change morality or governments throughout the world?

5. Analyzes the process of change over time and/or continuity (1 point)

Explain the *why* of something that stayed the same or changed—"this happened because…"

Subtotal: 7 points

EXPANDED CORE (excellence) 0–2 points

Expands beyond the basic core of 1–7 points. The basic core score of 7 must be achieved *before* you can get any extra points.

Examples:

- Has a "clear, analytical, and comprehensive" thesis, so remember to break down exactly what you'll talk about
- Mentions several changes and constants
- Gives lots of evidence

12. Analyze the continuities and changes of European Imperialism from 1800 to the present.

BASIC CORE (competence) 0–7 points

1. Has acceptable thesis (1 point)

The thesis has to be at the beginning or the end of the essay, though you can split it. The thesis must
- Be more than just a restatement of the question. DO NOT quote the prompt
- Clearly discuss both the things that change and the things that remain the same

2. Addresses all parts of the question (2 points)

To earn 2 points, address the changes *and* the continuities, but this is separate from the thesis. The thesis can never count for double points.

To earn 1 point, address the changes *or* the continuities.

3. Substantiates thesis with appropriate historical evidence (2 points)

To earn 2 points, at least FIVE pieces of evidence must be presented which illustrate change *and* continuities.
- At least one must explain a continuity, and at least one must explain a change
- Each example must be clearly appropriate to the task—facts illustrating how Europe controlled the region (economic, political)

To earn 1 point, write about at least FOUR pieces of evidence which illustrate change *and/or* constants.
- Think who was governing, how the resources of the region were used

4. Uses relevant historical context effectively to explain change over time and/or continuity (1 point)

Remember to mention somewhere in the essay something relating to the global aspects of these controls during the period that remained constant OR changed. For example, how did control of the government or the economy effect the country and its present or future?

5. Analyzes the process of change over time and/or continuity (1 point)

Explain the *why* of something that stayed the same or changed—"this happened because…"

Subtotal: 7 points

EXPANDED CORE (excellence) 0–2 points

Expands beyond the basic core of 1–7 points. The basic core score of 7 must be achieved *before* you can get any extra points.

Examples:

- Has a "clear, analytical, and comprehensive" thesis, so remember to break down exactly what you'll talk about
- Mentions several changes and constants
- Gives lots of evidence

13. Compare and contrast the reasons for the rise of extremist governments and their governance policies in the twentieth century in TWO of the following countries.

Germany
Italy
China
Russia

BASIC CORE (competence) 0–6 points

1. Has acceptable thesis (1 point)

The thesis has to be at the beginning or the end of the essay.
The thesis must
- Be more than just a restatement of the question. DO NOT quote the prompt
- Clearly state similarities and differences—"China saw a rise of Communism while Germany became fascist" is minimally acceptable. "There were some similarities and differences" is not

2. Addresses all parts of the question (2 points)

To earn 2 points, cover all FOUR parts (Region 1 + rise, Region 1 + governance, Region 2 + rise, Region 2 + governance)

To earn 1 point, write on TWO or THREE of the parts listed above.

No points are awarded if only one of the four is discussed.

3. Substantiates thesis with appropriate historical evidence (2 points)

To earn 2 points, present FOUR or more correct *and* relevant pieces of information (as in, historical facts).

To earn 1 point, TWO or THREE *correct/relevant* facts are necessary.

One piece of information can be used as evidence for both regions, but you need to explain *how* it's relevant to both. For example, "Failing economies played a role in both Germany's and Italy's moves towards extremism. Fascists in Germany said *x* and those in Italy said *y*."

4. Makes at least TWO relevant, direct comparisons between or among societies (1 point)

Make at least TWO direct, clear comparisons or contrasts between the two regions. One *has* to be about the rise of extremist governments and one *has* to be about the way those governments ran their respective countries. If you contribute examples of only one or the other, you don't get this core point.

Comparisons obviously have to be relevant and pertinent to the question.

SUBTOTAL: 6 points

EXPANDED CORE (excellence) 0–2 points

Expands beyond the basic core of 1–6 points. The basic core score of 6 must be achieved *before* you can get any extra points.

Examples:

- Has a "clear, analytical, and comprehensive" thesis, so remember to break down exactly what you'll talk about
- Shows a balance between similarities and differences
- Provides balanced information on both regions
- Proves balanced information on philosophical and religious effects
- Provides ample historical evidence to support thesis
- Includes comparisons related to the global impact(s), for example
  - "Germany's fascist government was expansionist and began taking over parts of the continent."
  - "Russia's rise of Communism eventually led to confrontation with the United States."
- Makes direct comparisons between regions regularly

14. Compare and contrast the reasons and impacts of nuclear weapons development in TWO of the following countries

    The United States
    The USSR
    Israel
    Iran
    North Korea

BASIC CORE (competence) 0–6 points

1. Has acceptable thesis (1 point)

The thesis has to be at the beginning or the end of the essay.
The thesis must
- Be more than just a restatement of the question. DO NOT quote the prompt
- Clearly state similarities and differences—"The world responded differently to the United States' and the USSR's possession of nuclear weapons, though the countries developed the weapons for similar reasons" is minimally acceptable. "There were some similarities and differences" is not.

2. Addresses all parts of the question (2 points)

To earn 2 points, cover all FOUR parts (Region 1 + rise, Region 1 + governance, Region 2 + rise, Region 2 + governance).

To earn 1 point, write on TWO or THREE of the parts listed above.

No points are awarded if only one of the four is discussed.

3. Substantiates thesis with appropriate historical evidence (2 points)

To earn 2 points, present FOUR or more correct *and* relevant pieces of information (as in, historical facts).

To earn 1 point, TWO or THREE *correct/relevant* facts are necessary.

One piece of information can be used as evidence for both regions, but you need to explain *how* it's relevant to both. For example, "Neither Israel nor Iran has admitted to the existence or development of nuclear arsenals, though Israel's nuclear program *x* and Iran's nuclear program *y*."

4. Makes at least TWO relevant, direct comparisons between or among societies (1 point)

Make at least TWO direct, clear comparisons or contrasts between the two regions. One *has* to be about the reasons and one *has* to be about the impact of the development of these weapons. If you contribute examples of only one or the other, you don't get this core point.

Comparisons obviously have to be relevant and pertinent to the question.

Subtotal: 6 points

EXPANDED CORE (excellence) 0–2 points

Expands beyond the basic core of 1–6 points. The basic core score of 6 must be achieved *before* you can get any extra points.

Examples:

- Has a "clear, analytical, and comprehensive" thesis, so remember to break down exactly what you'll talk about
- Shows a balance between similarities and differences
- Provides balanced information on both regions
- Proves balanced information on philosophical and religious effects
- Provides ample historical evidence to support thesis
- Includes comparisons related to the global impact(s), for example
  - "Iran has become a popular target of the IAEA, and the UN sanctions placed on the government have severely affected the Iranian middle class."
  - "North Korea is known to use its nuclear arsenal to scare and coerce regional powers."
- Makes direct comparisons between regions regularly

15. Analyze major continuities and changes to the impact of global institutions and governance from the eighteenth century to the present.

BASIC CORE (competence) 0–7 points

1. Has acceptable thesis (1 point)

The thesis has to be at the beginning or the end of the essay, though you can split it.
The thesis must
- Be more than just a restatement of the question. DO NOT quote the prompt
- Clearly discuss both the things that change and the things that remain the same

2. Addresses all parts of the question (2 points)

To earn 2 points, address the changes *and* the continuities, but this is separate from the thesis. The thesis can never count for double points.

To earn 1 point, address the changes *or* the continuities.

3. Substantiates thesis with appropriate historical evidence (2 points)

To earn 2 points, at least FIVE pieces of evidence must be presented which illustrate change and continuities.

- At least one must explain a continuity, and at least one must explain a change
- Each example must be clearly appropriate to the task—facts illustrating the move from world powers who dominate foreign economies to institutions such as the UN and EU

To earn 1 point, write about at least FOUR pieces of evidence which illustrate change *and/or* constants.

- Think how the economies are structured, who is benefitting

4. Uses relevant historical context effectively to explain change over time and/or continuity (1 point)

Remember to mention somewhere in the essay something relating to the global aspects of these developments during the period that remained constant OR changed. For example, did European imperialism affect economies of that era, and how does the EU affect global economies today?

5. Analyzes the process of change over time and/or continuity (1 point)

Explain the *why* of something that stayed the same or changed—"this happened because…"

Subtotal: 7 points

EXPANDED CORE (excellence) 0–2 points

Expands beyond the basic core of 1–7 points. The basic core score of 7 must be achieved *before* you can get any extra points.

Examples:

- Has a "clear, analytical, and comprehensive" thesis, so remember to break down exactly what you'll talk about
- Mentions several changes and constants
- Gives lots of evidence

16. Analyze the social and political changes and continuities in ONE of the following countries or regions in the recent past

   The USSR (1917 to present)
   Iran (1979 to present)
   China (1911 to present)
   Africa (1950s to present)

BASIC CORE (competence) 0–7 points

1. Has acceptable thesis (1 point)

The thesis has to be at the beginning or the end of the essay, though you can split it. The thesis must

- Be more than just a restatement of the question. DO NOT quote the prompt
- Clearly discuss both the things that change and the things that remain the same

2. Addresses all parts of the question (2 points)

To earn 2 points, address the changes *and* the continuities, but this is separate from the thesis. The thesis can never count for double points.

To earn 1 point, address the changes *or* the continuities.

3. Substantiates thesis with appropriate historical evidence (2 points)

To earn 2 points, at least FIVE pieces of evidence must be presented which illustrate change *and* continuities.
- At least one must explain a continuity, and at least one must explain a change
- Each example must be clearly appropriate to the task—facts illustrating the roles of women, the type of government and economy

To earn 1 point, write about at least FOUR pieces of evidence which illustrate change *and/or* constants.
- Think how old traditions were folded into new realities or the responses to outside forces

4. Uses relevant historical context effectively to explain change over time and/or continuity (1 point)

Remember to mention somewhere in the essay something relating to the global aspects of these changes during the period that remained constant OR changed. For example, how did Soviet political decisions impact other governments?

5. Analyzes the process of change over time and/or continuity (1 point)

Explain the *why* of something that stayed the same or changed—"this happened because…"

Subtotal: 7 points

EXPANDED CORE (excellence) 0–2 points

Expands beyond the basic core of 1–7 points. The basic core score of 7 must be achieved *before* you can get any extra points.

Examples:

- Has a "clear, analytical, and comprehensive" thesis, so remember to break down exactly what you'll talk about
- Mentions several changes and constants
- Gives lots of evidence

DOCUMENT BASED QUESTION (DBQ) ANSWERS AND EXPLANATIONS

BASIC CORE (competence) (0–7 points)

1. Has acceptable thesis (1 point)

- The thesis must appear at the beginning, in the intro, or at the end, in the conclusion, of the essay
- The thesis can be found in multiple sentences throughout the essay. The thesis must refer to both the way in which women were viewed by men and how they viewed themselves, and the roles they played in their respective nations' revolutions
- A thesis that is split among multiple paragraphs is unacceptable
- Don't just restate the prompt; that doesn't count for this point
- The thesis CANNOT count for any other points

2. Understands the basic meaning of the documents (1 point) (May misinterpret one document)

- Make sure to mention all 8 documents
- Demonstrate the basic meaning of at least 7 of the documents
- Don't just repeat what's in the document. Give the document context—who is saying it and why

3. Supports thesis with appropriate evidence from all or all but one document (2 points)

For 2 points, evidence must be drawn from 7 of the 8 documents and address the question.

For 1 point, evidence must be drawn from 5 or 6 of the 8 documents and address the question.

4. Analyzes point of view in at least two documents (1 point)

Remember that POV means who the particular person is, why he/she may have that particular POV.
- Give more analysis than just who the person is—explain who he/she is speaking to (his/her audience), the tone, the context, and how all those elements may come together to explain *why* the author is writing this document

5. Analyzes documents by grouping them in two or three ways, depending on question (1 point)

- Group in at least two ways. Example: Peasants v leaders, philosophers
- Noting the Chinese and the Vietnamese documents does NOT count as a grouping, but noting social class or leadership roles *is* acceptable

6. Identifies and explains the need for one type of appropriate additional document or source (1 point)

- Explain how this extra document could contribute to the analysis as a whole
- Examples:
  - French viewpoints
  - Vietnamese or Chinese anti-Communist, pro-nationalist women

Subtotal: 7 points

EXPANDED CORE (excellence) (0–2 points)

Expands beyond the basic core of 0–7 points. You can't get these points unless you hit all of the 7 points above.

Examples

- Have a clear, analytical, and comprehensive thesis
- Show careful and insightful analysis of the documents
  - Put the documents in historical context
  - Analyze all 8 documents
- Use the documents persuasively as evidence
- Analyze the point of view of most or all of the documents

Think about the author's background, intended audience, or the historical context.

- Analyze the documents in additional ways—grouping, comparisons
  - Include groups beyond the two required
  - Contribute additional analysis of subgroups within a larger grouping
- Bring in relevant "outside" historical content.
- Explain, don't just identify, why additional types of document(s) are needed
  - Identify more than one kind of document that could give better context
  - Give a sophisticated explanation of why the addition is necessary
  - Mention why the additional documents are necessary are woven throughout the essay and part of the larger analysis
- Write a clear and comprehensive conclusion that brings the argument into a meaningful perspective

Subtotal: 2 points

TOTAL: 9 points

NOTES

NOTES

NOTES

NOTES

NOTES

NOTES

NOTES

NOTES

NOTES

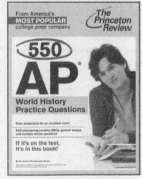